American Dreams, Hebrew Subtitles
Globalization from the Receiving End

Political Communication
David L. Paletz, Editor

Eastern European Journalism
    Jerome Aumente, Peter Gross, Ray Hiebert, Owen Johnson, and Dean Mills

The In/Outsiders: The Mass Media in Israel
    Dan Caspi and Yehiel Limor

The Holocaust and the Press
  Nazi War Crimes Trials in Germany and Israel
    Akiba A. Cohen, Tamar Zemach-Marom, Jürgen Wilke, and Birgit Schenk

Islam and the West in the Mass Media:
Fragmented Images in a Globalizing World
    Kai Hafez (ed.)

Mass Media, Politics, and Society in the Middle East
    Kai Hafez (ed.)

Governing from Center Stage: White House Communication Strategies
During the Television Age of Politics
    Lori Cox Han

Eden Online: Re-inventing Humanity in a Technological Universe
    Kerric Harvey

Civic Dialogue in the 1996 Presidential Campaign:
Candidate, Media, and Public Voices
    Lynda Lee Kaid, Mitchell S. McKinney, and John C. Tedesco

American Dreams, Hebrew Subtitles
  Globalization from the Receiving End
    Tamar Liebes

Mediated Women: Representations in Popular Culture
    Marian Meyers (ed.)

Business as Usual: Continuity and Change in Central and
Eastern European Media
    David L. Paletz and Karol Jakubowicz (eds.)

Women, Politics, Media
  Uneasy Relationships in Comparative Perspective
    Karen Ross

Public Opinion & Democracy: Vox Populi—Vox Dei?
    Slavko Splichal (ed.)

Gender, Politics and Communication
    Annabelle Sreberny and Liesbet van Zoonen (eds.)

War in the Media Age
    A. Trevor Thrall

Local Media Coverage of Congress and its Members: Through Local Eyes
    C. Danielle Vinson

American Dreams, Hebrew Subtitles
Globalization from the Receiving End

Tamar Liebes

The Hebrew University of Jerusalem

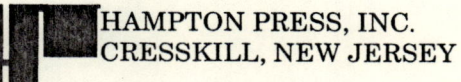
HAMPTON PRESS, INC.
CRESSKILL, NEW JERSEY

Copyright © 2003 by Hampton Press, Inc.

All rights reserved. No part of this publication may be reproduced, stored in a retrieval system, or transmitted in any form or by any means, electronic, mechanical, photocopying, microfilming, recording, or otherwise, without permission of the publisher.

Printed in the United States of America

Library of Congress Cataloging-in-Publication Data

Liebes, Tamar.
   American dreams, Hebrew subtitles : globalization from the receiving end / Tamar Liebes.
      p. cm. -- (Political communication)
   Includes bibliographical references and index.
     ISBN 1-57273-417-5 (cl) -- ISBN 1-57273-418-3 (pbk.)
   1. Mass media-Israel. 2. Americanization. I. Title. II. Hampton Press Communication series. Political communication.

P92.I79L54 2003
302.23'095694--dc21

                                                      2003040704

Hampton Press, Inc.
23 Broadway
Cresskill, NJ 07626

Contents

Acknowledgments ix
American Dreams, Hebrew Subtitles: An Introductory Note xi

1 "If You Will, It Is No Dream" 1
   Utopia in Hindsight 2
   Americanizing Local Culture:
     Is it the Message or the Medium? 6
   TV's "Mix-and-Match" Playground 8

2 Performing a Dream and Its Dissolution 17
   The Lost War Against Americanization, in Three Acts 18
   Why "Democratic Participation" is More Complex
     Than It Sounds 19
   Looking at "National Integration" and "Democratic
     Participation" in Context 20
   "Democratic Participation" May Be Conceived
     in Different Ways 22
   Giving Voice to Different Cultures Does Not Necessarily
     Enhance a Pluralistic Dialog 23
   Radio Days 25
   Enter Public Television 29

	The Decollectivization of Israeli Society: Can Television be Blamed?	35
	Reprise: Media's Role in Israel's Evolution From National Integration to Separatist Cultures	38
3	Failing Finger in the Dike: The Vulnerability of Public Broadcasting	**43**
	Problematizing Newsworthiness	47
	The Underlying Assumptions Made Explicit in the Construction of an Item: Possible Readings	53
	Did the PM Hear? Did the Story Take a Stand?	55
	Safra Square as a Watershed: The Politicization of Public Broadcasting	57
	The Place of Public Broadcasting in a Multichannel Commercialized Environment	59
4	"Disaster Marathons": The Danger of Action News	**63**
	Electronic Journalism on Time-Out	64
	Disaster Marathon: The Potential	66
	The Discourse of Routine News	67
	The Open Space of Live Marathons	69
	A Television Marathon Following the "The Helicopters' Disaster"	71
	Onscreen Reflection Over the New Genre's Possible Effects	72
	Television's Marathon Following a Series of Terrorist Bus Bombings	74
	Vacillating Between Populist Appeals and Normative Debate	77
	Crisis Marathons as Sites of Public Debate	79
5	Constructing Scandal: Whistle Blowing, Entrapment, and Spotlighting	**85**
	A Typology of Media Scandals	91
	Whistle blowing: betrayal by an insider	93
	Entrapment: Betrayal by the Journalist	98
	Spotlighting and Mainstreaming	103
	Scandal: Who Is Responsible?	108

Contents

6 The Americanization of Election Campaigns	**111**
The Media, and the Politics, Are American	112
The Media Are American, the Events Middle Eastern	117
Challenging Mainstream Television Campaign: Small Media and Cultural/Ethnic/Religious Communities	122
The Risks Of Adopting the American Model In Israeli Elections	127
7 Netanyahu Defeats Peres: The Victory of Style Over Substance	**131**
Peres Versus Netanyahu: Television Wins	132
Negotiating the Format	132
Modes Of Address: To Whom Do the Contestants Talk, and What Does It Convey	134
Constructing Political Personae	138
Responding to Questions	141
8 The Political Discourse of Authenticity: American and Israeli Style	**149**
A Close Look At The Political Strategy of Authentic Caring, U.S. Style	150
The Imagined Public That Calls For the Strategy of "Authentic Caring"	153
Conversation of "Trust" and the Creation of *Pseudo-Gemeinschaft*	154
Forms of Bonding: The Subgenres of Talking to the Public	155
Allying With Viewers to Expose an Opponent as Inauthentic, Israeli Style	156
"Look Me Straight in the Eye"	157
Mordechai, Clinton, and their Respective Communities	159
Why Is Pseudo-Sociable Conversation Dangerous?	160
9 Political Talk Shows: American and Israeli Style	**165**
The Emergence and Significance of Political Talk Television	166
A Typology and Analysis of Political Talk Television	168
Classic Journalists and Classic Citizens	169
Insider Journalism and Cynical Public	173
Therapeutic Journalism and Voyeuristic Audience	177
Ideological Journalists and Partisan Audience	179
Confrontational Panel Shows	181
Harmonious Panel Shows	185

10	Americanization Under Siege: New Media, Same Middle East	**189**
	Television Takes on a New Role	191
	The Changing Media Ecology: From *Intifada I* to *Intifada II*	192
	The Fight Over Whose Victims Suffer More	199
Epilogue		203
References		205
Author Index		213
Subject Index		217

Acknowledgments

Part of the original research reported in this book was supported by funding from the Smart Institute of Communication at the Hebrew University of Jerusalem. Particular thanks are due to Shosana Blum-Kulka, who collaborated in the study of the Peres–Netanyahu debate and was a co-author in the original version of chapter 7; Yoram Peri, who co-authored an earlier version of chapter 6; and Bruce Willams, who is the co-author of a later version, in progress, of chapter 9. Additionally, I have consulted colleagues at many points in the study. Most valuable was the generous advice of Elihu Katz, of great value throughout, not least for playing devil's advocate when needed. I would also like to thank Sonia Livingstone, Daniel Dayan, James Curran, Bruce Williams, members of the annual Ross Priory seminar, and the Israeli colleagues who took part in the seminar analyzing the Safra Square news story reported in chapter 3, Haim Beresheet in particular.

An earlier version of chapter 2, entitled "A Socio-Schematic History of Broadcasting in Israel," appeared in *De-Westernizing Media Studies*, eds., J. Curran and M.J. Park, 2000, 305–324, London: Routledge.

An earlier version of chapter 6, entitled "Electronic Journalism in Segmented Societies," co-authored with Yoram Peri, appeared in *Political Communication*, 15(3), 1998, 27-43.

Acknowledgments

An earlier version of chapter 7, entitled "Peres Versus Netnyahu: Television Wins the Debate," co-authored with Shoshana Blum-Kulka, appeared in *Televised Election Debates*, eds., S. Coleman, London: Macmillan, 2001, 66–92.

Chapter 9 presents a first version of a paper in progress, co-authored with Bruce Williams.

A portion from chapter 3, entitled "Inside a News Item: A Dispute Over Framing," appeared in *Political Communication, 17*, 3, 2000.

American Dreams, Hebrew Subtitles
An Introductory Note

Looking back, it seems that there is good reason to justify Ben Gurion's reluctance to introduce television in Israel. Launched only in the late 1960s, after the Six Day War, TV has managed to transform itself, together with its constituency, from a BBC-like public broadcasting system, intent on a national identity and dialogue with the Arabs, into a multi-channel system, featuring American values of individualization, privatization, and a premature sense of "normalcy" that followed the Oslo agreement.

Trying to capture the dynamics of this change, the book looks at a series of case studies. Starting with Theodor Herzl's vision of a Jewish state that would introduce classic European culture into the Middle East (chapter 1), it continues with the major role played by Public Broadcasting (first Radio, then TV) in the creation of national identity, and the reasons for its later marginalization (chapters 2, 3). The following chapters focus on the workings of privatized mainstream media operating in an increasingly segmented media ecology, in which national/ideological/ethnic channels are talking mostly to their own communities. A good occasion to see how it works is election time, with mainstream television conducting an American-style campaign while the particularistic sectors use the latest technologies to run their own campaigns in parallel (chapters, 6, 7).

Meanwhile, everyday life is punctuated by new hybrid genres of political entertainment. One form is the live coverage of terrorist attacks (chapter 4), considered by some as the hijacking of television. Another is the coverage of scandal, central to the yellowing of news (chapter 5), and the flourishing of primetime political talk shows (chapter 9).

As the book was being completed, the second *intifada* erupted. This reopened, with a vengance, the question of whether Americanized television, geared to individualistic sensation-seeking, can be reclaimed so as to address the needs of a collective with new shared concerns and acute common anxieties (chapter 10).

1

"If You Will, It Is No Dream"

The gentlemen would probably not want to see a play similar to those which can be seen in London, Berlin or Paris. A great French theater company and the best Italian company are visiting in Haifa this month, but I imagine you would be more interested in a Jewish play. . . . At the opera they are showing "Shabtai Zvi." Some popular theaters are staging Yiddish comedies. They are funny but in bad taste.
—Sara (in Theodor Herzl's *Altneuland*, 1902)

There is no chance of ever becoming an Israeli if you do not watch <u>Dallas</u> . . .
—A Russian immigrant to Israel (circa 1980)

Eighty years and the distance from dream to reality separate these two quotes. In Herzl's utopia, Altneuland (in German, "an old-new land") is situated in the heart of a lively, energetic, European environment of high culture, where Israeli authors and performers actively contribute to the cultural centers of Europe, Israeli audiences crowd the opera and theater halls, and a reserved concession is made to the popularity of Yiddish theater (admittedly "funny, but in bad taste"). Since the 1970s, with its reluctant embracing of television, Israel's cultural orientation has gradually shifted to the United States. Transformed by the technologies of reproduction and the need to feed TV's ravenous appetite and woo audiences, culture has become democratized and accessible and forms and contents have become mostly American, mostly commercial (what Herzl would consider "in bad taste"), and are wildly competing for global popularity. The U.S. entertainment industry has engulfed the world, demoting Europe (and the rest of the world) to the state of helpless, even if reluctant, receivers, and marginalizing "high culture" and local cultural production everywhere. From the perspective of the newly arrived Russian-Jewish immigrant (quoted earlier), all that Israelis had in common at the beginning of the 1980s were the shared fantasies cultivated in the viewing of American-produced capitalist dreams.

UTOPIA IN HINDSIGHT

Israel may be the only state on the globe that was conceived of in the form of a detailed working plan, or working fantasy, half a century before its establishment in reality. The planner, Theodor Herzl, a journalist and playwright operating in the cultural centers of Europe, was also aware of the centrality of religious tradition in the Jews' longing for national independence. The utopian model reflects his preoccupation with the question of the cultural character of the new state. Its portrayal in *Altneuland*, best described as a docu-novel, attempts to prescribe just the right mixture of the traditional and the modern, the imported and the locally produced, the cosmopolitan and the particularistic (with a strong preference for the highbrow over the popular). In Herzl's blueprint, all these elements work in perfect harmony.

Altneuland, that is, Israel in Herzl's vision, naturally becomes an integral part of European (then global) culture, with local theater and musical productions, a constant influx of European companies, and sophisticated audiences with the necessary command of languages. At the same time, Herzlian society does not neglect traditional texts, incorporating and recreating biblical themes and characters in modern, fashionable forms, such as drama and opera. The Jewish homeland in this idyllic portrait has created a civilized, postenlightenment society—liberal, humanistic, and secular. Religion is not seen as a threat. The ancient canon does not constitute a competing ethos. It is treasured in the form of "national heritage," protected and refurbished. From the vantage point of hindsight, Herzl attempted to do exactly what Hobsbaum warned against, that is, treat tradition as "heritage," thereby "draining tradition of its content and repackaging it as spectacle; it is a process of severing it from the lifeline of tradition, which is its connection with the experience of everyday life" (Giddens, 2000, p. 22). However, at the turn of the century, when the utopian state was invented, the utilization of biblical leaders (such as Moses), or ones who emerged in the more recent Jewish history (such a Shabtai Zvi), for contemplating the contemporary issues that concerned the newly born Zionist movement, seemed liked a good idea.

We can only guess what would have been Herzl's reaction to Hobsbaum's criticism. His description of the Passover dinner celebration in Altneuland is an important clue to the place of tradition in the life of the new Zionist society he had envisaged. The first thing to notice is that despite the fact that none of the participants (the fictional leaders of the society) consider themselves religious, it is a surprisingly emotional and ceremonious evening.

Herzl first describes the scene from the distanced view of Mr. Kingskurt, a non-Jewish elderly gentleman, representative of all that is humanistic and liberal in European culture. When the hostess instructs the reluctant Kingskurt to do what the others do as "this is the custom" (p. 145), he "stifled a few curses, but his sense of humor and good manners helped him to quickly imitate the strange habits of the other guests." Nevertheless, he slowly gets drawn in, as the celebration, "partly prayer . . . partly family celebration . . . evoked the strongest emotions of anybody who is capable of feeling respect towards the sublime." The event becomes most intense when "one of the guests" reads *mah nishtana*:

> One of the guests reads the Hebrew Hagada with the passion of a newly born, [and] with great efforts stops himself from bursting into loud crying. Almost thirty years have passed since, as a child, he himself asked mah nishtana; then, when he grew older, experienced enlightenment, the liberation from any Jewish traits, and finally, logically, the jumping into the void, as by that time he had nothing more to connect him to life. In this Passover night he felt like the lost son returning home.

Herzl does not identify this guest by name, but recounts his biography, which suspiciously resembles that of the author-in-the-text, and Herzl's own. Returning to Hobsbaum, it can (and should) be argued that this is not a case of draining tradition of its content and packaging it as spectacle, but of reintroducing tradition to people who, for reasons of expedience (fear of anti-Semitism), ideology (emotional and intellectual rejection of religious belief, and of religious observance's rigorous demands on daily life), and cultural environment (exposure to enlightenment), have already rejected it. For these people, "true" tradition is no longer an option. At the same time, it is both unrealistic and cowardly to deny the shared cultural roots as a basis for the creation of a state founded for the purpose of solving the Jewish problem.

Herzl's way of encountering anti-Semitism, obviously directed toward believers and nonbelievers alike, is to give back to the Jewish people (both assimilated and religious) the basic human dignity of which Europe at the beginning of the 20th century had deprived them. He intends to do so by creating a Jewish state based on universalistic, liberal principles. The founding of such a state would endow the Jews with a status equal to that of the Europeans, and liberate them from (economic, legal, and psychological) dependence on countries controlled by others.

A basic condition for the revival of a sense of self-respect within assimilated Jews is to acknowledge, rather than to hide or avoid, their common roots. Although Jewish tradition has been miraculously preserved for hundreds of years, it stayed alive mostly among orthodox Jews, for whom it remained a total life commitment (remember Hobsbaum). Zionism, however, was a solution for the need of Jews who had broken out of the orthodox community.

Hobsbaum's position on tradition leads to a the "all-or-nothing" attitude of the Yeshayahu Leibowitz-type, that says you either continue abiding by the letter of the Halachic law, in the way it was always done, or you are indulging in a phony, pathetic attempt, severing tradition from its live context, and emptying it of relevance and meaning. In Zionist utopia, tradition is rediscovered by a movement that had made an ideological break with religion, yet does acknowledge a shared history, based on acquaintance with shared texts. Paradoxically, only the break from the enslavement of religion makes it possible for Zionists to recreate tradition as part of a new way of life in a new geographic area, within a rejuvenated national experience. And because common heritage is what constitutes a link with the community's historical continuity, it is relevant and emotional.

It thus seems that although the reinvention of tradition within the Jewish state is paradoxical (in terms of adopting part of what one rebelled against), there is nothing phony or artificial about it. And, as we have shown, preserving the Jewish holidays is no spectacle, but an active reenactment with the participation of families and friends (and with the knowledge that the same ritual is performed by Jews everywhere).

Moreover, when heritage does take the form of spectacle in Herzlian utopia, there is nothing passive about it. First, there is the creative effort by the artists. Herzl is (in effect) calling on writers and composers to weave their plots and music around biblical characters. It is quite safe to assume that none other than Herzl himself would be hiding under the guise of Moses (the great national leader who was destined not to enter the land of Cana'an). No lack of relevance and/or involvement there.

Looking from Herzl's perspective at the cultural dimensions of global–local, cosmopolitan–Israeli, relevant–irrelevant, one must remember that at the turn of the century, the globe was much smaller than it is today, and Europe was its center. Herzl rather took for granted that his state would take part in that culture—both as consumer and producer. Unlike contemporary popular American culture, which targets the largest possible audiences, Herzl was mainly concerned with the unemployed Jewish academics who found themselves pushed to leave Europe, seeing them as the consumers and producers of European culture in Altneuland. By mobilizing, reviving, and recreating traditional texts, these artists and thinkers would establish a link between the heroic ancient past and the contemporary project. Thus, tradition becomes politically relevant, and the new media and cultural forms in vogue may even revive it.

Skipping 80 years to that Russian immigrant who sees Israelis as incorrigible *Dallas* consumers brings us to an era in which the model of cosmopolitan culture has been replaced by a global–popular–commercial model, dramatically transforming society through the technologies of reproduction and transmission. The center has shifted to the United States, and Israel has been wired to the American Tube of Plenty. Watching *Dallas* in the 1980s, on the single-channel television, with families gathering in their living rooms around the one TV set, Israelis could still share the imported dreams and at the same time negotiate their own cultural identity vis-à-vis the "capitalist," "materialistic," "glamorous," and/or "corrupt" characters (Liebes and Katz, 1993).

Two decades later, in 2000, even American dreams were difficult to share. With the shift of entertainment and politics from the halls and town squares to people's living rooms and bedrooms, and the introduction of cable TV and multiple channels, the consumption of entertainment and news was becoming an increasingly private, and isolated, pastime. Shared culture—of a kind that might compete with global commercial culture—could be found only within religious, and/or cultural/ethnic enclaves (Sivan, 1994) who define themselves in contradiction with the mainstream, Americanized, morally inferior environment. The resurrection of religion was becoming a serious rival to forms of secular culture and entertainment, both public and private. Herzl's view of the high–low dichotomy, given the transformed demography of the Jewish state, was no longer reflected in popular Yiddish comedy but in popular Sephardic comedy and music. And Yiddish passed through a period in which it was considered a threat by Zionism in its battle for the establishment of Hebrew as the national language, fading in the 1990s to become the subject for off prime-time documentaries on the High

Holidays (and enjoying a certain revival within the new Russian immigrant community).

In the postscript of *Altneuland,* Herzl posed two options for the future of his utopia: "If you have the will—this is no fairy tale, but if you do not—all I have told you is a fairy-tale and so it shall remain." Herzl chose to think in terms of "all or nothing." He was not going to entertain the possibility of spoiling the dream. Either there will be enough social energy to realize the project, or it would remain an (unspoiled) dream. But books and histories have a life of their own, and 100 years later, we are facing the imperfect reality of the would-be utopia of a Jewish state. At the beginning of yet another new century, Israel is horrifyingly distant from the fictional harmony of the model. In the throws of the fiercest culture wars in its history, while struggling internally to discover and/or reformulate its own identity (or rather its multicultural identities), Israel is facing the most massive invasion of globalized culture.

AMERICANIZING LOCAL CULTURE—IS IT THE MESSAGE OR THE MEDIUM?

It took a while for television to become a major force in transforming Israeli culture and politics. For better and worse. "Americanizing" the culture and "deideologizing" politics—the initial fears that have made Israeli leadership resist television during the first two decades of statehood—have turned out to be justified from the government's perspective, but not altogether negative for the society. On the up side, exposure to U.S. programs did introduce this geographically isolated society into the growing global cosmopolitan environment, and television journalism played a major part in "deepening democracy," in the sense of restricting the government's capacity to keep secrets from the citizenry. Censorship became a nonviable proposition (Liebes, 1997). At the same time, however, by trivializing and personalizing political issues, television has destroyed the existing public space in which the information revealed could be debated (Giddens, 2000).

But suspicion of Americanization was concerned not only with politics, but with the risk of "cultural imperialism." In the Israeli context, this fear was more acute than in Europe, where cultural traditions have long been established. In Israel, the flood of American popular culture meant intervening in the precarious assimilation of the newly revived Hebrew language, and in the attempts to create an "authentic" Israeli culture (a contradiction in terms, at best). Did the flood of commercialized, mostly American entertainment trample the budding of "authentic" creativity? As I argue here, there is no easy answer.

In the era before television invaded Israel, the dichotomies between "our" culture and the culture of others were easier to maintain. We had our own hard-won heritage, mostly in book form, and considered it authentic and relevant. American culture was encountered mostly in the form of the occasional Hollywood movie, seen as glamorous, phony, and fleeting fantasies. Even when Israelis did finally establish a national TV service (as late as 1968!), the leadership was naive enough, or unworldly enough, or idealistic enough (or simply socialized only to the book culture) to believe that a medium is only a vehicle for messages, and that television's messages could, should, and would be controlled. The kinds of content screened would naturally be decided by the country's policymakers, and it would consist of reflecting the state's life, its struggles, creations and achievements, and the cultures of the various Jewish "tribes" who have immigrated to the state. It would promote Hebrew and Israeli culture. Sounds unrealistic? Israel's Law of Public Broadcasting specifies all this and more.

But, as in the case of all new nations, where the establishment of television had built up high expectations for the flourishing of local culture, the necessity to fill the air regardless of whether you have something to show has taken the upper hand, making all ambitious planning irrelevant. Necessity has opened the gates for the flooding of mostly American commercialized culture, teaching us, "the people of the book," that when it came to the medium of television, we were no better than any Third World country. Thirty years later, Israel (and the rest of the world) continues to consume the products of the American entertainment industry right off the production line (granted, with a trickle of "counter-imperialistic" telenovellas and prestigious BBC miniseries), catering to the largest accessible audience. In the year 2000, this meant more action-violence, less drama and relationships (McChesney, 1999) so that language should not become a barrier for following the plot. To signal that the outraged opposition to "American cultural imperialism," rampant in Europe in the 1980s, has gone out of fashion, it is now labeled *global* culture. Europe did "fight back" somewhat at the time (Silj, 1988) but has since continued to lean heavily on U.S. imports.

Ironically, by imposing its forms and formats as the only economically viable ones on our own media products (as well as the rest of the world's), the U.S. industry has given a deeper, structural meaning to "cultural imperialism," leaving us (and others) to discover the extent to which medium and form end up determining the content. Can an Israeli-made soap opera have a local flavor, or would we find out that when all is said and done (mostly said, of course), a soap is a soap is a soap? Or, perhaps more distressing, can election campaign reporting rise above the practices of race horse coverage?

TV'S "MIX-AND-MATCH" PLAYGROUND

Media globalization at the receiving end looks as if it has confused the once obvious distinctions between what is genuine and has (artistic, intellectual, or human) quality, and what is merely entertaining, and between what belongs to "others" and what remains "ours." A good site for viewing these uncertainties is provided by press columns, where self-styled cultural observers-cum-local-anthropologists, try on various combinations of "local" versus "global," and "real" versus "phony." Television provides critics with a comfortable hunting ground for bashing the contemporary mishmash of current culture, streaming by in staccato rhythms.

Two pieces, written by the media critic of *Ha'aretz* (Israel's equivalent of *The New York Times*) on the same week, demonstrate the end of an era in which, by definition, "our" culture was regarded as "real" or "authentic," and the culture of others as "phony." It should also be noted that the columnist takes for granted that nationwide television, public and private alike, acts as an arbitrator between the Israeli and the global, the authentic and the phony, the relevant and the trivial, and carries the responsibility to do the right thing.

The Inventing of Zionist Heritage. The following piece was written on *Tish'a Be'av*, the date in the Hebrew calendar marking the annual mourning of the destruction of the (twice built and ruined) ancient Jewish temple. As in the case of other traditional Jewish holidays, or in commemorations of historical events, it is destined for heroic attempts by TV (the First Channel [public] more than Channel Two [commercial]) to enact its role as performer of public culture. As we will see, this proves to be a minefield.

In his piece, "To Each His Own Kick" (using the English word *kick*, for lack of a Hebrew equivalent; published July 22, 1999), TV critic Rogel Alper, a young, sophisticated, direct, funny, and often personal writer, starts on a autobiographical note:

> It reminded me of schooldays depression. It reminded me of annual school outings. It reminded me of [obligatory service in, T.L.] the army. It reminded me of the days in which there was only a single channel here, and when it started to blow the arid spirit of eternity, there was no place to take shelter, nowhere to escape to.

Leaving his readers in the dark as to which program he had watched the night before, Alper hurries to identify Israel's BBC-like public television as the institution under attack. It appears last on a list of failed institutions—school, army, public television—all regarded as making up the ideological apparatus in charge of socializing young Israelis into the Zionist ethos. From Alper's point of view, public TV, naively or cynically, has taken advantage of its 20 years of monopoly for packaging and selling some form of Zionist heritage, which it keeps recycling. For young Israelis, such scenes seem irrelevant at best, or an embarrassing form of rhetorically alienating ethnocentrism at worst.

These short opening lines indicate clearly and powerfully the speed with which the Zionist ethos has been transformed in the course of two generations. Alper's generation cannot tolerate the self-confident enthusiasm of the state's founders, and their nationalist tone, oblivious of conflicting moral rights (of the Palestinians). Alper's weariness of public TV's major efforts to cultivate "Israeliness" seem to express an Israeli variant of the notion obvious to any Woody Allan fan, that to be Jewish is to be a self-hater. It is almost as if many of the twentysomethings and thirtysomethings of this country would make a deal to fulfill their civic duties if only they could be spared the pathos of trying to convince them that justice is (only) on our side. Alper's next paragraph zooms in on the program under attack:

> The late Professor Ze'ev Vilnai [a nationally renowned geographer and tour guide, now dead]—a fanatic and a bore—in black and white archival fragments—guides a tour round the walls of Jerusalem. His sons, Oren and Matan [an army general and later politician], bring up a heaps of broken-up memories . . .

Alper takes no chances, hastening to tell us exactly what he thinks of the older Vilnai ("a fanatic and a bore"), "precontextualizing" the next anecdote to erase the possibility of any benevolent interpretations (Blum-Kulka, 2000). No more tolerance for sacred cows, is the message. No more tolerance for the nostalgic celebrations of Israel's ancient nationhood, with their implied, highly controversial contemporary claims to the historical rights for the land that this nostalgia entails.

> The hearty professor greets an Arab riding on horseback in Arabic and throws at him some "Keeff?" [Arabic for "How are you?"], closing with "Mabssut?" ["Happy?"]. The same Vilnai who has defined himself as "landscapist" (from landscape), which is about the complete opposite of "humanist." The same Vilnai who was a Jewish fundamentalist imperialist.

From his privileged position of post-Edward Said hindsight, Alper draws out the irony inherent in the encounter between Vilnai, the imperialist conqueror, and the disenfranchised, conquered "native," with the insensible Russian Jewish immigrant using his scant Arabic for an unselfconscious and (in his mind) sociable exchange. Such an exchange, Alper implies, requires an equal status of the interlocutors, so badly missing here. A "tour round the walls of Jerusalem" has nothing to do with scenic views. Broadcast on *Tish'a Be'av* it is a red flag, an ideological provocation, in the best Zionist tradition of "conquering" the land by hikes to ancient symbolic sites, intended to develop a physical intimacy with the earth (Gurevitch and Aran, 1991).

Having made the point, Alper still cannot let go. He is genuinely enraged at Vilnai's, or, better, at our blindness (as Jews, as colonizers, as powerful) to the inequality of the Arab contenders (an inequality far less obvious, it should be said, for the senior Vilnai's generation, who have lived in Palestine under Turkish, later British Mandatory rule):

> "Mabssut [happy?]?" Of course he is mabssut, the conqueror Vilnai, how can he not be mabssut? Best friends [with the Arab]. I shrank with shame. In the annual school outings too, that was always the moment I wanted to bury myself.

This personal critique encapsulates the trap in which young Israelis find themselves. Born into the success of Zionism, they are alienated by its offensive insensitivity to the Palestinians. Public broadcasting has delegitimized itself by clinging to a naive and archaic historiography, to forms that by now seem unacceptable, to cultural heroes who are incompatible with the times, and to what seems like a pathetic attempt to construct a Zionist "heritage" by linking biblical texts to contemporary landscapes. Since Herzl, the establishment of our connection to the land via biblical texts has become politicized. Now it is a dangerous game, used by West Bank settlers and right-wing extremists to refuse any compromise with the Palestinians.

Paradoxically, at the end of this text, Alper zaps to the liberating MTV, where he doesn't have to feel responsible for the channel (no need to hide himself), where he wouldn't be aggravated by claims to authenticity, belonging and relevance, all of which he finds phony and abusive.

> Matan Vilnai [the son] continues his thrilling tour in honor of *Tish'a Be'av* calling gayly, "Come on guys, let's continue to the graveyard." The only problem is that according to my diary, yesterday was July 21, 1999. After all, today there are options to Romema [Public Channel headquarters]. I switched to MTV. To each his own kick.

It is, however, premature to conclude that Alper sees himself as a wild supporter of the new commercial revolution of Israeli media. One advantage of having a daily column is the capacity to express multiple perspectives, and allow for subtlety and complexity over time.

TV's Import of American Obsessions. Another day on that same week (July 16, 1999) has brought together, by coincidence, the premature deaths of two men—John F. Kennedy, Jr. (whose plane crashed into the sea), and Meir Ariel, an Israeli singer and songwriter (who was misdiagnosed and died for lack of proper treatment). In his column, entitled "John-John, Where Are You?," Alper points out that the commercial Channel Two devoted a full 8 minutes, almost one third of the evening news program, to Kennedy—"an American obsession," at most—whereas only 3 minutes, "somewhere in its middle," were given to "the sudden, and no less brutal death of one, Meir Ariel, a very original and talented man, who influenced Israeli culture, and is much more relevant and important to the viewer than Kennedy Junior." "Let's be grateful," Alper adds sarcastically, "that he (Ariel) wasn't turned into a component of the synoptic weather map."

These two somewhat parallel events provide Alper with an opportunity to comment on what television news should be doing, as compared to what it actually does. His piece dwells on the conventions of the news genre, its global and local aspects, and, most revealing, the relationship it has (compared to what it should have) with the local public sphere.

It turns out that despite Alper's relief about the introduction of commercial channels as a refuge from public television's force-feeding of concocted "heritage," he does believe that television in Israel belongs in some form to the Israeli public, not only to advertisers and individual viewers. He also believes that it should provide some kind of shared space, in which Israelis can witness and contemplate the heroes of their culture, and be presented with the weighty political issues confronting the state. In short, we rediscover Alper as feeling the need to view television not only in his capacity as a private individual. At least when it comes to news, he expects to be addressed as an Israeli. As such, he sees the Second Channel's decision to devote a major part of its evening news edition to John-John as a demonstration of that channel's whole-hearted adoption of American news culture, and of American-turned-global stars—drawing Israelis away from news that matters and into irrelevant, empty gossip, and the voyeuristic pleasures of melodrama. The irony of the opening lines says it all:

> Ya'akov Eilon [the news anchor] breathed a lot of air through his teeth, as is his manner when bearing bad news; what happened? "Well, this evening we will provide extensive reporting. . . . This is a great shock . . . after the national trauma of the Kennedy assassination . . . the most senior anchors are choking as they mourn the loss . . . the sexiest man in the world."

Eilon would not wear his sad face when informing us about thousands of Chinese farmers killed in floods, or about thousands of Japanese who died in earthquakes. Such an item may not even pass the threshold into the program. But John-John was a different story. We all knew him, well, knew all about him. In the commercialized environment of global media, with the acceleration of synergy among media institutions and other entertainment industries, tabloid-style celebrity gossip has become legitimate news.

Even in Israel, where audiences still have high concern for "real" news, print and electronic press have become increasingly dependent on mediators such as spokespeople and public relations agencies, who deliver camera-ready texts. In between terrorist attacks, war threats, and ethnic and economic tensions, Israelis sink into viewing news as another genre that allows them to escape into lives of the rich and famous, the globe over, and wallow in victory and tragedy that are not their own. That is not to say that all global news is phony. But Kennedy was the story of the day, whereas large-scale global disasters followed the well-known rules of relevance.

Of course Kennedy was a news item, which merits reporting somewhere in the program. But 8 minutes? Channel Two news would not devote 8 minutes to disasters from all over the globe. Instead these are latched on to the weather forecast, as exotic *piquanterie:*

> As these massive disasters are not relevant, that is, not close enough for "our" public to be threatened by, and/or to identify with the victims, they are relegated to maximal marginality, that is, allocated minimal fleeting seconds, usually the ones at the end, which, if necessary, may be edited out. And Kennedy? Why, we know him from the time he attended his father's funeral, we can remember his girlfriends, know which ones his mother approved of. We were surprised at his choice of wife, curious about the success of his magazine. As someone who was born as a prince into the celebrity circle, started life as a little hero in a tragedy followed closely by global media, and certainly looked the part, how could we not be interested?

TV's Annihilation of Authentic Israeli Stars. But as fate would have it, on the same day in which John-John died after his plane sank into the Atlantic Ocean, Meir Ariel had died in a hospital in Tel Aviv, due to medical negligence. Ariel was "ours," not a character in a virtual, global, popular fantasy, but an active participant (sometimes controversially) in the Israeli reality of making popular music and lyrics. As an artist, says Alper "He was relevant, and important to the viewer much more than Kennedy Junior, but he gets only 3 minutes, somewhere along [the program]."

By now, Alper's criteria for inclusion and salience in the news are unequivocally stated. A major part of the news should have been allocated to Ariel—as "ours": an original, authentic, relevant artist, one who has had an influence on the culture. But when it came to the test, Channel Two did not rise to the occasion, but chose the easy way out so as to use the spoonfed visuals of the Atlantic, transposed by photos of the glamorous American and his wife. No need to make our reporters sweat.

The coincidence makes blatant the paradoxes of commercial TV. Orit Shohat, a prominent columnist, joined in the protest, and used it to express her view on the relationship between commercial television and Israeli popular culture:

> Meir Ariel died because of negligence on the same week in which Kennedy died. Was there a good reason to chatter about the Kennedy family for hours as if they were a part of our culture?. . . The death of Ariel was more important and more disturbing, and did not get enough attention on TV. First of all, Ariel is ours, and he is not a product of the Children's Channel [a label for the route all of commercial TV has taken]. He symbolizes an annihilated Israeli culture which does not even have a small corner on TV. (Orit Shohat, *Ha'aretz*, July 23, 1999)

Shoaht also sees what's "ours" as important by virtue of cultural authenticity and relevance, situated at the opposite pole of commercial, infantile television. And this kind of culture, she claims, is annihilated by commercial television.

Shohat expresses the concern of cultural critics such as Gadi Taub (1998), who claimed that we have had enough trance and dance and grange and camp (all imported, global escapism) to allow ourselves to look at our own singers without fear of drowning in provinciality. As much as we admire Israelis who have made it in Hollywood or on MTV, or try to nurture a local X generation, body piercing or platform shoes,

> [W]e are first of all Israelis, first of all Hebrew speakers. And that includes strong sun and crowding and Arabic and Russian and Rumanian and Polish and Moroccan, and development towns . . .

and Ultra-Orthodox and settlers . . . and popular [Oriental, "lowbrow"] singers . . . and basic army training and war with another people over the same piece of land.

The ensuing public debate following the news show reflects the position of TV news as the shared arena of "breaking news" (pseudo or not), with the printed press watching and commenting on TV's social and cultural role, situated, as it is, along the seam between political, current events and culturally significant events.

The debate reflects confusion about what culture Israelis belong to. The Zionist attempts at creating "Israeli" culture are considered hegemonic and phony. New Israeli popular culture does need nurturing, but TV, with its need for safe-bet superstars and maximum ratings, is in no position to encourage anything that does not ensure a mass market. Is commercial TV indeed contributing to the "annihilation" of original Israeli popular culture? And if, indeed, the adoption of the cultural myths of others and the tabloidization of the news are part and parcel of media privatization and the easy access of global TV, does public broadcasting stand a chance of revival in this new environment?

In an attempt to sort out these comments in terms of American versus Israeli, and "real" or "authentic" versus "phony" or trivial news, we classify TV news items that make their way past the threshold as belonging to a combination of two "phony" types and two authentic types. Kennedy is a metaphor for a product of global TV, entertaining (in ritualistic or scandalous ways or both), supplying emotional voyeuristic kicks under the respectable label of "information." The dramatic deaths of John-John or Princess Diana, the OJ Simpson trial, anything to do with Julia Roberts, and the "survivors" of the new "authentic," real-life, *Big Brother* type docudrama, are daily TV fodder, in and out of the news. Moreover, the same familiar faces do the rounds of the almost interchangeable news editions, talk shows, teasers, and ads.

A second kind of phoniness implied by Alper is typical of national holidays and other ceremonial occasions. Accordingly, Public Channel's documentary on *Tish'a Be'av* is a locally produced attempt at authenticity, pompously claiming to resurrect cultural "roots," or to reinforce a national ethos, but is out of synch with the public that judges it to be irrelevant, phony, and irritating, even enraging at times.

Although phoniness of the first kind is the result of a world system of commercial television, promoting, as it were, the celebrity heroes of globalism, tied to the worlds of fashion, sports, politics, and the entertainment industry, the phoniness of the second kind is part of the contrived efforts of the outdated type of public television, faced with the possibly unfeasible mission of preserving and recreating a local tradition that may never have existed, or, once gone, cannot be resurrected.

In this environment, authentic, or "real" news, whether imported or locally produced, stands less of a chance to reach the screen, and even lesser to make a mark. Foreign news such as a mass disaster hitting Chinese farmers does not stand a chance because although undoubtedly real, it is happening far away. As such, it is not threatening enough, and does not evoke enough empathy as do disasters that happen close by—possibly affecting people from "our" country, town, neighborhood, or ethnic group. Local disasters stand a better chance—especially if victims are found to tell the woeful tale. The Israeli girl saved by an Israeli rescue team at the earthquake in Turkey was given endless time on Israeli TV—right after the rescue, at her homecoming, at the hospital, at a party for the rescuers, and so on. The masses of Turkish victims, and the enormous magnitude of suffering in this neighboring country, were but a fleeting shadow.

As for "authentic" Israeli news, it is no surprise for Alper that on the Second Channel, Kennedy won over news stories such as the continuing political battle between the leader of the orthodox Sephardic party and the leader of the civil rights party over Israel's civil and pluralistic identity, as well as over news regarding the talks carried out by Prime Minister (PM) Barak and President Clinton about Israel's future. What does manage to surprise Alper is that even the death of a local star of popular culture barely makes it into the news. How is it possible, he asks, that the death of Meir Ariel, a local authentic, admired singer, makes the news only marginally?

The speed at which what has been considered an authentic Israeli experience slips away, becoming irrelevant from one generation to the next, can be demonstrated by the words of Yehuda Amichai, an Israeli poet who died in 2000. Viewed by many as Israel's most genuine voice of literate, humane Zionism, Amichai expressed his amazement in an interview to *Yediot Aharonot,* about the selection of Aviv Geffen, the king of pop singers for young Israelis, to sing in the peace rally at the end of which PM Rabin was assassinated:

> They took the little Geffen to the terrible evening in which Rabin was assassinated. This is the person who made a celebration out of not having served in the army. They took him as a symbol, and did not take one of the thousands who have served in fighting units. Why choose this copycat of American culture?

2

Performing a Dream and Its Dissolution

During the winter of 1998, celebrating 50 years of national independence, Israel's public television produced a 24-episode documentary series on the history of the state since its inception. At the end of the episode on the Six Day War, my son, who had made a point of watching the episodes covering the first 20 years, remarked: "Now the sad part begins; there is nothing worthwhile left to watch."

Despite its producers' reflexive and sometimes critical view, the first two "good decades" shown on TV have provided viewers with an uplifting pride and a sense of witnessing a great, at times heroic, story. These were also the years when Israel had no television, and Israelis, not knowing what they were missing, gathered around one "radio set" in the living room to listen to the one radio channel, which was officially part of the prime minister's office, and politically controlled to the hilt. During the next two decades, radio diversified somewhat but there was only one TV channel. Not knowing what they were missing, Israelis gathered around one "television instrument" in the living room, to view the First (and at that time only) Channel, which had been established (now together with public radio) as an independent public institution (Public Broadcasting Authority—PBA). From the beginning of the fifth decade, Israelis have split into different rooms to select from an abundance of mostly commercial TV channels—national, transnational, sectoral. Israelis are told by a government that calls itself "nationalist," that they have *too little* choice, a deficiency that would be remedied by the law of "open skies" already passed in the Knesset.

I suggest here that the changing technological and institutional character of the electronic media, as well as the choice of their formats and contents, is emblematic of the successive stages in the evolution of Israeli society, expressing, and bearing witness to the widening cracks within its hegemonic culture. Media provides a reflection of the shifts in this culture—charting its lightspeed course from a naive, nonreflexive, national solidarity, to an emaciated "consensus" in which government and media hold a tattered umbrella over a society segmented into a variety of cultures openly competing for political domination, with the ethos of the secular, Western-style democracy wearing thin.

THE LOST WAR AGAINST AMERICANIZATION, IN THREE ACTS

The infiltration of American popular culture, with its media technologies, commercial structure, and formulaic content, should be seen in parallel, perhaps in competition to, the attempts of a budding new nation to promote a language and nurture a culture that would give it cohesion. A look at the social history of broadcasting in Israel shows a national broadcasting institution that attempts to assist in (and give voice to) the development of "authentic" local culture, while confronting two types of threat: that of the internal multiplicity of cultural enclaves, and that of the external Americanized culture. On the Americanization front, Israel's public broadcasting conducted a series of losing battles, starting with 20 years of postponing altogether the establishment of television (a symbol of Americanization). For the next 20 years, there was only one TV channel that desperately tried to follow the British tradition institutionally as well as culturally, but finally succumbed, during the 1990s, to a technological, institutional, and cultural invasion, which overturned the hegemonic restraint of the preceding four decades. Now, at the beginning of the 21st century, Israel is opening up new cable and satellite channels, all strictly commercial, with an overwhelming mass of imported, American content. Moreover, Israeli-made programs, among which news, talk shows, and quiz shows are paramount, closely follow American forms and formats.

Looking back at the five decades of Israel's short life, the first two decades seem an era of enthusiastic innocence, when radio reflected the benevolently paternalistic, taken-for-granted belief in the instant integration of masses of immigrants (mostly from North Africa) into a secular, Western style "Israeli culture," a culture that soon after independence had (numerically) become a minority culture.

Television entered the scene a moment after the euphoria of the Six Day War, at the onset of an era in which repressed messianic-religious and ethnic-religious forces were gradually unleashed, and a process of rejuvenation of primordial-tribal identities was relentlessly at work. These were also the years in which the protest over nonconsensual wars took place, and mainstream Israelis became less committed to the collectivity. But television, no more self-reflexive than the political establishment it supported, mostly ignored all this, continuing to protect the society's sacred institutions and integrating the country around *Dallas* and *The Love Boat*, but also around *The Column of Fire*, a history of Zionism styled after the BBC's *World at War*, and, most memorably, around a number of great historical moments that lifted the national spirit.

During the third stage of its evolution, in the 1990s, the media reflect the hegemony of a government presiding over bitterly contestant groups. Reconciled to the idea that national unity is a dream of the past, government chose to marginalize national television by opening up an enormous choice of "entertainment" channels—offering sex, violence, and vulgar talk—perhaps in order to neutralize political debate, and thus to contribute to further depoliticization. This process has reinforced the entrenchment of separatist cultures in their own enclaves, around their own, segmented media, condemning the rest of us to zapping among indistinguishable transnational channels or turning off the TV set altogether.

WHY "DEMOCRATIC PARTICIPATION" IS MORE COMPLEX THAN IT SOUNDS

As historians and social scientists have learned, any story can be turned upside down, and my description of Israeli history as a failed attempt to create a unified nation is no exception. Thus, what for many Israelis, brought up on Herzl's utopia of a secular-liberal community, seems like the shattering of a dream, may, from another perspective, be regarded as a positive development. This is the perspective implied by Hallin (1998) in his critique of the role of broadcasting in fostering "national integration" in new nations. Hallin's juxtaposition of the key concepts of "national unity" and "democratic participation" suggests that he may see the current stage of segmentation in Israeli society and media in a positive rather than negative light. As his arguments are central to my image of what is happening to

Israeli democracy and media, I consider them before going into the detailed presentation of the Israeli case, arguing that the terms of the debate are oversimplified, and not necessarily generalizable, as an in-depth analysis within a specific context may demonstrate.

National Integration Versus Democratic Participation

Hallin re-examined the classical studies, conducted in the 1970s, that sought to define the role of the electronic media in the establishment of new nations in what was then labeled "the Third World." The problem with these studies, he argued, is that although they hold media's role in "national integration" in high esteem, they disregard media's failure to provide a public sphere in which diverse voices (mostly the less privileged) can be heard. One study explicitly states that certain African countries were not yet ripe for democratic participation, whereas other studies do so implicitly, by equating media with modernity ("progress") in contrast with tradition ("backwardness"), and by emphasizing the importance of media for communicating from the center to the periphery, not vice versa. Katz and Wedell (1977), Hallin noticed, do acknowledge the need for preserving native cultural heritage, but he deemed their concern too narrowly focused, constituting a romantic gesture rather than an attempt to take the possible contributions of pluralism and periphery seriously.

The subtext of these studies, Hallin concluded, is that media democracy may stand in the way of the truly important tasks of mobilizing society for economic development. In their zeal to see modernization and economic growth, and in their wish to generalize their findings beyond specific countries, these scholars have ignored the political context—failing to consider the implications of media operating, in some cases, in the service of dictatorial regimes, or, in other cases, of neo-populist, corrupt democracies. In short, these studies are to be reprimanded for disregarding the potential of media in cultivating a pluralistic society. By analyzing the Israeli experience, I point out a number of problems in this critique.

LOOKING AT "NATIONAL INTEGRATION" AND "DEMOCRATIC PARTICIPATION" IN CONTEXT

In considering Hallin's critique in light of the Israeli experience, I make three arguments. First, I address Hallin's warning that the role of broadcasting in national unity should be looked at within particular contexts.

Moreover, I would add that in democratic nations this should include empathy for the "natives'" perspective, and for the norms and beliefs of the times. Second, and in line with the first, I argue that democratic participation may be understood in various ways, not always prioritizing the participation of a plurality of voices in the public debate. Third, I propose that the participation of different cultural groups in the public debate does not necessarily mean that such participation is "democratic," in the sense of joining in a multicultural dialogue.

To begin with, as Hallin noted in his first point, the issue of media's role in national integration should be seen in the context of the kind of regime in which they operates. Judging the effectiveness of media must depend on whether one is considering a dictatorship, a corrupt democracy, or a society operating according to democratic principles. The media policy of what one considers a bona fide democratic state should be considered, first, within its social and cultural context and, equally important, from the normative perspective of its chosen elites. Following Geertz's (1983) advice to any outsider who interprets another culture, here too it is useful to form an open-minded understanding of the founders' own perspective of what an enlightened democratic society should be like.

Naturally, in hindsight, 50 years later, we may point to failings and shortsightedness in any policy, as long as we remember that our own criticism too may seem irrelevant or naive 50 years from now. Theoreticians and scholars are sometimes the first to advocate a change, but by the time the new meanings take root and their vision is adopted, they may have changed their minds again, or regret what has been lost, or realize that they have not meant it so radically. One should remember how scholars' criticism of BBC elitism, monopoly, and hegemony, quickly turned into mourning over its possible demise, and an adamant defense of the principle of public broadcasting.

Bearing in mind the importance of the "natives'" perspective, let me sketch the cultural (r)evolution of Israeli society, which is crucial for an understanding of the complex (and formidable) tasks Israeli media had to perform.

The Cultural Evolution Of Israeli Society. The roots of the Western-style democracy that characterizes Israel, perhaps not for much longer, can be found within the secular-socialist-Zionist core of Jewish immigrants, mostly from eastern Europe, who settled in Palestine at the beginning of the 20th century. This pioneer wave of immigration, responding to the call of Herzlian Zionism, gathered momentum when the British officially established a "national home" for the Jews in Palestine. These were immigrants who wished to leave behind the traditional Jewish occupations in the various diasporas, to settle and work the land. Israel's central social institutions (such as the Jewish Agency, the Workers' Union, the ideological newspapers) were established by this secular-socialist Zionist leadership in the pre-state period, and later harnessed to the needs of the young state. Shortly following Israel's independence, at the beginning of the 1950s, the newly established state, with a population of 600,000 Israelis, was faced with task of absorbing a new, mass Jewish immigration from Asia and Africa, more than twice its own number. These new immigrants had not gone through the processes of secularization and modernization, and were suddenly faced with an unfamiliar country and culture.

Fifty years later, on a somewhat apocalyptic note, Kimmerling (1998), a prominent revisionist sociologist, described the current state of Israel as "a cracking of the political and cultural hegemony of the Labor party version of secular, Western-style 'Israeli-ness' [*Yisraeliut*]," which had developed within a secular middle class, now third-generation Israelis, who have ostensibly absorbed the Oriental immigrants, as groups and as individuals, and Israel's Arab citizens (currently 20% of its population) as individuals and families. This hegemony is threatened by a number of almost autonomous subgroups and cultures—the national-religious settlers (in the occupied territories), the orthodox Orientals, the Ashkenazi Ultra-Orthodox, the Israeli Arabs, and perhaps the new Jewish immigration from the former Soviet Union. Unlike pluralist societies, where the various subcultures accept the universalistic principles according to which their society operates, these Israeli subcultures seek self-determination for their own brand of particularism and/or wish to replace Israel's Western-style democratic norms with their own. Having reached a critical mass due to high birth rates, immigration, and the acquisition of social and political skills, these former "enclaves" have "sharpened existing social boundaries" and created new ones "by recycling and reinforcing histories and collective particularistic memories, (and) retelling the history of the state and . . . their place in it, in a way that differs from the accepted version" (Kimmerling, 1998).

"DEMOCRATIC PARTICIPATION" MAY BE CONCEIVED IN DIFFERENT WAYS

Second, I argue that the concept of "democratic participation" may be conceptualized in different ways—not only in Hallin's "plurality of voices," but also as closely related to "national integration." Seen from the perspective of Israel's founding fathers, national integration is directly connected to the idea of "democratizing" the society. Democratic participation, however, was not understood so much in terms of providing a stage for a plurality of subcultures, but rather in terms of providing equal access to what they perceived as universally accessible cultural riches. In this, the policy of *Kol Yisrael* ("The Voice of Israel")—Israel's public radio network—was not much different from that of the BBC's early idea of democratic policy, as described by Cardiff and Scannell (1987):

> The policy was democratic not in the sense that it bowed to popular will or sought to cater for the tastes and expectations of the average citizen, but in the sense that it tried to bring within the reach of all those cultural goods which had previously been available only to the privileged. (p. 158)

Democratic access in the Israeli case may have been even more difficult than in Britain. In Britain, broadcasters have failed to take into account the differences in cultural resources of the various classes (Cardiff and Scannell, 1987), whereas in the Israeli case one had to consider not only class and education, but a much wider cultural diversity, including various degrees of the mastery of Hebrew, and of the distance from the European cultural heritage that had been incorporated into Israeli culture. Israel's image as a self-evident Western-style democracy notwithstanding ("the only democracy in the Middle East"), it is a country in which the majority of the population consists of first-, second- or third-generation refugee immigrants from Asia and Africa, who had had to rebuild their lives and learn a new language at the same time as they were expected to start appreciating Mozart.

Regardless of how hegemonic, or overambitious, this may seem to us, the goal of providing access to cultural goods seemed unquestioningly important at the time. What today's scholars have lost in our postmodern, multicultural postmillennium times, is the conviction (or the courage) that allows for determining that certain cultural goods are inherently enriching and should be accessible to all members of society. The relativism, which, as Curran (1998) argued, has been reinforced by the academic development of the field of cultural studies, has paralyzed our capacity to judge, inadvertently serving commercial media by making it difficult to call for the improvement of quality.

GIVING VOICE TO DIFFERENT CULTURES DOES NOT NECESSARILY ENHANCE A PLURALISTIC DIALOG

Beyond the various ways of interpreting "democratic participation," there is the third issue, of whether participation necessarily means *democratic* participation. The interpretation according to which a plurality of voices means the creation of dialogue, is based on the understanding that these voices accept the rules of the game, and are interested in listening to others and in contributing to the common culture. Hallin's interpretation does not take into account the possibility that some groups may appear on national TV with their own agenda, not necessarily in order to put in their own voice into the dialogue. One has to consider that certain cultures appear in the national arena with the aim of missionizing for their own brands of particularism—fundamentalist religion, for example. Appearing on the national scene helps such groups to reinforce their own group's legitimacy in the eyes of their members and of potential joiners whom they attempt to recruit.

Thus, "giving voice" to peripheral social groups does not always fulfill the expectation that these groups begin to listen to each other. This may be better understood by expanding Katz's scheme (cited in Gross, 1998), in which minority groups can either speak *for* themselves (e.g., Ultra-Orthodox rabbis in an Ultra-Orthodox synagogue), *of* themselves (about the content of the weekly Biblical sequence), or *by* themselves (the preaching rabbi belongs to the community). They may also present themselves *to* the rest of the society (*of* the minority, or *by* the minority *to* the rest of the society), in order to promote better understanding toward their group and to contribute elements of their culture *for* the general reservoir. The possibility not covered in this scheme is a minority that speaks *to* the majority in order to exploit it *for* that minority's interests. In this case, participation becomes a struggle over the principles of the mutual tolerance that strives for and makes multicultural coexistence possible, leading to a culture war rather than dialogue. Such interaction may only lead to the splitting of the audience into opponents and possible new recruits.

In a society based on a large enough majority, which supports democratic principles, giving voice to absolutist groups may not constitute a risk to society as a whole. Israel, however, is in a paradoxical situation, in which separatist cultures are battling against the Western-style secular democracy, sloganizing about fighting the ruling elite when that elite has already lost its political power and is fast becoming a (numerical) minority. This creates a scramble among the fundamentalist religious militant groups advocating the scrapping of the principles of equality and democracy, and the individualist, therefore less organized Israelis, who lack the challengers' zeal. In view of Israel's changing demography, this contest may end with the disappearance of pluralist society. This brings us back to the well-known dilemma of the difficulty democratic societies have in defending themselves against anti-democratic rhetoric, which is risky even in societies that are better established than Israel, with a long-standing tradition of internalized democratic values. This is the dark side of "participation," which serves as a reminder against seeing it only in glowing but oversimplified terms, as the road to enhancing pluralism.

Having pointed out the problematics inherent in the expectation that "national integration" can be maintained (in an improved, less hegemonic manner), while bringing in the "participation of multiple voices," I propose to demonstrate this point in greater detail by looking at Israeli society and media in the era of monopoly radio, the era of TV monopoly, and the era of the multiple commercial channels.

RADIO DAYS

As a child in Jerusalem in the 1950s, I spent hours listening to sounds coming out of our radio, a massive piece of furniture imported from Germany, which occupied the center of the living room (Hartley and O'Regan, 1992). An avid listener to "The Children's Corner," I became acquainted with British miners, children in pre-revolutionary Russia, slaves and masters in the American South, and young local heroes who helped to throw the British out, played host to disheveled, displaced, orphan refugees from Europe, and unraveled ancient treasures in Palestine's countryside. I remember my attentiveness when the voice of Moshe Hovav—the grim announcer assigned to rituals and major crises—was heard reading the news. I can still recall the tears in father's eyes when Adolf Eichman's arrest was announced, the panic aroused by PM Eshkol who sounded too "hesitant" during the anxious days before the Six Day War, Israel's most brilliant war, and the last in which radio alone had been in charge of "us" civilians. And although I missed the live broadcast of the voting in the UN General Assembly on November 29, 1947 on the division of Palestine between the Jews and the Arabs— the most poignant media event in the state's history—I have listened to that poor, quaking recording many times since.

Hebrew radio was established a decade before the state, under British Mandatory Rule, and regarded by the Zionists as a vehicle for rallying the community around the revolutionary goal of self-rule. As *Kol Yisrael*, it continued to perform, single-handedly, for the next 20 years (1948 to 1968), the important national missions of creating common ground for the new state: introducing the disparate groups to a new language, shaping the form and content of the society's High Holidays and its everyday life, and providing the common agenda. *Kol Yisrael* kept the public informed and preserved public morale in times of crisis, made Hebrew into the common operative language and invented and cultivated a common "Israeli culture"—injecting new content into traditional Jewish holidays, shaping the new "civil" holidays (notably the Day of Independence), incorporating everyone in "great historical moments." Radio was the arbitrator of taste, picking out the songs that would become popular nationwide. The radio network, commissioned and produced music, formed and reinforced the nation's collective memory and its national myths, and looked after the waves of immigrants—the Russian and Ethiopian waves are the most recent—by speaking to them in their own languages, as well as teaching them Hebrew, so that they could be incorporated in the general broadcasts. With the arrival of television (at the beginning of the 1970s), radio had to adjust to the loss of its monopoly status as the society's center stage for collective ritual, building on its technological advantages of immediacy, accessibility and interactivity to address listeners individually and intimately. Nevertheless, it still maintained its prioritized place at times of war and lesser crises.

Reporting From the Field and Keeping Up the Nation's Morale in Times of War. Called "The Voice of Jerusalem," the name came as a compromise between the British suggestion of "The Broadcasting Service of Palestine" and that of the Jewish leadership's—"The Broadcasting Service of the Land of Israel" (Caspi and Limor, 1992). (Ironically, in 2000 Palestinians were broadcasting on "Radio Palestine"; Israeli media refer to the Palestinian territory as "The Palestinian Authority"). The service received its highest ratings during World War II, in the 15-minute weekly commentary on the international situation, aimed at sustaining the morale of the Jewish population and its Jewish-"Palestinian" soldiers serving in the British army, who, in 1942, watched the Nazi army's arrival in Alexandria. This role of military interpreter (something between a government propagandist and an independent commentator) became an important wartime institution. During the Six Day War, and even more crucially during the tense eve-of-war period, Israelis rallied round the daily radio commentaries by (Ret.) General Haim Herzog, later Israel's president.

Radio's essential role in wartime has been sustained during the entire period of Israel's existence, even after the introduction of television has deprived it of most of its ceremonial and integrative functions. Its accessibility and immediacy, both for reporting from where the action is and for being heard everywhere (by people at work, in cars, etc.), and the freedom of movement provided by transistors, ensured its continuing centrality in times of crisis. During wartime (the Yom Kippur war, the Gulf War), the country's radio channels (*Kol Yisrael* and *Galey Zahal* ["IDF Waves"–the Army Radio]) are united into one channel, both for symbolic reasons and in order to maximize the potential of professional reporting. Although at such times (as in lesser security crises), reporters are torn between their roles as citizens and as professionals, reporting has generally proved credible (Liebes, 1997). Wartime radio also carries out sidelines jobs, such as interactive advice programs, soldiers' recorded messages to their families, and even nighttime " silent broadcasts" for sleeping citizens, invented during the Gulf War for the purpose of broadcasting the alarm signal and siren sound in missile attacks. In war, radio is the most authoritative medium, that is, what in peacetime we would term *hegemonic*.

Wrongly Imagining the Audience, and Self-Consciously Inventing "Israeli Culture." In its first years, the radio was engaged full time with updating and defining canonic Hebrew, inventing and cultivating "Israeli culture," and simultaneously integrating new immigrants into that language and culture. Radio's way of turning immigrants into Israelis had been established during the first years of independence, when the new state received more than twice the number of its original inhabitants. As mentioned earlier, the new immigrants were Jewish refugees from Morocco, Yemen, or Iraq, who came after the 1948 war, when their home countries were no longer safe for them. In temporary makeshift housing in Israel, they joined displaced, homeless Jews from eastern Europe, who had inhabited Nazi concentration camps and had no place to go. The project of integrating these people into a society that had yet to find its own footing, was a formidable one indeed, and, in retrospect, may have been doomed from the start.

A look at the program scheduled for one weekday in the 1950s illustrates the radio's hierarchical organization of the widely disparate national, religious, ethnic and cultural groups living in Israel's 20,000 square kilometers. *Kol Yisrael* was now broadcasting on two channels—one nationwide channel and another devoted to programs for immigrant groups, by them, and about them, in their own languages. This channel broadcast in French (suggestions of sites to visit, a weekly play, news), Yiddish (political commentary, seeking displaced relatives, "Postbox"—answering listeners' letters, news), Rumanian (news, greetings from Israel abroad), Hungarian (news, greetings), Espaniol ("With Our Editor"—talking to listeners, "In the Workplace," news), Polish (news), Mugrabi ("The Government in Israel"—political commentary, news), and news in English. The same channel also featured Hebrew lessons and a daily "News in Easy Hebrew" program, offering a first step for the immigrant groups to enter the larger society. In terms of our earlier definition, this program was broadcast *for* the minority, *by* the majority, *of* the majority. An extended program in Arabic, and a program of church music entitled "a Special Program for the Christian

Communities," acknowledged the legitimacy of separate communities which are not destined as targets for incorporation, but are recognized as deserving nurturing in their own separate languages and cultures.

The main channel, mostly addressed to mainstream society, opened at 6:30 a.m. with a liturgical singing of psalms, blessing the "Tents of Israel," and ended at 11 p.m. with the Zionist national anthem (its unrevised lyrics still expressing religious longings from the Diaspora), demonstrating how religious rhetoric is deeply ingrained in modern day secular Israel, entwining the two in a way which would be impossible to disentangle (Kimmerling, 1998). As the expression of the desired "Israeli-ness," and a (self) conscious effort to socialize to this culture, the radio offered instruction in "everyday Hebrew," talks about local heroes, teaching of Hebrew songs (entitled "Sing a New Song"), requests for Hebrew songs, "visiting" various sites and settlements, and a prominent time slot for children and youth programs.

As part of the overall mosaic of very short programs (many lasting only 5 or 10 minutes), within the effort to create a common mainstream language and culture, the radio's main channel also provided programs such as "Oriental Music" (sometimes in the form of "Listeners' Requests"), readings from the Bible, and cantorial singing. Such programs gave voice to what was perceived as minority cultures, acting as windows for "minority" cultures to present themselves to majority listeners (*of* and *by* the minority, *for* the majority). But the bulk of broadcasting on prime time, and on prestigious days such as Saturdays and holidays, featured classical music (with an effort to incorporate Israeli composers, especially on holidays), radio drama and literary programs (featuring writers and academics who occasionally also discussed Russian or French writers).

A look at the schedule thus supports the argument that there was a strong sense of hierarchy of cultural expressions to which radio has attempted to provide equal access. Even so, programs such as "Oriental Music," or a "Program for the Yemenite Immigrants" demonstrated that broadcasters were not only "integrating" mindless masses into a united whole, but were performing a duty to give voice to the "ethnic" cultures of different groups, seeing these as contributing to a ("pluralistic") social dialogue. Indeed, the stars of "Israeli" songs were Yemenite singers, whose music often expressed the (misguided?) attempt of east European composers to create "oriental" music, in a style that was thought to befit the mosaic of the new country.

Being There When History is in the Making. Preceding television in performing secular and religious holidays, and in transporting listeners and viewers to the heart of major ceremonial events, radio's greatest days will be remembered as the bringing home, live, of the two constitutive events in the birth of the state. The first was the live transmission of the voting in the UN General Assembly (on November 29, 1947) on the division of Palestine into Jewish and Arab states. Captured on newsreel film, at the receiving end, the long-awaited moment is evident in the tense faces of future Israelis, glued to their radio sets, marking down each "yes" and "no" vote, and, at long last, hugging and kissing each other, tears shining in their eyes, when the decision was announced. The second major historical occasion in which Israelis participated in real time thanks to radio, was the Assembly of the leadership of the Jewish community in Palestine, in which David Ben Gurion, Israel's first prime minister, announced the establishment of the state.

During Israel's first 20 years, while television was kept out of bounds, the military parade starred as the high point of the annual Independence celebrations. Ironically, just as the right medium for showing off the state's prowess had finally arrived, military parades went out of vogue, and were considered vulgar at best. The first broadcast of the new television, a few months before it went regularly on the air, was a live broadcast of Israel's last military parade, following the 1967 war. Independence Day celebrations then moved into the outdoors, and later still, into the home, and to the substitutions offered by television (Katz, 1998). During the early collectivistic years, it was radio alone that brought the military parade to Israelis who could not be there, making them see the tanks rolling by, and the airplanes demonstrating their acrobatics.

Of the four functions of media in holidays proposed by Katz (1998), Independence Day radio may be said to have supplied the *phatic* function, of transporting listeners into the experience (perhaps even creating a more powerful experience by invoking the imagination, and, perhaps, by causing listeners to participate more actively than if they had watched the parade on TV). Radio also *complemented* the holiday, embellishing it with documentaries, specially written radio dramas, and the singing of Israeli choirs. The radio did not attempt to *substitute* for the event, however. This was not even an option in those early days, when people still felt they wanted to share their enthusiasm in person, enough to mingle and dance in the streets on the eve of the holiday, and fight for a vantage point to view the parade under the scorching Israeli sun. Dusty, sometimes awkward, it was the real thing.

ENTER PUBLIC TELEVISION

Late for the Right Reasons? Television took over radio's collectivistic role only in 1968. It made its entrance, as its first director tells us, through the back door, and for all the wrong reasons (Katz,

1971). What was it, then, that made Israeli leadership reject television for 20 years, and what has made it change its mind in haste? The bona fide ideological objections of the political leadership to television, according to Katz, were that it would subvert the effort to renew Hebrew culture, undermine reading, and Americanize and secularize society (as argued by religious politicians). There was also fear of the personalization of politics. For 20 years the arguments for television, which pointed to its usefulness for nation building and integration, had not been strong enough to overcome these objections.

What finally tilted the balance in favor of TV, as in the case of radio, was what the political establishment regarded as immediate security needs. In the wake of the Six Day War, the Israeli government, apprehensive about leaving the Palestinians exposed only to Arab TV from neighboring countries, introduced TV in order to safeguard its newly acquired domination. (Ironically, a similar rationale—i.e., safeguarding their rule by venting steam off the Jewish community—has led the British to allow the Zionist leadership to establish "The Voice of Jerusalem").

Defining the Role of Public Television in Enhancing Integration and Multiculturalism. Like radio, then, television broadcasting was introduced for political reasons, but quite opposite to those of radio. While radio has come into being as the voice of a revolutionary movement, television in its early days had embodied the naive hope of heading off a revolutionary movement (in the Occupied Territories). But realism prevailed, and by the time regular broadcasting began (in 1968), the pretense of broadcasting to the Territories had been dropped, and television took its place alongside radio under the aegis of a new (1965) PBA, mandated by law. The law clearly illustrates the legislators' belief in the power of the media, as well as in the reconcilability of the values of "national integration" and "multiculturalism." Accordingly, public media were expected to perform the improbable feat of reflecting "the life of the state, its struggle, its creation, and its achievements"; cultivating good citizenship, strengthening ties with the Jewish heritage, reflecting the lives and cultural properties of all the "nation's tribes [sic!] from the various countries." It was also expected to broaden knowledge, reflect the lives of Diaspora Jews, advance Israeli and Hebrew culture, broadcast in Arabic "for the Arabic-speaking population, and for the advancement of peace with the neighboring countries," broadcast to Jews abroad, provide space for the different opinions and perspectives in the public, and broadcast credible information. Notice that religion is framed here in terms of "Jewish heritage" and "values," indicating that religion was entirely discarded, nor considered a threat to the liberal, pluralistic values postulated by this ambitious law.

The hierarchical order implicit in the serial mention of Jewish religion, "tribal" culture, and Arab culture is striking. First, broadcasting should act to "strengthen ties" with the Jewish heritage, meaning that it should urge the incorporation of traditional religious values by the Zionist majority. Next, it should "reflect" the cultures of "all the nation's tribes" in order to provide recognition and status to the minorities in the larger society. Israeli Arabs, lowest on this list, are spoken to in their own language, but lawmakers have not included their culture among the cultures of "the tribes" that should be reflected by the broadcasts, either for the benefit of the society at large or for the enhancement of the minority's status.

The high expectations created by television, and its salience in the public eye, made for harsher criticism and bitter controversy. Radio, which had preceded the state, was there from the start, and seemed less threatening, but television has never been taken for granted. The debate it had generated twenty years before its actual establishment, has continued throughout the years of its operation. TV was, and continues to be, attacked politically for towing the government line; its reporters were, and still are, attacked for being a "leftist mafia"; it was, and is still, attacked for giving voice only to western music and culture, or for not giving enough space for Jewish tradition. Also, there was, and still is, a constant debate about the advantages and disadvantages of having more TV channels. Incidentally, radio has benefited from the fact that television was drawing all the fire, and could be freer to explore more subversive avenues without serious repercussions.

Why did television become the focus of such bitter debates? First of all, because of its magical power of transporting viewers to other places, and of making them intimate with real and fictional characters, as if they were together in the same room (McLuhan should have labeled television as emotionally sweeping and "hot," rather than cognitive and "cold").

Second, by the time television arrived in Israel, everybody—from majoritarian politicians to religious and cultural minority groups—was much more sophisticated about its social centrality and the ways in which it could be used. Thus it immediately became the focus of culture wars. One example is the battle over broadcasting on the Sabbath, which was begun over the protests of the religious parties; it was finally decided by a private citizen's appeal to the Supreme Court, and considered a victory for the secular majority. Another example is the protest of singers of "oriental" music (in the beginning of the 1970s) against their alleged discrimination on TV's hit parade, and the accusations that producers exercised "racist discrimination" against them. These indications, that cultural groups were considering themselves outside the general cultural space, seemed peripheral at the time. For most people, however,

TV did provide a common ground for meeting, in the sense that viewing was accompanied by the knowledge that most other Israelis were also viewing. TV's power to unite was particularly evident on ritual ceremonial occasions, and, daily, on the evening ritual of watching the news.

Gathering Israelis Around the "Campfire." The symbol of the power of public TV (The First Channel) to integrate the nation has been the prime-time evening newscast (Williams, 1974), with 70% of Israelis regularly tuning in. Israelis did not telephone one another during the news, and viewing was perceived as obligatory in the sense that it was a precondition for joining the conversation the next day. Nevertheless, although television provided a shared agenda for discussion, it did not influence the public's political attitudes, which, from the 1977 election onward, have remained split down the middle into "hawks" and "doves" concerning the Arab-Israeli conflict (Liebes, 1997).

The centrality of the news (and perhaps of other prime-time current affair programs) is evident also in a study (Katz, Gurevitch, & Haas, 1997) that found that in the beginning of the 1990s, Israelis still regarded TV as a medium that served their needs to be informed on current affairs rather than as a medium for entertainment. Radio, with its qualities of immediacy and accessibility, continued to fulfill the collective needs in times of war, by mobilizing reserve units, reporting from the front, instructing the civilian population, keeping up morale, and fighting off rumors. War (the Six Day War) has brought about the establishment of a popular "open channel," carrying unprogrammed chat and music, always ready to be interrupted by breaking news. In between wars, radio's fall from dominance in the era of television has brought about its segmentation to a number of channels, cashing in on its qualities of intimacy, informality, and interactivity.

Mobilizing National and Group Identity in Opposition to Dallas. Paradoxically, during the era of the single channel monopoly, national integration could also be conducted around the viewing of programs such as *Dallas* (Liebes and Katz, 1993). Despite the fact that prime-time drama was mostly American, viewing was collective, in two senses: in the viewers' awareness that everybody else was also watching, and in the social and interactive family viewing, which took place mostly around the one TV set. Sue Ellen's morals thus became a nationwide topic for debate, discussed as heatedly as the pros and cons of retreating from the occupied Palestinian territories. *Dallas* served as a site for debating one's values vis-à-vis those of the series' characters, or, with more sophisticated viewers, vis-à-vis those of its producers. As a study of the decoding of *Dallas* within different cultural communities demonstrates, certain ethnic groups had early defined their identity in particularistic terms; more in terms of these groups' religion and/or ethnicity, than in terms of individual or overall national identity. Thus, although the news integrated the nation (against the rest of the world), *Dallas* and similar "provocations" may have contributed to the integration of the specific identity of traditional and religious groups, distinguishing them not only from the capitalist, materialist Americans onscreen, but, more significantly, from the Western, nontraditional rest of Israeli society that regarded them as role models.

Bringing Israelis to Participate in History-Making Moments. The most emotionally uplifting moments in which viewers felt at one with the collective entity, have been media events, when TV has brought history-making into the home (Dayan and Katz, 1993). Except for events such as the Entebbe rescue and Sharansky's landing in Israel, and some minor events such as winning international soccer matches or the Eurovision song contest, almost all of these media events had been highlights in the otherwise grim narrative of the Arab–Israeli conflict. The emblematic event was the Egyptian president's visit to Jerusalem, to enact the public phase of Israel's peace negotiations with Egypt. This was the case which triggered Dayan and Katz's insight, according to which leaders who are seeking change may use the power of television to appeal directly to the people over the heads of parliaments and political establishments, circumventing the mediating institutions, both on one's own side and on the other. Sensing Israelis' longing for peace, Anwar Sadat had done just that, giving television its greatest moment. Other moments were less perfect (Liebes and Katz, 1993). The signing of the peace treaty with Jordan's King Hussein was less dramatic (since there was already a de facto agreement in place); the signing of the Oslo accords had been more ambivalent on the sides of both leaders; Rabin's funeral was much more painful. Yet these, too, were moments in which television has turned Israeli citizens into participants, witnesses, sometimes judges, of major events in the country's history.

Television has also invented its own ritual events, notably, election night celebration, starting with the "television's polls" predicting the outcome and staying on to prove that they were correct (once the real results start pouring in); the prime ministerial debates, in which viewers play judges; and marathonic campaigns for good causes. All these are but Israeli versions of what television does elsewhere.

Transfixing Israelis in TV-Declared Disaster Marathons. Another unpremeditated, live genre, which may have displaced the ceremonial events of the 1980s, brings everybody to the set for breaking news. "Disaster marathons" have become TV's standard format for reporting national traumas during the 1990s, a time in which the First Channel had lost its monopoly to a second, competing commercial channel (Channel Two), and to cable and satellite broadcasts. Live marathons grip the country during or in the wake of a major news event, mostly following terrorist attacks, but also after the assassination of PM Rabin, and throughout the one-day mini-war with the Palestinians following the opening of a tunnel in Jerusalem. On these occasions, television interrupts its schedule, clearing the screen for a disaster marathon that continues long beyond its newsworthiness wanes. This seemingly integrating broadcast may develop into a disruptive rather than uniting event, because of television's need to respond to public feelings by mounting a neo-populist production. At such moments, the public returns to the nationwide channels, and television is looking for scapegoats on whom to put the blame, adopting simplified positions, losing the political context while infuriating large sections of the population (Liebes, 1998). This giving in to a populist public mood has less to do with journalistic considerations, or with the political convictions of editors, and more with the new capacities of the technology coupled with the demands of cutthroat commercial competition, which affect public broadcasting as well.

The Era of Multiple TV Channels. Monopoly public TV exploded at the beginning of the 1990s into a multiplicity of channels—with a second over-the-air channel, financed by advertising but supervised by a separate public council, and a variety of cable channels (specializing in sports, children, music, films, etc.). TV's emphasis on news and current affairs now shifted to more light entertainment. Talk shows, which replaced news as the main prime-time public space (Liebes, 1999), were fast sinking into sensations, scandals, celebrities, and provocations. At the end of the 1990s, these programs dropped all pretenses to discuss public issues. The formula for the selection of participants for these programs in 1998 was a celebrity, a singer, a comic, and pretty girls and boys ("hormones," as they are called by one production team). Ironically, the addition of a rival news program brought down the overall viewership of news on both channels to less than its level when there was only one channel, ending the era when Israelis felt "obliged" to view the news. A new law of "open skies" opened Israel to hundreds more channels, completing the transformation of TV from a medium that had involved Israelis in the political and social agenda, into a video shop of indistinguishable, cheap diversions, each seeking a maximum number of viewers.

THE DECOLLECTIVIZATION OF ISRAELI SOCIETY: CAN TELEVISION BE BLAMED?

Two major trends within Israeli society gradually became apparent in the last two decades. In the 1990s, they were at work transforming Israeli society by leading away from a sense of commitment to the polity in two opposite directions. One was the move, within secular mainstream Israelis, away from collectivism, toward individualism. The other was the move of religious and immigrant cultures in Israel toward separatism or, in some cases, to an attempt to actively substitute for the hegemonic culture. Television could not be the cause of these trends, of course, but the dynamics of its interacting with various groups in the society seems to have contributed to these trends in more than one sense.

Television and Individualism. The shift in values of mainstream Israeli society from mainly collectivist norms to individualist pursuits is expressed by the new legitimacy granted to hedonistic concerns, engaged more with the present and less with the future, and more with worrying about oneself than about the society and the nation. Katz et al. (1997) argued that the First Channel, in its monopolistic era, slowed down this process by providing a shared agenda to the whole of the society. On a deeper level, however, a number of less obvious aspects of the message (the patriotism, the existential tension of living under the constant threat of war), and of the medium (splitting the audience, personalizing the issues) may have backfired, and worked in the opposite direction (Avraham and First, 2003).

Nor can one ignore the impact of television on the undermining of traditional political institutions (parties, meetings in the town square), disintermediating them, as it were, by bringing the political leaders directly into the viewers' living room. Although this new type of public involvement does give access to weaker groups, it contributes to the political passivization of the public (Lazarsfeld and Merton, 1948) in the sense that political involvement remains confined to the living room, never feeding into the public sphere outside. Eventually, this may create a feeling of inefficacy and indifference, and reinforce individualism. Television's widely noted effect on the personalization of politics has contributed to the revision of the election law, under which the prime minister is elected personally (see chap. 6) and pushed both candidates to the middle of the political spectrum instead of stressing their ideological differences (Liebes and Peri, 1998). The fears of the medium harbored by the first generation of the political leadership thus proved right in the long run. The combination of media technology advances and their economic potential proved strong enough to overcome the initial political intentions of its founders.

In the political climate of the 1990s, the new reality of segmented, entertainment-oriented media was in line with the political designs of a right-wing government intent on preventing a serious political debate, by providing Israelis with the voyeuristic, visceral pleasures of choosing between *The Ricki Lake Show* and *Take off Your Bikini* (a highly popular Italian program). To complete this mission, PM Netanyahu, in his capacity of minister of communication, neutralized the First Channel by appointing a director general who hastened to announce that the pubic was tired of politics, and proceeded to act accordingly. Concurrently, the process of marginalizing the public role of media continued through the creation of yet another over-the-air channel to compete with the existing franchisers that make up the nationwide commercial channel (Channel Two), so that they would no longer be able to afford the fair number of still existing quality programs, including a fine news program, and a number of original drama and documentary series.

Television and Separate Cultures. The second trend away from national integration, which developed into a real threat to the hegemony of "Israeli-ness" in the 1990s, was the rise of a number of countercultures, mentioned earlier, which are actively working toward changing the state's dominant culture. Strengthened by the decollectivization of the general public, these groups construct their identity vis-à-vis the rest of society, some even mobilizing for the struggle of taking it over.

The gradual empowerment of these groups is a result of a number of causes (Kimmerling, 1998):

1. The inherent difficulty of Zionist nationalism to separate between religion and nation, so that most of the national slogans and symbols are drawn, selectively, from the reservoir of Jewish religion.
2. The unselective mass immigration, mostly from Asia and Africa, in the early 1950s, which had not gone through the process of secularization.
3. The opportunity presented by the Six Day War to the national-religious movement for territorial annexation of the original Land of Israel, as a basis for the creation of a new community according to Halachic Law.

4. The acknowledged autonomy of the Israeli Arab community and the new wave of mass immigration from the former Soviet Union in the 1990s, who, regardless of their instrumental adaptation to the country, came to view themselves as "Israeli persons" who nevertheless hold separate cultural and emotional identities. These societies lead a separate existence in terms of habitation, lifestyles, language, and so on, and are supported by institutional and sociopolitical systems of their own (such as schools, synagogues, religious, and civil beliefs).

How do media enter into the process of empowerment undergone by these groups? First, the technological revolution that made media accessible (first audio and videocassettes, then radio, then time-sharing on satellite TV), could be exploited for integrating separatist communities and enticing new followers. The most striking example of media use for such goals is that of the Ultra-Orthodox-Oriental Shas culture. Quick to realize the effectiveness of electronic media and its compatibility with this group's oral tradition, Shas started out with the distribution of audio cassettes of sermons by populist rabbis, went on to establish the movement's own interactive radio channels, and is currently transmitting special satellite broadcasts of the weekly Biblical commentary by their spiritual leader to packed halls of believers.

The use of particularistic, mostly pirate media channels for recruitment and internal cohesion does not mean that these groups shun nationwide television. Prime-time talk shows have made the representatives of these groups popular, first as curiosities, for their shock value, and later—with the incorporation of the Shas party, the Ultra-Orthodox and the Russian immigrant party into the new political power elite of right-wing coalition government—for the real threat that they represent. From their perspective, these groups are taking advantage of nationwide TV for their needs. All of them, including the Ultra-Orthodox who prohibit TV viewing altogether, appear in advertising spots during election periods. The political leaders of all of these groups regularly give interviews on nationwide television and participate in talk shows, yet usually make no concession in the direction of acknowledging universalistic norms in an attempt to be liked by the rest of the society. They are there for gaining political power by reinforcing their status within their own group, and among its sympathizers, soliciting additional followers. Thus, for example, Ultra-Orthodox politicians make their mark by announcing on nationwide TV that they are not Zionist, that "secular" means "sick," and that their Talmud-studying sons, exempt from the military service all non-Ultra-Orthodox men are obliged to do, are serving the country by studying ("killed in the tents of the Torah"), not by serving in the (compulsory) military.

Could the rise of separatism have been brought to public attention earlier? Did public TV miss the warning signs? Has it failed in the job of reinforcing national integration by failing to give voice to peripheral groups, and thus in bringing them to the attention of the political establishment? Alternately, did TV contribute to the postponement of the society's gradual disintegration? Or, perhaps, did it have an indirect effect of undermining the existing political parties, leaving groups that felt disempowered no other recourse but to start their own separate political institutions? Or are these forces far stronger than anything the political leadership or electronic journalism could be held responsible for? In examining the workings of public television, we may only speculate on what could have gone amiss.

REPRISE: MEDIA'S ROLE IN ISRAEL'S EVOLUTION FROM NATIONAL INTEGRATION TO SEPARATIST CULTURES

In examining the role played by Israeli media with regard to national integration and pluralism, I proposed that Israel's 50-year history divides roughly into three periods, each characterized by its dominant media: National Radio in the first two decades; public television in the next two decades; on which the 1990s have superimposed an array of multiple, mostly transnational TV channels, plus a parallel system of various versions of religious separatist pirate radio.

My main claims are as follow:

1. During the first two decades of Israel's history, National Radio was in charge of the crucial (and, in hindsight, probably impossible) task of "national integration," whereas the political debate was carried out in the mostly ideological, partisan press.
2. Albeit hegemonic, radio has conceived its mission as creating a common ground—on both instrumental and ideological levels—for the different ethnic, religious, cultural and ideological groups, mostly newcomer refugees from Europe and North Africa, culturally shaken by the transition, for many of whom the language was incomprehensible, and idea of democracy new.
3. Radio was the central agent for developing and diffusing a shared "Israeli culture"—based on a Western-style democratic, secular ethos. It was in charge of updating the Hebrew language, defining its "canonic" pronunciation, diffusing existing and new "Hebrew songs." It molded the observance of national (and even traditional) holidays, with contemporary heroes and national myths, drawing on symbols taken from Biblical texts and religious traditions.

4. "National integration," in the first years, mainly offered the diverse cultural groups with access to an odd mixture of the developing "Israeli culture," blending together the riches of Western culture (mainly classical music, world literature, and drama) with daily scheduling of liturgical singing, Bible reading, and commentary, as excerpts of Jewish religion, conceptualized as "heritage."
5. In addition to providing broadcasts (on a separate channel) for immigrant groups who had not yet mastered the language, radio also made room on the main channel for "ethnic" music and culture. Although intended for the minorities themselves, these slots also gave status to minority cultures and exhibited them to the rest of society (with the idea that mutual acquaintance would eventually breed mutual recognition and respect).
6. On an instrumental level, radio undertook varied missions such as daily morning physical exercise instruction, a lunchtime program for housewives, tips for farmers, daily press overview, and, in the 1950s, a "relatives search" for family members lost in the Holocaust.
7. Radio brought Israelis into the state's great historical moments, and into national ceremonial events, notably the military parades that marked Israel's independence in its first two decades.
8. In times of war, radio was there to report from the front, combat rumors, raise national morale, and tell civilians what measures to take.

During its monopoly era, public TV displaced radio's role in national integration, albeit in a different form:

1. Although radio has delineated the daily routine and performed an enormous variety of tasks, TV was originally limited to evening broadcasts. Relying on the by now multichannel radio network (broadcasting all day and quick to get to where the action was), TV did what it could do best, leaving the radio to take center stage in wartime, interacting with its listeners and providing different channels to cater to (mostly musical) multicultural tastes.
2. With TV, the focus of national integration shifted to the shared agenda of the daily evening news, which, during the single channel era, had operated as a "tribal campfire," with most of the country tuning in.

3. Television also took over the performance of traditional and national holidays—in transmitting and supplementing ritual events, inventing its own traditions, often encouraging private, less interactive, modes of celebration by moving Israelis into the home.
4. Ironically, TV's form of cultural integration was limited to gathering Israelis to view mostly American programs. Because these programs had been watched within the family, and (simultaneously) by most Israelis, they soon became an important site of struggle over the definition of Israeli-ness. Local drama was missing from the screen, partly because all production efforts went into the unsurpassable drama of the news.
5. TV did "write the history" of Zionism and of the state of Israel onscreen, in two series which gave rise to bitter political-cultural debates, uncovering the internal rifts.
6. With the technological facilitation of live broadcasts, TV embraced the new task of performing national crises, alongside preplanned ceremonial events, thus introducing the genre of marathonic broadcasting (in times of terrorist attacks, the Gulf War, the Rabin assassination). Such events may also become the focus for unity, but equally often they seem to reveal and egg-on irreconcilable internal conflicts.
7. In terms of its impact on political involvement, TV undermined political parties by virtually bringing political leaders into the living room. What looked like providing access to politics, especially for weaker groups, also meant that political involvement began and remained in the private sphere of the home.
8. The ensuing passivization of the public has been exacerbated by the de-ideologization and personalization of politics, in itself the product of television.

In the 1990s, when monopoly gave way to a multiplicity of mostly global channels, the national integrative function eroded and the extent of news viewing declined dramatically. Viewers zapped between channels just as they would roam in a video store (Katz, 1996). At the same time, the internal integration of separatist groups (for some of whom TV is religiously prohibited) and their reaching out for larger audiences was reinforced. These ethnic-religious cultures appealed to publics who were increasingly diverted from the general media into their own segmented radio and TV channels. These channels (many of them illegal) were emerging as the new media of subgroup integration, reinforcing particularistic identities.

Having revealed the end of the story at the beginning, I can only reiterate my admittedly subjective perception that either "national integration" and/or a "pluralist " society in Israel, have not lasted "forever," or, worse, have always been an illusion. Looked at from the perspective of the interaction between a society and its media, it may be that the superimposition of the media and their institutional forms over the corresponding social and cultural forces in each phase of the state's development, has accelerated the processes of what at first looked like successful "national integration," and later, in a matter of a few years, burst at the seams. Radio may be the most dramatic accelerator, both in the stage of the establishment of cohesion, and in the current fragmentation of Israeli society into disparate groups.

In the overall context of the Americanization of Israeli culture, broadcasting should be seen as one link in a chain of mutually influential social institutions. Thus, for example, the disintermediation of the political institutions by TV, brought about the Americanization of politics, which, in turn, gave rise to the establishment of primary elections within political parties, and to the revision of the election law. These legal changes in turn exacerbated the personalization of politics, making the patchwork of an American model superimposed on a multipartisan system unpredictably unstable, for no fault of the original.

Another example of the damage caused by transplanting a system from one society to another was the multichannel revolution of the 1990s, which, combined with a conservative government not interested in public debate (and criticism), caused the marginalization of public broadcasting that formerly provided a common space for the political debate. The weakening of public broadcasting pulled the carpet from under a channel that (theoretically at least) had, as part of its mandate, a commitment for nurturing Israeli culture by supporting local productions.

Chapter 3 traces the process of the vendetta against the First Channel, which adopted publicly committed Western journalism, with an independent spirit, but was saddled by the original sin of the Broadcast Law that keeps the appointment of its director general in the hands of the government. The case analyzed in chapter 3 demonstrates the commitment of public broadcasting to the public interest, and the crucial need for preserving a public channel (and for amending the law to insure its independence). If Americanization means that market economy is the sole regulator of broadcasting (with PBS playing in the margins), then Israel is not ready for it yet, as this model discards the public functions of broadcasting, still crucial in Israeli society.

3

Failing Finger in the Dike: The Vulnerability of Public Broadcasting

Looking back from the vantage point of the year 2002, the idea of financing broadcasting by a license fee still seems sound, even brilliant. From the point of view of public interest, nobody has yet come up with a better solution for the establishment of nationwide electronic media committed solely to the citizenry, and liberated from both the constraints of ratings and the dependence on government.

That said, it should be noted that, particularly in a multichannel media environment, this model poses major problems. One such problem arises from the ambiguity inherent in the definition of *public interest.* Who knows, and who is to determine, what are the needs, or interests, of the public? What criteria apply to issues such as how to define *quality*? How to allocate space to various "voices" in the society, various broadcast genres, and so on?

Moreover, assuming all this is agreed on, up pops the next problem of how to deal with the likely discrepancy between what has been prescribed for the public interest and the actual preferences of members of the audience at any given time. Obviously, the predefined needs of the "public," based as they are on an idea of a collective entity, have little to do with the individual manifestations of this generalized client in the form of particular audiences, at specific moments, with individualized needs (as well as collective ones). True, the underlying assumption of public broadcasting is that broadcasters are professionals, trained to serve the public good, and therefore know better than their clients—"the public"—what is good for them (Katz, 1989). But who is the client? Unlike patients or criminals who have clearly defined needs when they come to the doctor or the lawyer, audiences are by no means committed to their collective identity or their normative roles. Thus, the relationship between journalists and audiences is not completely similar to that of doctors and patients or of lawyers and clients (physicians in the public health service do, however, have to look after the health of individual clients and the society as a whole). When they turn on their TV sets, real audiences may be oblivious to their membership in civic society. Even when they are aware of their duty in theory, they may believe that they are free to choose between viewing in their "public" or private capacity. And they choose the latter most of the time. (This second possibility would account for the fact that polls show that people favor support for public broadcasting even if they personally do not watch it.) Thus, as the client of public broadcasting, "the public" is a prescriptive concept, situated somewhere between the needs and aims of real audiences, and the needs and aims of the collective, as defined by its policy planners. A third (theoretically soluble) problem is how to secure the independence of the broadcasting organization so that it remains free of political pressures.

The Demise of Public Broadcasting in the Era of Multiple Channels. For as long as it was the only player, the First Channel was faced with the very real problem of how to preserve its independence; the problem of defining its social role remained theoretical. In the multiple channel era, however, the clash became clearly manifest. The PBA and its TV channel, the First Channel, now had to tread the thin line of producing the kind of (public interest) programs that for-profit channels cannot or will not deliver, and yet, at the same time, make sure that it did well enough in the rating race so as not be pushed to the margins as a minority or elitist channel. This is a very tricky game in the best of cases, and it should be remembered, that as the number of channels and, with it, the audience fragmentation, increased, the definition of success itself changed (the definition of success sunk from 30% in the beginning of the 1990s to a mere 17% by the end of the millennium). This means that the expectation of bringing together a large section of the population had to be lowered.

One would think that 20 years of monopoly offered Israel's public broadcasting network a good chance to consolidate its hold on the public, plus a head start toward maintaining its centrality on the new media map. Indeed, considering its structural vulnerability, the First Channel did manage to maintain professional standards and provide the public with information that the government had been reluctant to provide. A clue to this argument is the car stickers of Israeli right-wingers, crying "The people are against hostile media" (i.e., against giving voice to "leftist" and defeatist" concerns). Unfortunately, being the only player in the field, and the illusion that this situation would last forever (or at least for a very long time), also gave the First Channel a false sense of security.

Sadly, this chapter is concerned with the failure of Israeli public broadcasting to remain relevant and to develop into a viable alternative to commercial broadcasting in an almost completely Americanized media environment. In its present state, following its fast decline (reported in what follows), it is incapable of operating as a buffer against a media system that, as elsewhere, is aimed only at making profits. The channel known until the early 1990s as "the tribal campfire," is fast becoming increasingly marginal in Israel's fast-changing, multichannel media environment.

An indicator of the decline is the fact that the First Channel news (or any of its other regular programs) is not listed in the weekly ratings of the 20 most popular TV programs, whereas Channel Two evening news, broadcast at 8 p.m., regularly scores, delivering a clear message that Israelis aren't tired of news, they're just tired of First Channel news. This is particularly upsetting to the First Channel's news department, its flagship, in view of the efforts it has made to regain its audiences. Rescheduling its news from prime time (9 p.m.) to compete with the new news program in its own time slot (at 8 p.m.), and reinstating a veteran anchor, acknowledged for decades as "Mr. Television," did nothing to bring back viewers (and the aging news star's fat contract only increased his colleagues' frustration over their own salaries). Another (not unrelated) indicator of the First Channel's decline is the constant migration of its star professionals to Channel Two (and the ensuing transformation of journalists into entertainers), motivated by both financial reasons, the First Channel's fast declining popularity, and the heavily bureaucratic work environment. The PBA's hope of reviving the magic of the first two decades, in which the 9 p.m. news had gathered around 70% of Israelis nightly, has thus been crushed.

Moreover, the reputation of the First Channel's news suffered a further damaging blow as a result of the blatantly political appointment of a PBA director general who applied himself to crushing its independence and professionalism. Uri Porat was appointed to the post in 1998 by Binyamin Netanyahu, the minister in charge and prime minister at the time. As discussed later, Netanyahu regarded the PBA, and its former director general (appointed during Yizhak Rabin's administration), in particular, as a political enemy, and brought Porat in as soon as the former director general's term expired. A quarter of a century after PM Levi Eshkol led the legislation that got PBA out of the prime minister's office, Porat was determined to push it right back in. In an interview to Israel's most popular tabloid on his entry into office, Porat explained that public broadcasting, translated at the time of its establishment as *shidur mamlachti* (state broadcasting), should be understood as "nationist" (of the nation state), not as "public" (*tziburi*). His interpretation of *mamlachti* indicated that his understanding of public broadcasting's role would prevent it from fulfilling its public mission effectively.

Indeed, it soon became clear that Porat's semantic distinction contained more than a hint of the mission he had defined for himself. It was to bring PBA back into the bosom of government. He also made clear that there were "good" or "bad" journalists in the First Channel's news department, and that he was going to discontinue employing the ones whom he did not hold in high regard. This marked the beginning of a sustained effort to destroy the delicate balance between government interests and professionalism in the newsroom. It also demonstrated in the most dramatic way that the only effective means of ensuring the future and independence of public broadcasting was to change the law, so that the PBA's director would be appointed by an independent public body.

The following case study portrays a major crisis in the director general's attempt to break the professional spirit of the news department. On the face of it, it seemed as if the director general had lost this battle, as he was prevented from fulfilling his declared intention of firing two veteran news editors. But the imminent threat of losing one's job was sufficient for creating an atmosphere of fear in the newsroom. Reporters and editors began to think twice about broadcasting any statement or item that may be regarded as "controversial" (by the minister in charge and his appointee). At the end of the affair, no actual firing was necessary. The workers had internalized the lesson, and Israel's public broadcasting has lost its capacity to act as watchdog.

One Case Study, Two Competing Frames. Interestingly, the case study itself may be read as an exercise in demonstrating that "news value" is not inherent in an event, but lies in its editorial framing. Thus, it is the editor's interpretation of the material that determines its news value. Moreover, a conflict over interpretation can be (and often is) a legitimate debate in the newsroom. Putting context aside, I begin with a bona fide examination of the event as a clash between two legitimate editorial positions—that of the news editors and that of the director general in his role as "chief editor," and go on to ask whether this approach can be defended.

PROBLEMATIZING NEWSWORTHINESS

The belief in serious journalism—whether printed or electronic—is based on trust in the professionalism of journalistic practice. This means, first of all, that we expect the main evening news, say, to select the most significant events "newswise" out of the infinite mass of events that occurred in the previous 24 hours, and to recount them from the studio or from the field, in a fair and accurate manner. Quality journalism and academic research agree that news value, or newsworthiness, should be the principle guiding selectivity, but that principle is rarely spelled out in detail. From an empirical viewpoint, occasional attempts have been made to infer these values from (the relatively high consensus on) the stories of the day among similarly situated newspapers or broadcasters (Galtung and Ruge, 1970; Gans, 1980), and one might learn even more from an enumeration of items that were *not used* (Meyrowitz, 1994). Yet, even such results conceal the process of negotiation and disagreement that goes on among professionals not only in the selection of events but also in framing them.

The case study presented here aims to problematize this taken-for-grantedness of the concept of *newsvalue*, by reconstructing the uneasy process through which the choice of a particular story and its transformation into a news item is carried out. Although this is perhaps an unusual case, it shows that newsworthiness is not independent of framing, or, better, that it is often a function of framing. A story may be chosen for its intuitive newsworthiness, but it is likely that the reporter or editor has a frame in mind. It may be that the same story evokes several frames, even competing ones. We would do well to collect more systematic evidence about items that barely make it into the news because the editor does not concur with the reporter's framing, and, equally interesting—as in the case presented here—to collect case studies of debates within the newsroom, or between the newsroom and external authorities (representing the interests of private or public ownership), over how to frame a story or whether to present it at all. The itinerary of such controversial stories makes explicit the issues at hand.

Negotiation in the Newsroom

The core practice of TV reporting—the selection of a fraction of reality to be presented as a 2-minute story on screen—means, almost by definition, extracting a part of a sequence of ongoing events out of its original context. The question of how to create a new context without distorting its original meaning (or even planting a meaning that was not there before), defines the daily work in the newsroom of responsible journalism, and may become a major bone of contention. If the debate remains among professionals in the culture of the newsroom, the kinds of questions that arise are: "Is there enough evidence to support the story?" "Is there enough taped material—on audio or videotape—for turning it into an 'item,' and if so, what is the right context in which to present it?" In the most common case of conflict (or of a story that has two sides), debate can focus on the kind of reaction the "fairness" doctrine demands.

We viewers put our trust in editing as carrying the advantages of journalistic work. Editing puts journalists in charge, giving them time to crosscheck sources, receive reactions, and investigate motives. It precludes the pitfalls of live broadcasting, where politicians can disintermediate reporters by creating pseudo-events to enforce their own agenda, and dissident groups or individuals can "highjack" the virtual space for their own aims, demoting the press to the role of traffic police (Dayan and Katz, 1993).

Unlike other conventions of TV news presentation, the problem with editing is its invisibility. Viewers may happily suspend disbelief, knowing somewhere in their minds that when the news anchor is looking them straight in the eye, conveying honesty, directness, and frankness, he or she is merely reading from the teleprompter, and that the heavily accented Russian voice is but a simulation of Yelzin's voice (Scannell, 1996). The reason for this is that the conventional devices of presentation are in the open, and may be considered relatively free of ideology. The stitches of a supposedly "seamless" editing, on the other hand, are meant to be unobtrusive and invisible. Anyone wishing to stop suspending disbelief would quickly discover that the elements of editing are inaccessible. In the case of the announcer, a visit to the studio would lead to the teleprompter, but checking the selection criteria of the news agenda would imply establishing the range of all alternative agendas (Liebes, 1994). Similarly, to retrace the steps in the editing of a story would mean retrieving all the film or videotape that never made it to the screen.

Editing is thus potentially much more manipulative than the rest of the performing devices, precisely because of the characteristics for which it is valorized—its unobtrusiveness and transparency. Editing by its nature has to include "substance." The point (or message) of the story is what dictates the way in which its intelligibility is constructed. But, if, as Scannell wrote, "[E]diting is a highly effective and efficient, motivated way of conveying meaning without having to say it," its effectiveness must lie exactly in covering its traces, leaving no clues to alternative editing, something the more ritualistic conventions of presentation cannot do, and are not trying to.

Thus, although the conventional devices of presentation are in the open, and may be considered relatively free of ideology (not always—remember the BBC's insistence of employing an actor for producing Jerry Adams' voice), we have no way of knowing what items were excluded from the news program, what footage of an item ended on the floor (Meyrowitz, 1994). It is the very seamlessness that ensures the intelligibility that makes it impossible to determine where professionalism ends and the hegemony of power begins. Rules of professional news editing such as "objectivity," "neutrality," and "balance"—themselves a product of ideology (Hallin, 1994)—all hover on this borderline between conventions of presentation and ideological belief ("investigative" or "public' journalism, for example, conveys alternative models). Moreover, even if an agreed set of rules is adopted, applying these rules in practice is still far from automatic; sometimes it is the source of bitter debate not only within the broadcasting organization, but also between the organization and the public.

Recently our faith in bona fide editing has suffered a number of serious blows, from various directions, weakening our taken-for-granted trust in broadcast news. This is particularly noticeable in countries with a strong tradition of public broadcasting, where trust in broadcasting institutions has been remarkable. Sometimes we have the opportunity to gain more awareness of the risky potential of the editing process to hide alternative stories, but more often, we become disillusioned with the gradual abandonment of traditional news editing, with its capacity to create coherence and credibility.

Negotiation Between Newsroom and Management

A problem that figures in everyday news editing occurs in the very process of selective perception, which leads to alternative framings that are necessarily tainted with ideology, witting or unwitting. The taken-for-granted public faith in the editorial function of broadcasting news is further weakened when suspicion arises, that the broadcasting institution has fallen prey to political pressures. Such intervention creates the need to reconcile differences not only among newsroom professionals, but between the newsroom culture and external demands. In privatized press and broadcasting systems, such demands are put, directly or indirectly, by the owners, who are motivated by economic and/or political considerations, such as not alienating advertisers or politicians whom they depend on, or refraining from clashes with their own competing business interests. In public broadcasting, such demands may be brought on (directly or indirectly) by the institution's director (sometimes "editor in chief"), looking after the interests of the politicians who may influence his or her appointment. Any news item that may criticize or put the political masters in a bad light, is thus in danger of becoming the focus of a debate between unequal participants. Such a debate may, of course, masquerade as a perfectly legitimate negotiation over applying particularly meticulous professional standards.

What follows is a close look at the problems of the preservation of credibility of broadcast news, by analyzing a recent case of a confrontation between the director general of Israel's PBA and its news editors. The controversy was made public by virtue of a formal action, whereby the director general dismissed senior news editors on the grounds of "unprofessional editing." The ensuing struggle exposed the problematics of delineating the boundaries of "legitimate" editing, which, as elaborated above, necessarily means "taking out of context." By now we all know that news is a construction of reality, but this cliché term serves to cover up the problem rather than to highlight it.

What Are They Telling Us About the PM?

The Start of a New Era In Public Broadcasting. As mentioned earlier, in April 1998, Netanyahu, Israel's prime minister, who also happened to be the minister in charge of public broadcasting, nominated a new PBA director general (DG). Since his election, Netanyahu had repeatedly attacked the PBA and its former lame-duck director general (nominated by the former government), and carried out various kinds of sanctions, which intensified considerably following the First Channel's coverage of the apparent collusion of Netanyahu in a conspiracy surrounding the appointment of the attorney general. Uri Porat, the new director general, began his reign by announcing plans to cut down on news and current affairs (which, he claimed, "the public was bored with"), in favor of more entertainment, promising to produce additional chapters in a series of 24 documentaries on the history of the state, completed before his appointment. His aim was to control the damage done by the series to the Israeli cause, and demonstrate that "Justice has been on our (Israel's) side." He went on to threaten the news department with "cleansing" it of "bad journalists who had somehow infiltrated it." The affair analyzed here occurred 1 month into Porat's term.

The DG's Report. On May 9, 1998, the First Channel's evening news included an item on the victory revelry by fans of a Jerusalem football team, the idols of the right-wing Likud party. During the revelry, jubilant mobs in the town square were observed rhythmically shouting "Death to the Arabs," while PM Netanyahu was waving and smiling at them from a balcony above the square. The item was not based on on-the-scene reporting, but rather was an excerpt from a videotape of the event, recorded from its live showing on a tiny public channel (which, like the

American C-SPAN, transmits live from the Knesset) the night before. The audio recording came from microphones situated in the crowds, on the actors stage, and on the VIP balcony, via four entries from the public address system responsible for handling the various entry channels. The next day, Porat announced that he was going to examine allegations of manipulative editing of the item, which included tampering with the sound of the screaming and superimposing the prime minister's shots over the square scene. Three weeks later, Porat published a report concluding that the item was designed to distort the truth, and, specifically, to present the prime minister in a bad light. The report also announced the removal from their posts of the two veteran editors who were responsible for the item. The editors went to court, demanding their demotion be canceled on procedural grounds, and the two sides finally settled on a compromise, in which the DG had to reinstate the editors in their jobs, and had to retract his allegation of manipulative (i.e., ideologically motivated) editing, whereas the editors had to admit they had edited the item irresponsibly, but without intentional manipulation.

The struggle brought the hidden assumptions of news editing into public debate. People, including academics, vehemently discussed the rules of editing, and Israelis emerged as more sophisticated about what goes on behind the scenes, that is, they became more enlightened viewers. It became clear that there was no way to tell the "facts as they are," and that the only course of responsible journalism is routine methodology.

Here, then, are the competing stories read into the item. Each framing delineates its own boundaries (field vs. field and studio), addresses its own implied viewers, and makes its own point.

The Story: Prime Minister, Football Fans, and "Death to the Arabs." This much scrutinized news item was broadcast during the 45-minute main evening news of the First Channel, which consisted of 30 minutes of general news, with the last 15 minutes devoted to economic news and sports. The item was the next to last in the opening headlines (followed only by the victory of Israel's Dana International, a drag queen, in the Eurovision song contest), and was given the following promo: "*Beitar*'s fans are celebrating the team's championship also by shouting 'Death to the Arabs'." The item itself was placed next to last in the general news section, and consisted of 18 seconds of edited film, framed by live reporting from the studio. News anchor Geula Even said in her opening statement:

> Beitar Yerushalaim fans celebrated the winning of the championship in Safra Square last night. But not only cries of joy were heard there, but also cries of "Death to the Arabs," which resounded clearly.

On film, the camera showed the masses of fans filling Jerusalem's city square (at the culmination of a 3-hour victory celebration), the prime minister appearing on the balcony of Jerusalem's new municipality building looking over the square, accompanied by Mayor Ehud Olmert. Rhythmic cries of "Death to the Arabs" are heard from the crowd, while Netanyahu, oozing smiles, happily waves his hand at the fans (9 seconds). Netanyahu then says: "I came to say only two words to you: Yalla ["onward" in Arabic] Beitar." Following this film sequence, Even said:

> The response of the PM's office this evening is that from the place in which they were standing, the PM and the Mayor did not hear the shouts "Death to the Arabs." The PM, the announcement said, adamantly condemns these cries and absolutely objects to them and to their content. This is the announcement of the PM. (22 seconds)

The sports supplement of the news program that evening opened with a 108-second item devoted to the personality of Beitar's manager, which incorporated a repeat of the fans' racist welcoming of the prime minister. The opening exchange in the studio (lasting 72 seconds) between Even and sports presenter Meir Einstein went as follows:

> Even: Shalom Meir,
> Einstein: Good evening Geula
> Even: These were the Beitar championship celebrations, but we also saw the shouting "Death to the Arabs," and I am ready to bet you that there will be someone who will say "It's only a handful; it's not serious [unclear] like the Hapoel Tel Aviv fans at the time, why do they hang everything on the masses?"
> Einstein: We already heard that the PM who stood there at the top of the municipality building did not hear these shouts, and he of course most forcefully condemns the shouting.
> Even: The mayor too
> Einstein: The Mayor Ehud Olmert too. But it is worthwhile mentioning that this is nothing new in the repertoire of Beitar fans. This is not the first time that they sound these ugly shouts [Takes a breath, moves on to a new item]. A new holiday from the training camp for the players of Beitar Yerushalaim . . . Amir Bar Shalom was today with the man who was not there last night, but deserves a large chunk of the championship's celebrations [Beitar football club manager]. The celebrations as we said took place last night and a large part of the audience accompanied them by swearing at the Arabs at the time in which Binyamin Netanyahu was there.

The film section on the Beitar manager begins with a repeat of the 18 seconds of Netanyahu and the fans, then moves to manager Dadash, shaking hands with fans on the street, accompanied by the reporter's voiceover:

> These dissonant chords, which were voiced in the fourth championship celebration of Beitar Yerushalaim, did not make the team's management happier. The morning after, Moshe Dadash tells us that the next day, in protest over such behavior, and in order to promote closer ties between Jews and Arabs, the champion team would play a friendship match in Baka'a el Garbia [an Arab townlet in Israel].

THE UNDERLYING ASSUMPTIONS MADE EXPLICIT IN THE CONSTRUCTION OF THE ITEM: POSSIBLE READINGS

What constitutes a news event? The first major question that should be asked in explicating the implied (and often taken-for-granted) assumptions of news editing should be whether there is news value to the item. The DG's report criticized the editors for choosing "5 seconds of the 3-hour (videotaped) celebrations." Apparently, the DG's underlying assumption was that the subject of the item was "the celebration of Beitar's fans," and as such, the representation had been inadequate. The editors did not do justice to the event nor to the fans; their "sample," so to speak, was flawed.

It is clear, however, that the news editor did not choose these seconds in order to provide a fair representation of the event, but rather chose it for its newsworthy moments. (As it happened, it was a viewer who watched the live broadcast and called the First Channel's news department to tell them that this belonged in the news.) Because one major characteristic of newsworthiness is its deviation from norms, in that sense news often does not do justice to the big chunks of reality that it does not show (leading to the familiar complaints against showing only "bad news"). For example, the large range of incidents in which Israeli soldiers did not clash with *intifada* demonstrators did not make the news. The ones in which they did clash were presented as an aberrant phenomenon, which could, and did, develop into a major uncontrollable downhill slide. Paradoxically, once a phenomenon such as racist shouting becomes so prevalent that it is regarded as routine, public opinion cannot be roused by its exposure, and television news no longer has a role to play.

To begin with the most elementary interpretation, I suggest that the newsworthiness of the event lies in the very presence of the PM at a gathering in which the loud, rhythmic cries of racist incitement are sounded, regardless of whatever else was happening there. Regardless of whether Netanyahu heard the cries and did not want to spoil the warm welcome that he received, or preferred to wallow in his own glory and chose not to notice, or actually did not hear, it was still important to broadcast these images and sounds.

Going one step back into the process of news editing, we looked at the recording of the live broadcast that served as raw material for the news item. Sixty seconds prior to the PM's appearance, the crowds are seen filling the square, a singer with a guitar is performing, when the mayor's voice is heard:

> Look up to the balcony for just one moment. There is a fan of Beitar here who came to congratulate you. Gentlemen, you recognize him. His name is BB Netnayahu. I give you the PM.

During Mayor Olmert's last two sentences, the shouts "Death to the Arabs" begin to be heard, and they are heard more soundly when he ends his words, during the 9 seconds in which Netanyahu is smiling and waving. Thus, it is the appearance of the PM on the balcony, that triggers the shouts, which then take off to become the most prominent welcoming greeting.

What Connotative Strands Were Evoked? Two lines of connotation connect the event to the cumulative knowledge of editors and viewers, thus constructing the item's "biography" for the editors and the viewers (Barthes, 1975). Both histories reinforce its value as news. One context is the history of Beitar fans, the other is the history of the prime minister. The fans are known to have behaved similarly in the past, on a series of occasions, usually during or following games. The characteristics of the current incident as a familiar recurrence is referred to in the news item, and later, by the sports anchor ("This is not the first time they sound these ugly cries"), and again by the sports reporter in the mention of a Jewish-Arab game planned as a gesture of friendship over a prior incident of the same kind. This recent history lends added significance to this latest outbreak, turning it into one event in a menacing series, which stands in the way of the ongoing attempts to control the damage. Ironically, the editors were reprimanded by the DG for inaccuracy, because he heard them say that the "friendship" game had been planned following this latest incident in the city square, when in fact it had been planned prior to this event, in response to a previous similar incident. He ignored, however, the connection between these two events in terms of coherence—as parts of the same pattern, with the current incident undermining the planned reconciliation efforts. This history of the event adds to its news value, making it part of a disconcerting trend.

The second connotative strand evoked by the event leads to the role of the PM in political incitement. In the minds of the DG, the editors, and the public, the current pictures brought to mind a Likud party rally, organized in opposition to the Oslo accords, which had taken place in Jerusalem's Zion Square (the central city square prior to the completion of the new one) in 1996. On that occasion, Netanyahu, then the Likud candidate for PM, appeared under a large poster featuring a doctored photograph of Yitzhak Rabin, then PM, dressed as Yassar Arafat. That rally ended in a mock funeral featuring a black coffin covered with PM Rabin's photograph. As in the current case, Netanyahu had vehemently denied having seen Rabin's photograph. This connotation does pull the story in the direction of "Did the Prime Minister hear?" The deja vu makes it a better story, and the editors should not be required to protect the PM from the analogy that these pictures might bring up in the viewers' memories; the contrary may be true.

DID THE PM HEAR: DID THE STORY TAKE A STAND?

What did the cutting and pasting do? The DG's allegation of manipulative editing that was designed to make the viewers believe that the PM did hear the shouting was based on the cutting out of 40 seconds from the excerpt of the original recording. As described earlier, the edited film begins with the 9 seconds of Netanyahu's appearance on the balcony, during which the rhythmic shouting clearly resounds, then cuts to the congratulatory message, declared by him as the purpose of his visit ("I came to say only two words to you: Yalla Beitar"). The original film contains more racist shouts that continue intermittently, now mixed with other cries, such as "Heide ["Onward"] BB," and "He is Great," while the PM continues to wave and smile at the public. Then the mayor, his body language conveying discomfort, bending over to the PM, telling him that the crowds will quiet down if he begins to speak, and the beginning of the PM's greeting, where he praises the team's manager. As viewing the original and the edited film makes clear, the loud rhythmic shouting (ironically, louder in the original than in the news item) begins when the PM appears, and continues as he waves and smiles to the crowd. In the best of all worlds, one might have been concerned about the possibility that cutting out the sentences which separated the loud shouting from the PM's greeting, would necessarily impose on viewers the notion that the PM's statement ("Yalla Beitar") was in support of incitement. It remains doubtful, however, whether retaining these sentences could have reassured viewers who did suspect that the PM was capable of of such silent acceptance, or other viewers, who were concerned about those who might harbor such suspicion.

Studio and Field: What Constitutes the Boundaries of a News Item? The allegation that the item was edited in order to give viewers the impression that the PM heard the shouting, reframes the story, both from a commemorative story about the celebration, or from a story about racist shouting in the presence of the PM, to one about the PM's possible collaboration. The DG's criticism was based explicitly on the editing out of the 40 seconds in the tape of the recorded live event, and, implicitly, on the DG's own definition of "the item" as only its filmed part, and not the (much longer) section where the anchors supplied their framing of the footage. In excising the studio segment, Porat defined the film part as "real," endowing it with the authenticity of "being there" (Barthes, 1975), and, therefore, with the power of impressing viewers. Yet such a reading (intentionally or not) leaves out half the story, and all of the interaction between the stars of the show and their daily public.

From the point of view of telling the story, its framing and its coherence are given in the opening statements from the studio, from the perspective of the anchors, which they share with their implied readers. In this case, the studio title was the racist shouting of Beitar's fans, following which the anchor shared the documentation of this behavior with us viewers. After the "documentation" from the field, Even went on to let us know that the PM's office stated that the PM had not heard the shouting and ardently condemns it. This means, that the editors did their jobs in seeking a reaction and delivering it. In the following sports section, in the context of the tension between Jewish and Arab football teams, that denial is already fully internalized. The anchor brings the PM's reaction in the form of "facts." Gone is the neutral form of "a response from the PM's office." Now "not hearing" becomes taken for granted, adopted by anchors who reiterate: "We already heard that the PM, who stood there at the top of the municipality building, did not hear these shouts, and he, of course, adamantly, condemns them . . . So does Mayor Ehud Olmert."

Ignoring the studio framing, as did the DG in his report, whether intentionally or not, edits out the "reading instructions" to the viewers. The question mark left by the film footage about the PM's nonresponse is addressed by the studio, leaving only those who would not find it incongruous that this PM could ignore racist shouting to their doubts.

What Each of the Players Learned. All the participants in the Safra Square affair were taught something. It got news viewers into a public debate. It made the public more sophisticated by exposing the practices of news making, thereby clarifying that objectivity is not possible.

The lesson learned by the First Channel news department was less commendable: The repeat broadcast of the celebrations on Channel 33 (where the original live broadcast was aired), cut out the racist shouting ("so as not to offend viewers," its director explained). In another of the PM's visits, this time to a West Bank settlers' rally in Jerusalem's Breichat Hasultan open-air theater, where similar racist shouts were heard once again, they were censored out by TV's editors. And, worse, when a protest group of unemployed citizens shouted abuse at the PM during his ceremonial visit to the opening of an exhibition celebrating the state's 50th anniversary, only (commercial) Channel Two had the story. But despite the clear signs that the First Channel news department had learned to "keep out of trouble," they still continued to pay a price. In May 1999, in a farewell ceremony (following Netanyahu's resignation from politics after he lost the 1999 elections), the woman reporter who exposed the story of Netanyahu's conspiracy to appoint an accommodating attorney general, was beaten up by fans of the PM.

For his part, the DG has learned that the public was not as gullible as he had believed it to be. He realized that professionals could not be treated as bureaucrats, and that the manner in which they practice could be defended. And the PM? On a rightwing settlers' rally 6 weeks later, Netanyahu was heard on radio reprimanding the crowd from the podium: "Not 'death to the Arabs,' not 'death to the Arabs'."

SAFRA SQUARE AS A WATERSHED: THE POLITICIZATION OF PUBLIC BROADCASTING

From the scholar's perspective, this is not just a titillating incident in the history of (Israeli) journalism. Nor is it simply a backstage view of a newsroom. Rather, it seeks to use public exposure of the details of this incident—abetted by our access to the original tapes (including the portions that weren't used in the news), as well as by unstructured discussions among a group of scholars and editors (including the editor of the program in question)—to call attention to certain basic problems in the conceptualization of professional praxis everywhere. Thus, this chapter addresses problems related to: (a) judgments concerning newsworthiness, and framing in the studio and at home; (b) professional bureaucratic and ideological constraints on framing, and rules governing the autonomy of professionals within bureaucratic organizations; (c) genres of presentation of news, especially when there is conflict over newsworthiness and framing inside the newsroom itself; and (d) the bearing of all the above on the maintenance of journalistic authority and credibility.

The Case Study Ofers a Glimpse into Certain Criteria of Newsworthiness. Is celebration of the cup finals by a local team with massive support worthy of national attention? Does the PM's presence at the event enhance its newsworthiness? Does the disruptive racial shouting, albeit by a minority, change the newsworthiness of the celebratory event? Does the disruption change the framing of the event, from celebration to racial incitement? Does the presence of the PM change the frame yet again, from incitement at the sportsfest to incitement presumed to flatter (not provoke) the PM? And would the frame change yet again had there been reason to believe that the PM did hear the racial slurs without reprimanding the offenders?

The journalists in the newsroom edited the story to leave open the possibility of either of the latter two frames; they left the celebratory frame to the sports desk. They were guided in this by a hierarchy of beats that gives priority to the national leader, but also the two frames—the resultant of an earlier incident—in which the PM (then leader of the opposition) was thought to have ignored or condoned a case of rabid incitement at a political rally in which anti-Arab sentiment was redirected against Yitzhak Rabin.

In contending with these judgments, the DG took issue with the downgrading of the celebration frame, and the upgrading of the incitement frames, accusing the editors of unprofessional and ideologically tendentious editing. The event had been a celebration, he said, disrupted by a small group of rowdies having nothing to do with PM—who was there for only a few moments out of the 3-hour rally, and who had not (or could not have) heard the cries.

Case studies of this kind reveal professional praxis, in which judgments are made about how to map the world in "beats" or "desks" (Epstein, 1973), where to look for trouble (Katz, 1989), and how to determine the hierarchy of beats (whereby the presence of the PM overrides the sports beat) and of frames (where the scent of conflict overpowers expressions of solidarity).

Framing is Subject to Various Kinds of Constraints: Professional, Bureaucratic, and Ideological. The DG crossed over from his bureaucratic role (although he also formally serves as editor in chief) to dismiss the news editors, going over the head of the editor of news, accusing them of the high crime of ideological framing.

The professionals, on their part, pointed to the code of beats and frames that constrained their judgments, the inclusion of the PM's denial, but the primacy of the critical frame nevertheless echoed their experience of the earlier incident (the balcony in the anti-Rabin rally). By implication, they were invoking the professional obligation of serving as an early warning system to the clients (Katz, 1989).

Along with the debate over competing frames, at issue here is the autonomy of professionals working within bureaucratic organizations (as most professionals do nowadays). What, in practice, is the editorial chain of command? What are the rights of owners and CEOs?

Conflict Within the Newsroom Over Competing Frames is Probably Infrequent. Yet an argument can be made—as we do here—that it may be useful, and even enhance the newscasters' authority, if viewers and readers were made privy to these dilemmas. Indeed, compared to the "narcotizing dysfunction" of American newscasts, the "openness" of Italian news (its lesser authoritativeness) is associated with far more participation in the decoding process, according to Hallin and Mancini (cited in Hallin, 1994). This should be true, a priori, if journalists were to bring their own differences to the screen. In presenting all the sides of an issue—including the competing frames of participants—the norms of journalism support this direction. But the implication of the present case is that a further step would reveal the competing frames of the journalists themselves—when there are such—rather than try to resolve them in order to tell a seamless story. Scannell (1996) may have been wrong in asserting that common ground between producers and viewers is a function of "leaving no clues to alternative editing." Our case study illustrates how the anchor was used against the grain of the filmed story, both to allay, and, at the same time, to question, the more radical of the two framings.

THE PLACE OF PUBLIC BROADCASTING IN A MULTICHANNEL COMMERCIALIZED ENVIRONMENT

Having analyzed the case in terms of conflicting framings, I now return to the issue of the functioning of public broadcasting in an increasingly Americanized media environment.

The failure in the functioning of public broadcasting in Israel, as argued previously, is no evidence to the weakness of the model. On the contrary. It points to the dangers inherent in Israel's partial and deficient implementation of the idea. As I argued in chapter 2, the BBC model had been adopted in a modified version, which curtailed the means of ensuring its independence from the political system. The question, then, is how it did as well as it has despite its vulnerability, and what made it lose its status in recent years.

The answer is that whereas the Law of Public Broadcasting is imminently vulnerable to politicization, even severe critics of the First Channel would agree that throughout its history it did manage to function better than could be expected. The explanation for this relative independence is simple: A succession of ministers in charge, with the authority to appoint the DG, mostly kept to a tradition of professional appointments, and did not blatantly abuse their right to install a politically motivated DG with an unabashed commitment to serve his political bosses. This meant that, on the whole, public broadcasting has managed to provide credible information about the way government functions, and has created an arena for dialogue among various voices in the Israeli public. Bearing in mind that broadcasting expresses the climate of the times, with changing definitions of what is deemed a "security risk," or "private" rather than "public," and so on, and the relative importance of various types of public issues, Israeli public broadcasting did not do badly. (It was much less successful in other tasks, such as the production of high-quality drama and documentation, as these were always regarded as less prioritized).

And, as the Safra Square case demonstrates, the accessibility of information and the new style of framing from the studio, are themselves part of the new multichannel media environment in which the channel operates, signifying a new openness and flexibility in the work of news reporters and editors. First, the plurality of channels, including a C-span-like channel documenting the legislative process, means access to a lot of public information, 90% of which is not used but can be resurrected when needed. News editors no longer have to rely solely on a team sent by the news department in anticipation. Second, the presentation in the studio has moved from the model of the neutral, classically British presenter, who effuses objectivity by being one with the news (Scannell), to the adoption of the chat mode between man and woman presenters, including sarcastic comments ("I can hear them say it's only a few . . ."). Third, the easy interactivity with viewers, which became common in radio phone-in programs, making it thinkable for the caller in the Safra Square case to call the department in order to point to the newsworthy item.

Thus, the combination of a professional news department with a watchdog mission and the new open environment, has proven creative. It was this effectiveness that boomeranged. Although the PM may not have thought that he needed to reprimand the football fans, who were wildly enthusiastic about him, he was not so keen on seeing himself in the background of the racist screaming on prime-time news.

What brought about the demise of public broadcasting, then, was the erosion of a tradition that kept politicians from blatant visible abuse of political power. The personalization of politics, and the destabilization of the political system (causing governments to fall more frequently) made politicians desperate to control the media, and the law provided an easy way of doing so. The establishment of a long-standing political tie (almost 50:50) within the electorate, which in turn sharpened the confrontational aspects of election races, made the role played by television in those races more crucial, contributing further to the temptation of the government in power to control public broadcasting.

It could be argued that the issue of public broadcasing's politicization is less threatening to the Israeli public since the establishment of a second commercial TV channel. That is not the case. The existence of an effective and relevant public channel is crucial, because it can hold the other channels to journalistic standards, and balance the pressures of their advertisers and owners for censorship that is aimed at avoiding issues that may interfere with their own commercial interests.

4

"Disaster Marathons": The Danger of Action News

The multichannel environment has transformed the rules of the broadcasting game, most dramatically so in the case of news. As the public justification for Channel Two was based on the idea that a plurality of channels would bring about a plurality of opinions, the commercial channel was to establish its own news department (financed by its three broadcasting companies). The evening news on Channel Two is 30 minutes long, airs at 8 p.m., moves much faster than the First Channel news and replaces its traditionally pompous presentation with an informal chatty dialogue between the (man and woman) anchors. Thus, since 1993, Israeli public broadcasting has been faced with a competing news broadcaster modeled after the commercial U.S. networks, which has transformed the news. This evening ritual of Israeli society was now shifted to the margins of prime time, frequently interrupted for advertising, with only a few traces left of the neutral BBC-style presentation.

In an era when only commercial TV can afford to buy *ER* and *Ally McBeal*, the strength that the First Channel should have cultivated was its lead in electronic journalism. Free of rating considerations, it could have built on its prestige as a news provider seasoned in public issues, and on the well-established habits of Israeli viewers. Instead, as fate would have it, the First Channel suffered what may have amounted to a mortal blow, shortly after the establishment of Channel Two.

Tragically, the demise of the public channel was not a result of failing in its role of watchdog. On the contrary, by exposing a major scandal that implicated PM Netanyahu in a conspiracy to appoint an accommodating attorney general, the First Channel tested the limits of its professional independence. It soon became clear that either the PM would resign, or the channel would pay the price. The investigation ended with severe criticism of the PM's behavior, and a praise for the First Channel for its service to the public, but stopped short of prosecuting the PM. As chapter 3 recounts, the channel's original sin—its vulnerability to politicization—revenged itself. The Safra Square affair became the watershed, following which the channel's news department lost its spirit, and was made a lame duck by a government that it almost managed to topple.

The First Channel's new weakness gave an advantage to Channel Two, structurally less subservient to the government, and more to its shareholders. And it soon became clear that for Israel—violence-ridden, struggling with its neighbors, maneuvering between waves of riots, war, terrorist attacks, internal strife—"normalization" was a wish rather than a reality. And like it or not, news was still a highly popular genre.

Because the owners of Channel Two understood that news was worth investing in, they proceeded to do so. Able to offer appreciably higher salaries than their publicly owned competitors, it did not take them long to have the First Channel's star reporters and editors desert to their channel. The growing popularity of Channel Two news meant that they were now calling the shots. Soon it was the First Channel that had to adapt to the competitors' new practices in order to retain some of its viewers and to remain relevant.

ELECTRONIC JOURNALISM ON TIME-OUT

The need of both channels to prove their popularity with viewers grew particularly prominent in times of national crisis. This was a major reason for the practices they adopted, since the second half of the 1990s, in the wake of massive disasters, notably mass terrorist attacks. Both channels now interrupt their schedule, switching into live broadcasts, in the style of CNN's "breaking news," for long hours, sometimes for days. The resulting broadcast, obsessed with the drama at hand, is a mixture of voyeuristic fascination with tragedy and the amplification of populist feelings of revenge, with little or no news. Despite the fact that it was often suggested that the two channels would join hands at these moments, it is the sign of the times that they remain competitive, and refuse to work together. Each is too concerned with its own record. Ironically, it is Channel Two—constrained by the loss of advertising money in declaring a "time-out" (ads do not go well with disaster)—that thinks twice before getting into the crisis mode, and returns to normal schedule much earlier.

The genre of disaster marathon has the markings of the new media environment—a long, intermittent personal talk show, moving in and out of the studio and various "on-site" spots. No censorship can be exercised and serious consideration can be given to the issues at hand, as there is plenty of time and only the one agenda at hand. It seems that in such moments, when both nationwide channels must address the collective and create some kind of public space, the mixture between considerations concerned with public interest and the ones concerned with competition over ratings is most striking.

The problem for reporters is that when everything happens "live," the basic tools of traditional journalism are lost. In purely professional terms, crisis marathons are perhaps the best demonstration of the change in norms undergone in the era of electronic journalism. These are moments when public issues dominate the national agenda, but, at the same time, professional mediation is minimal. There is no time to check the facts, confirm or corroborate information, or edit the material before going on the air (Katz, 1993). The work is carried out live, up front onscreen, and control in the studio is further decreased by live interruptions from reporters in the field with more "witnesses," "reactions," or speculation.

On the other hand, marathons liberate the media from routine constraints, thus providing an opportunity for the kind of intensive, if not rational, debate that theorists of civil society are seeking (Alexander and Jacobs, 1998). When this happens, are journalists reduced to the technical role of facilitators? The evidence from cases such as the 1966 bus bombing marathon in Israel indicates that professionals play a crucial role in creating the conditions for a genuine debate by selecting the participants, framing the issues, and ensuring that participants observe the rules. The risk of losing control may lead to being swept by populist emotions.

As we know, routine practices of electronic journalism do not allow for much normative debate. Commercial competition, and the professional norms that have developed to befit them, require focusing on events, not on processes; on strategies, not on values; and constructing the news in the form of stories, not of issues (Hallin, 1994; Iyengar, 1991). Although there is a potential for normative debate in genres of entertainment, they too abide by the rules. For example, when talk shows host political figures, they tend to focus on their personalities, and prefer peeping "behind the scene." Sitcoms, too, sometimes touch on normative issues (Fiske, 1994), but overall, are subject to stricter constraints than the news.

As a possible exception to the rule, I call attention to the contribution to public discourse of a new genre, whereby scheduled broadcasting is interrupted in favor of the live broadcasting of crisis or disaster. Nationwide and public channels, traditionally the carriers of preplanned live ceremonies (Dayan and Katz, 1993), tend to resist switching to live marathons for reasons of responsibility to their public, their scheduled programs, and their advertisers, as well as a result of a general aversion to sensationalizing news. This reluctance nevertheless gives way at certain moments. I propose that such disaster marathons—the site of the high drama of action news—further enhances the erosion of the norms of electronic journalism, but may sometimes also constitute a liminal space for public reflection over social norms and values.

The examination of two disaster marathons on Israeli television serves here as a basis for exploring the conditions under which editors and anchors on live broadcast, following a national trauma, may choose to adopt the neo-populist mood of the public, or use the format of an open-ended, single-issue broadcast as an opportunity for conducting an in-depth genuine debate over national failures and public policies. But let me begin by putting some order in the arguments that point to the reasons why routine news is only concerned with the heuristics of the story, and why disaster marathons may be different.

DISASTER MARATHON: THE POTENTIAL

The decision to interrupt scheduled programs means that routine journalistic practices undergo a change, liberating journalists somewhat from everyday pressures. How this unexpected vacuum gets filled depends to a large extent on the type of crisis at hand. At such moments the establishment is weakened by definition, but the extent to which the government is delegitimized varies. And the debate over the label—a disaster, an accident, mismanagement, or a blatant violation of norms—constitutes a central part of the marathon itself.

A live marathon moves through a number of phases. Starting with dramatic (or melodramatic), ongoing, live "action," the broadcast may enter its most significant stage once the riots, or the fire, or the rescue operations, come under control. Dayan and Katz showed how, in crises such as the assassination of a president, or a prime minister, a ceremonial event such as the funeral, and/or the swearing in of the new leader, provides the final closure of the event, embracing the public in the shared grief, and the sense of taking part in history. But the occupation with media events has shifted attention from events that do not have "natural" recourse to such ritual closure, and neglected the role of media during the crucial period following the crisis, and prior to its ceremonial closure (initiated either by the establishment or by the media) or to its gradual or abrupt disappearance. This period, after the first wave of action has subsided, which constitutes an unstructured, emotionally powerful, shared public space, is the concern of this section.

The traumatic unraveling of structural failings, and having enough time to discuss them, means that journalists are tempted to rise above the usual "technical" discourse. Surrendering their responsibility for the debate over norms or public policies to the government, another routinely used strategy (Hallin, 1994), may also be unacceptable if the government has just been proven at fault. Media professionals thus often engage in a debate with the relevant public participants, deconstructing the crisis to get at its roots, to probe its political and cultural implications, and to question the norms (or deviations from norms) that it exposes. In short, it is an effective moment for raising fundamental issues because the government has lost control of its image (Molotch and Lester, 1974), because the whole constituency is watching, and, most important, because the human cost of ignoring structural ills is flaunted at the face of the public.

But such situations may also lead elsewhere: The government's temporary loss of control, the high drama of the moment, and the emotional state of the public, may push journalists to prefer to cater to popular public sentiments of disappointment, outrage, sometimes cries for revenge. This means that instead of conducting an open debate to probe the social significance of the event, or the inadequacy or abuse of norms, journalists may yield this prerogative altogether to government or to opposition parties, depending on which way popular sentiments are blowing, and relinquish their own professional role. This type of resorting to neo-populism takes the form of celebrating hegemonic sentiment in government-led crises, such as the Gulf War, or of wallowing in anti-establishment sentiments, in cases such as the Watergate hearings. Thus, television's virtual space may be transformed from a town hall meeting into a mass rally, capable of instigating a field trial against whoever is marked as responsible for the failure—the person, the institution, or the government. Disaster marathons thus hover dangerously between the rare moment in which journalism can "play its role in the normative dialogue" (Hallin, 1994, p. 6) and, at the other extreme, the endangering of the possibility of rational discourse (Carey, 1998).

THE DISCOURSE OF ROUTINE NEWS

Should the media play a role in shaping society's normative views or should it be restricted to the gathering of information? Hallin, for one, believes that the media "rightly and inevitably" have a normative role to play. The price of the historical shift from the early political press to modern, commercial, mass media, explained Hallin (1994), was a shift from engagement in the norms and principles of public policy to a focus on "facts." Even while there has been an appreciable improvement in collecting and disseminating information, this shift has taken the form of asking questions at the level of technique and strategy.

A similar view of why journalists stick to the stories at hand, and why they shy away from the long-term issues and processes that underlie them, is offered by the more classical hegemonic approach. According to Edelman (1988), the seemingly technical tendency to emphasize events hides the convenience of having to deal only with "pseudo-crises," which can be shown as "solved" or "solvable," and, as such, helps to give the impression that things are under (the government's) control. The long-term processes that slowly accumulate to create major crises do not have to be dealt with.

Government control over its image in routine reporting is also the central argument made by Molotch and Lester (1974), who go a step further and inquire as to when politicians lose control over their image. Their answer: in events which are not meant to become publicly known (scandals), or were not meant to happen at all (accidents). These occasional cracks in routine control provide opportunities for journalists to peek into the way the affairs of the state are run "behind the scenes" (Goffman, 1974). But because journalists depend for their routine work on their sources, they are often reluctant to pick up these opportunities, the more so the more powerful the politicians, and the more established the journalists involved.

Although their model is still relevant and insightful, Molotch and Lester wrote too early to take into account two recent developments in the journalism of "disruption." One is the growing prominence of live electronic media in the treatment of crisis, including the centrality of live coverage and the use of amateur videotapes. The second, not unrelated development, is the increased control of the initiators of "disruptive events" over their media coverage (e.g., in cases of holding hostages or in suicide terrorist attacks), and their increased sophistication in utilizing live media (Danner, 2000). For Molotch and Lester, activists of disruptions may always be co-opted, or some concessions may be made, or the police may be instructed to deny access to the press, turning all these events into "routine" items.

A similar point is made by other scholars in the 1960s, 1970s, and 1980s who have observed media coverage of political processes in the United States (e.g., Gans, 1980; Gitlin, 1980), in Britain (Glasgo, 1976; Murdoch, 1988), and elsewhere (Liebes, 1997; Wolfsfeld, 1997), all of whom have shown how hegemony works in the coverage of "disruption." We see how soldiers or policemen were only doing their job, whereas dissidents, ghetto demonstrators and *intifada* rioters acted arbitrarily and irrationally, noisily, and or violently. Routine news coverage does not allow for deeper insights into the underlying issues of racial and class prejudice, police brutality, labor relations, or the effects of military occupation. As late as 1997, in a systematic attempt at describing journalistic routines, Lance Bennet (1997) found that journalists need a good reason to focus on nonestablishment figures.

Television's takeover of the news from the printed press—with its mad rush from one story to the next, and its emphasis on personalities, visuals, and ongoing drama—has only made things worse. Routine programs have to faithfully follow the accepted conventions of covering of political issues, mostly in the form of horse racing contests, and evaluating moves in terms of gain or loss to the competing politicians rather than to the cause (if there is one). And yet, the technology of live transmission from multiple points and the capacity to evoke powerful images, in moments of crisis, and with lesser time constraints, have the power to strike home, exposing what people normally prefer not to see.

THE OPEN SPACE OF LIVE MARATHONS

TV's daily news programs are organized in uncompromising time slots, between commercial breaks. Every story receives the standard sound-bite allocation, or, at most, a 10-minute "in-depth" report in an investigative format such as *60 Minutes*. In the daily bombardment of TV news, any accident, crime, and scandal has a moment of glory before sinking into oblivion. The standard narration of each item in one of three or four recognizable formulas, and the tight mold of the news program as a whole results in all stories—whether about polluted water, a new health fad, or a law for school reform—sounding equally important, leaving the viewer feeling that nothing is really important (Booth, 1982).

I propose that the same media environment, normally under ever increasing commercial pressures to further erode traditional journalistic norms, may nevertheless, at particular moments, allow for the type of discourse that penetrates from the immediate crisis to the deeper level of structural issues it uncovers. This may happen when disaster strikes, and broadcasters decide to stop all scheduled programs to focus only on the crisis at hand. Which events merit such a treatment in various societies constitutes a fascinating study in itself. It is the mix of pressures—the need to be popular and socially relevant while still competing with rival channels, the evaluation of what the public expects, the strength of a tradition of public broadcasting, or its equivalent—that determines whether street riots, a natural disaster, a lethal accident, or a terrorist attack, merit an interruption of the routine in a given culture. Thus, for example, in the United States, the networks interrupted their evening schedule for long hours in order to broadcast live the chase and arrest of OJ Simpson (Fiske, 1994). Yet though business as usual would be inconceivable in the case of the assassination of a leader, or a major terrorist attack, it is far from certain that the BBC would interrupt its schedule for a police chase after a British OJ. (Although my own analysis draws on the Israeli variation of the genre, I do examine this new format in light of examples from other democracies, mostly the United States.)

Once the event has been declared as deserving a break, it is expected to occupy viewers non-stop, often without any commercial interruption for hours, sometimes days. Events such as the L.A. riots, the San Francisco earthquake, Watergate, or Anita Hill's testimony in Congress, all caused the major networks to interrupt programming schedules (adopting CNN's breaking news format), for a live coverage of the developing event or its aftermath, commuting between the studio and various transmission points—for 4 days (October 11-14, 1991) in the Anita Hill case, 72 hours on Israeli TV following a series of terrorist attacks in winter 1996. While the Watergate and Hill–Thomas affairs enter into the genre that Dayan and Katz labeled ceremonial *media events*, these particular instances belong to the least ceremonial and most democratic subgenre, that of "contests" (which, in our examples, assume the form of confrontational debates), and to the least chaotic, most structured subgenre of crisis marathons.

Notwithstanding the historical, cultural, and institutional differences among countries, and the implications of the globalization of some of the broadcasts (Scannell, 1996), marathons everywhere elude the major weaknesses of routine coverage.

In the space of a disaster marathon, media journalists can make an all-out effort to experience the event, and, once the story has been told, to reflect on its public meanings. In its instant, gestalt manner, television collects victims, witnesses, experts, and whoever may be blamed, or is authorized to tell the tale. As the narrative coheres, anchors and their producers are free to decide on what constitutes the agenda, and on the manner in which the issues would be framed. In addition to the usual politicians, commentators, and relevant experts, in Israel and elsewhere, this is a time when intellectuals and writers are invited to consider the affair, speculate over causes and effects, and reflect on its deeper historical, social and cultural meanings. In the process, the event (rightly or not) is transformed into a metaphor or symbol for deeply rooted maladies of the society (Fiske, 1994).

The next section looks at two recent crisis marathons on Israeli television—one in which existential dilemmas and problematic national idiosyncrasies were exposed, and another that became an occasion for a "high-tech lynching" (to use Judge Thomas' phrase) of the political leadership at the time, and caused the government's downfall in the upcoming elections. Analysis of the first case demonstrates how media marathons may provide an occasion for articulating undercurrents of unsolved dilemmas, historical traumas, and intergroup tensions that are normally so disturbing, that people choose to disregard them.

A TELEVISION MARATHON FOLLOWING "THE HELICOPTERS' DISASTER"

On the evening of February 3, 1997, two army helicopters took off to transport troops on a routine exchange of personnel positions in Israel's "security zone" in southern Lebanon. (Ironically, transport by air was due to safety considerations.) The two helicopters flew close together, with their lights turned off in order not to attract terrorist fire from the Lebanese side. Approaching Israel's northern border, over a village, the two helicopters crashed into one another, killing everyone on board. Seventy-three soldiers died instantly.

As in the case of recent national disasters, the two nationwide television channels, and radio channels both public and commercial, interrupted their regular schedule, canceled all advertising, and, during the following 2 1/2 days, focused entirely on the event. The broadcast proceeded in three phases. First, it reconstructed the event, moving between the site of the disaster and the helicopters' air force base, reporting the fact that there were no survivors, and the decision to set up an investigation committee. Second, television turned to the mourning—reading the long list of names, showing photographs of the young men—almost boys—interviewing families and friends to describe them, attending a number of the funerals, discussing the decision to proclaim the day of the disaster an official national day of mourning. The totality of the disaster—no witnesses, no injured survivors, hardly any debris of the helicopters—created an absolute divide between the event and the marathonic broadcast. The chaotic stage was missing. The mood was heartbreakingly sad but solemn. The gloomy Hebrew songs on the radio were interrupted only by interviews with bereaved families and friends in their homes.

Since the assassination of PM Yizhak Rabin, the nation had not been so united in grief. President Ezer Weitzman, a former air force commander himself, interviewed at the outset, hurried to establish the right note by reminding the nation that "we have the best air force in the world," that the rate of air accidents had dropped appreciably in the last decade, and that accidents cannot be totally prevented. And indeed, the general atmosphere was one of controlled sadness; the usual automatic journalistic drive to search for fault was missing. Only in the third phase of the marathon, after the funerals, did the marathon broadcast move on to conduct a public debate. It was not an obsessive search intended to allocate individual blame but a discussion to examine chronic maladies that underlie everyday news events, but are rarely discussed in the media (Edelman, 1988).

The disaster had brought to the surface three fundamental problems that gradually undermine the unity and resilience of the society. These were discussed on the screen (and reverberated in the printed press), with past and present air force commanders, military historians, technical experts, political figures, bereaved parents (including some who lost their sons on previous military operations), and friends and colleagues of the dead soldiers.

One issue was the price paid for the reliance on what is generally believed to be an Israeli skill for creative improvisation in crisis, which supposedly characterizes the Israeli army. This belief in resourcefulness, originating from the 1948 war, when the army was small, hardly equipped, and inexperienced and yet managed to win the war, results in a reluctance to enforce strict detailed regulations, which may cramp the style of officers, forcing them to act like bureaucrats, "by the book."

Another issue placed on the agenda was the blatantly unjust (but legal) division of the burden between the majority of Israeli youth, who join the army for 3 years of compulsory military service, and the Ultra-Orthodox youth, who have full rights as citizens, yet are not called for army service.

The third issue debated was the rationale for the continued presence of the Israeli army in the security zone in southern Lebanon, where, since the evacuation of Lebanon following the 1982 war, it has been fighting against Hizballa terrorism to protect against Katyusha attacks on Israel's northern towns. And, as is the case each time this issue comes up, the public was once again reminded that the Lebanese problem is part of the larger problem of a peace agreement with Syria.

POSTMORTEM ONSCREEN REFLECTION OVER THE NEW GENRE'S POSSIBLE EFFECTS

On air, the slow departure from the event was characterized by self-reflection. Journalists asked how the event had affected public opinion, and how their own practices during the marathon might reflect or affect cultural norms. These onscreen musings (granted, away from prime time) gave viewers the illusion of peeping backstage. Thus, for example, the answer to the question, what effect did the event have on public opinion, and/or on policy concerning withdrawal from Lebanon, was given by a military historian. This expert believed that the disaster-as-media-marathon could be used "with a little bit of demagogy" to convince the inhabitants of the Golan, the main pressure group against a compromise with Syria, to consider "the overall blood-calculation" in their campaign for keeping the Golan. Thus, the event-on-screen may provide an argument to a "third party," although for the wrong reasons. A public opinion specialist explained that public opinion is affected by historical processes but that the effect presents itself slowly.

In a cultural vein, another "meta-reflection" was concerned with the way the marathon itself, with its invasion of the most private grief, reflected on the changing culture in Israeli society, on the one hand, and on changing journalistic practices, on the other. The PBA's DG expressed concern over TV's increasing lookout for melodrama, which he attributed not only to the need to compete, but also to reporters' evaluation of what 1997 Israelis (unlike 1987) expected them to do. He pointed to an interactive spiral, in which television's thirst to expose personal grief legitimates and encourages victims and families to express unreserved grief, something that was unacceptable heretofore in the culture.

On the whole, the helicopter disaster marathon was a powerful and insightful moment for debating the unsolved social, cultural, and political dilemmas that the accident so brutally brought to the surface. From the perspective of media practices, it was a rare moment in which there was time enough for serious deliberation. Viewers were involved, both personally and in their role of citizens, as the force of the tragedy united Israelis around the screen, dwarfed all other issues, and became the only relevant agenda for public and private discussions. Third, and most important, it was a moment in which the potential cost of specific public policies and practices in human lives became only too real.

The disaster was a moment when private and public concerns became one, and when journalists were involved not only as professionals but also as citizens. But, in character with the postmodern era, and unlike ceremonial media events (Dayan and Katz, 1993), the shared mourning around the set led to a debate, in which contradictory interests and ideologies of various groups were sharply contrasted and negotiated, proving that an emotional communal experience does not necessarily exclude a bitter debate, as Katriel (1998) has shown to occur in a historical unmediated context of pioneer groups. The shadow cast by the disaster influenced the rhetoric of the discourse, holding in check the usual demagogic tricks and easy scoring of rating points with the public. Framed by media professionals, it was a rational debate, in the sense that it was "not opposed to passion, but to tradition and authority, to coercion . . . [and] to the strategic pursuit of ends that are not themselves subject to dialogue" (Hallin, 1994, p. 9). It was a liminal space that sought to clarify social norms and deliberate over possible change in public policy within the mood of communal spirit that formed around the tragedy.

TELEVISION'S MARATHON FOLLOWING A SERIES OF TERRORIST BUS BOMBINGS

And yet, the very openness that makes a media marathon an opportunity for national soul searching, often provides a vacuum that invites a different kind of voice, the likes of which are restricted on ordinary days to the Rush Limbaugh-type of programs. The live broadcast of disaster may be exploited by the government or its opponents for making easy gains with the public. This is a moment for demagogic accusations, for the stirring up of emotions, even for the symbolic lynching of political candidates, leaders, or parties. The intensified drive at such a moment to search for scapegoats may be manipulated by power groups with a vested political interest, allowing the parties or politicians who stand to reap easy gains to transform the discourse into a populist rhetoric aimed at destroying political opponents. In such a case, the chance to gain a deeper understanding of the roots of the crisis at hand is lost.

Television journalists, it should be remembered, are careful not to create their own frames, but to look for the legitimate authority of the moment to latch on to (Alexander, 1981). Crisis may mean that the government, temporarily or permanently, loses the legitimacy to provide the framing (Molotch and Lester, 1974). At the same time, the unscripted marathon broadcast pressures media journalists into adopting instant framing. They are far more vulnerable than usual, as they have to reorganize their resources, establish a marathon routine while the broadcast is going on, and are constantly aware of their responsibility to the large public anxiously watching, often waiting for an explanation. Moreover, these are prestigious moments, in which television leaves its position of wallpaper to dominate the scene—competition is fierce, and the ratings are closely monitored and well publicized.

At the same time, television producers and editors are largely neutralized, receiving, as they are, live reports from the field and having to make instant on-camera decisions. They are captives of the visual drama at hand, trying to gauge the public mood as they go along, hav-

The Danger of Action News

ing to keep up dramatic tension for long hours (sometimes days), and careful to tell the story of whoever seems to be the winner of the day.

All this means that the easier it is to blame a political power—an individual leader, the government, or the opposition—the easier it is for media professionals, who are trained to adopt the current "hot" story, and are in dire need of an appropriate frame for the live broadcast, to succumb to the mood of the moment. In contrast with the helicopter disaster, in which television was not forced to chose between competing versions of the event, the live coverage of a bus bombing in Tel Aviv demonstrates how, when the manipulative version of an interested party gains legitimacy, media professionals collaborate in the melodrama of a "high-tech lynching" of a public figure—a president, a prime minister, a judge, the chief of staff, or the head of police, or a number of figures—who, for that moment, symbolize the evil forces that had caused the disaster (Alexander and Jacobs, 1998; Carey, 1998).

In February-March 1996, two months before the 1996 general elections, Israel was shaken by a series of terrorist attacks, carried out by Hamas fundamentalist groups, on buses in Jerusalem and Tel Aviv. In Jerusalem, two Line 18 buses exploded on two consecutive Sundays, followed, on the following Monday by a bomb causing a massacre in the center of Tel-Aviv. Fifty-four people were killed. As in the case of the helicopter disaster, both channels of Israeli television went into marathon mode. The right-wing opposition, who, until the attacks, had lagged behind in the polls (see chap. 5), framed the events as the outcome of the government's peace process with the Palestinians.

The live broadcast recycled the sights of dead bodies, crying witnesses, screaming mothers searching for their children, injured victims on stretchers, relatives in waiting outside operating rooms. In their worst hour of grief, victims and their families—least fit at that moment to formulate a well thought-out evaluation of the situation—were chosen as public representatives, and interviewed on what policy the government should conduct. Dubious security experts-cum-politicians such as Ariel Sharon, an opposition member of Knesset at that time who had failed as defense minister, and Rehavan Zeevi ("Gandi"), the leader of a small party calling for transfer of the Palestinians, were accredited with status, hosted for long hours in the studio, and permitted to freely exploit the disaster for a vicious attack on the government. Media journalists willingly adopted this framing of the disaster. Had journalists chosen to take a critical distance from the tragedy, it would have called for an analytic examination of the context of the event, along with the alternatives to government policies so heavily criticized. Instead, interviewees selected for their political radicalism, joined hands in wallowing in the disaster, pretending that there were quick solutions at hand, and irresponsibly making the massacre into a black hole, which swallowed the context of the Oslo agreements, the continuation of which was threatened by the terror. Thus, for example, a reporter waiting outside the government emergency meeting was given time to speculate on the measures the government was supposed to decide on—including the military reoccupation of the Gaza strip—"perhaps tonight." When an exhausted junior minister finally emerged to report about a coordination committee for the military and the intelligence forces, he was scolded for the meekness of the solutions. The reporters sensed that their public was looking for blood. Even Israel's president, known for his steady support of the peace process, was carried away by the hysteria enough to announce on TV that these were the most difficult days Israel had ever known.

The TV marathon worked to maximize the impact of the attacks in several ways. First, it decontextualized the attacks from their historical context, recontextulalizing them in a series of "tiger leaps," which connected the current event only to structurally similar incidents, without regard to the immediate reality in which it occurred (Benjamin, 1985). Thus, the onscreen story of the attacks wiped out all the achievements of the Oslo process—the young people's rising hopes of not having to fight any more wars, the opening of the Arab world to Israel after almost 50 years of isolation, the economic boom with the new surge of foreign investments.

Second, the marathon pushed the government to instant response by creating public expectations to "act" while "we" on television are waiting to conclude the story with a happy end. The drama on air ignored all the rules of decision making according to which governments do not make decisions in synch with live broadcasts. Worse, it ignored the fact that there were no immediate solutions—perhaps no long-term solution either—to terrorism. There was, therefore, no way the government could come up with the immediate macho decision demanded by its critics on the screen, even after a whole night of deliberation.

Third, the marathon space fell prey to a cynical opposition, which exploited the show, with the all too eager assistance of media professionals, as a free stage for their election campaign. (Ironically, having won the elections on the demagogy of "there cannot be peace as long as terrorism does not stop," a year later, following a terrorist suicide attack in the Mahane Yehuda market in Jerusalem, Netanyahu admitted that terrorism was not connected with the peace process).

Why did media professionals, not known for their right-wing sympathies, play the game of the opposition? The answer must lie in their sensing that this kind of story satisfied the public's urgent need for finding someone to hang the blame on, and befitted the mood of anger and frustration, which demanded a quick-fix solution, coupled with distrust for more complex, more realistic, answers. In aligning themselves with populist sentiments, thereby exposing their own need for being popular with the crowd, journalists found it easier to squeeze the event for all its emotional kicks and forgo a serious discussion of the issues it might have raised.

Following the marathon, political scientists and media scholars did accuse television's producers and anchors of collaborating with the Hamas terrorist faction in its attempt to destroy the peace process, by discouraging the Israeli public, raising doubts about the chances of the Oslo process, and pushing for the election of a hawkish, right-wing government.

Terrorists produce such events hoping exactly for this kind of coverage (Gerrits, 1992), and, wittingly or not, the commercial competition, the new technologies of live transmission, and the marathon genre have precluded the use of traditional journalistic practices, making it much more exploitable politically. It was a classic moment where extremists on both sides used the media for a common cause, and both were assisted by media professionals. The polls confirm that the bus bombing turned the tide against the Labor party, helping the Likud opposition back to power.

VACILLATING BETWEEN POPULIST APPEALS AND NORMATIVE DEBATE

Generalizing from these two marathons—the helicopter disaster and the bus bombings—suggests that the chances of conducting a normative debate depend on the answers to three questions:

1. Did the event end before the broadcast began or not?
2. Was the threat it generated perceived as continuous and/or existential or not?
3. Could a political leader, a public institution, or a political party be easily blamed?

The first question relates to the syntactic aspect of the story, asking whether the event is over, leaving broadcasters free to investigate the causes that led to the tragedy, or is the event still an unfinished business when it moves on to the screen. (In Tuchman's [1978] terms, from the journalists' perspective—is it a developing or a continuing story?) Heuristically, our two examples are strikingly different. When the first reporter got to the site of the helicopter accident, it was already completely, heartbreakingly, over. The death and destruction were total. No one was left to tell the tale. There was almost nothing to be seen on the ground—the bodies were burned, the helicopters exploded into bits over a vast area, the village where the crash occurred was left undamaged. Thus, there were no messy bits to pursue—no reporting from hospitals, no looking for survivors or chasing after culprits. In contrast, when television arrived on the sites of the terrorists' attack, the story was in no way neatly over. There were horror-struck witnesses, victims in the hospitals, relatives searching the morgue, damage to the shops in the center, security measures taken against further attacks. The public mood was a far cry from the solemn reserve following the helicopters disaster.

Second, as a tragic mistake made by a pilot, now dead, the helicopter accident did not constitute a direct, immediate, or existential future threat, although it did raise fundamental value issues. The air force was entrusted with doing what was necessary to prevent such an accident from ever happening again. The bus bombings, conversely, acted as a reminder of the continual, arbitrary, external threat that could not be controlled, and would unpredictably strike again at any moment, anywhere. Television played along, never missing out on the melodramatic cliches repeatedly heard in disaster marathons on the chance element of individual survival ("I happened to walk out of the bank 2 minutes before it blew up"). And, after three attacks in 2 weeks, nobody could reassure Israelis that the nightmare was over.

Third, the extent to which the event could be exploited politically was also very different in the two cases. In the case of the helicopters, shouldering the blame could mean, at most, unintended negligent action on the part of the military, and was certainly not exploitable on a political level. The terrorist attacks could be blamed on the government, and were consistent with the right-wing campaign line according to which the Labor government was too soft on Palestinian leader Yassar Arafat.

The combination of ongoing onscreen drama, with its emotional appeal, the threat of more attacks in the offing, and the ease of putting the blame on government policy by adopting the right-wing opposition line, offered the right wing an easy political victory, but prevented an open debate that could move from the event to its context.

During 1996-1997, a number of disaster marathons in Israel may be shown to have followed these rules. Real-time coverage of the collapse of a temporary bridge over the Yarkon river, on the opening night of the Maccabia games, an international Jewish sports event, occurred as the cameras were there to record the ceremony. Turning on the set to watch the celebration, Israelis witnessed a mass of people falling into the heavily polluted water on top of each other, as the bridge collapsed. The disaster caused the death of four Australian athletes but there was no existential threat to the society, no political gains to be made, and the extent of the disaster was not yet discovered. Although live broadcast was limited to the duration of that evening, it made its mark, operating similarly to the helicopters' disaster in raising public awareness to the high cost of two failings in the national culture. One is a reluctance to abide by the rules, another version of the failings which emerged in the helicopters' accident, expressed in sloppy, unprofessional execution of tasks while reassuring the client with the by now notorious words, "trust me" or "it will be OK," before going off to the next bungle. The second national flaw highlighted was the tendency of Israelis to uncontrolled hysteria in moments of disaster, which could benefit from the example of self-control demonstrated in the politeness and reserve of the Australians' reaction.

Another disaster—the assassination by a Jordanian soldier of eight girls from Beit Shemesh, a small town near Jerusalem, on a school trip—did not constitute an existential threat, as it was supposedly carried out by a single, "mentally disturbed," Jordanian soldier. It could not be exploited politically because the government and the opposition had a common interest in preserving the peace with Jordan. Moreover, the public wrath the event might have stirred was circumvented by King Hussein's royal gesture of coming to pay his personal condolences to the victims' families in Beit Shemesh; by initiating a ceremonial media event (Dayan and Katz, 1993) the King created a closure to the marathon. Thus, both the option of stirring an emotional public cry for revenge and the option of debating the possible roots of the tragedy were overridden in favor of responding to the grace and humanity of a king who was shown kneeling on the floor before a bereaved mother in mourning.

CRISIS MARATHONS AS SITES OF PUBLIC DEBATE

A number of issues for further study are offered in lieu of recapitulation.

Crisis Marathons and the Public Sphere. I have pointed out that crisis marathons are perhaps the best demonstration of the change in professional norms undergone in the era of electronic journalism. Live broadcasting prevents journalists from invoking their professional practices (corroborating information, checking sources, editing), thereby robbing the media of its potential capacity to serve as a shared arena for public debate. At the same time, provided that anxiety is not overwhelming, the temporal space cleared from all else in such moments does create an opportunity for an in-depth discussion of endemic issues that are usually swept under the rug.

Crisis Marathons and Media Events. What are the most memorable moments on television? Dayan and Katz made a convincing case for the live broadcasting of public ceremonies. Alternatively, it may be argued, as Scannell (1996) did, that the magic moments of television, which linger in memory long after the event, are not the carefully preplanned celebrations that Dayan and Katz exult in, but events such as the explosion of the Challenger space shuttle, Nelson Mandella's release from prison after 30 years of invisibility, or the downfall of Mrs. Thatcher (a choice that reminds us of the extent to which highlights are culture-bound). According to this view, what television does best is destroy the charisma of leaders rather than promote it, and TV's great moments are therefore those which demystify heroes (or, as in the case of Mandella, assist in the birth of new ones), not the ones that glorify them.

Even if live ceremonial events were the highlights of TV during the 1970s and 1980s, crisis seemed to be the dominant media event of the 1990s. Whether this was brought about by mobile equipment, competition, the struggle against cable television, or a new evaluation of what the public wants to see, live marathons certainly fit Scannell's description of television's forte. Although formally the new genre fulfills a number of the conditions stipulated by Dayan and Katz—constituting an interruption of the ordinary schedule by an external event (not initiated by the media), which becomes the sole focus of the broadcast for hours, sometimes days, and which typically attracts large audiences—it is characterized by conflict and, sometimes, by fierce debate, not unity and reconciliation. Although events such as the royal wedding (1981), Anwar Sadat's visit to Jerusalem (1977), or the first landing on the moon (1969) are initiated, controlled, and starred in by the establishment, this new genre originates in those moments in which the establishment temporarily loses control, and, as such, may serve as an opportunity for an independent and open public debate.

But disaster and media events sometimes constitute phases in one sequence, or cycle: routine, the sudden eruption of disaster, the ensuing chaotic crisis, a return to some form of control, and, sometimes, to a collective ceremony (which calls for further mourning), and a return to routine. Although disasters call for blame and therefore provide an occasion for critical journalistic discourse, ceremonies restore hegemony, call for appreciation, causing journalists to lose their independence. Hence, the desire of the political establishment to end disasters with the closure of collective ceremonial events. And the more they are to blame in the public's eyes, the stronger this need (e.g., PM Peres' initiating the Sharm-el-Sheich Conference following the 1996 bus bombings, King Hussein's visit to Beit Shemesh, the Royal family's decision to arrange a royal funeral for Diana). In cases where such ceremonial closure occurs, careful study of the live marathons that precede them shifts attention from the ceremony back to the debate.

Crisis Marathon as Co-optation of a Media Event. I have suggested that marathon events are triggered by loss of control. Accidents are, typically, are a disruption of routine (although a number of famous disasters, such the Challenger, or the Titanic, started as media events), yet disruptions are often planned to subvert or coopt a pre-planned ceremonial event. From the initiators perspective—typically terrorists or assassins—this is a moment where the cameras are already there, and maximum public attention can be counted on (Gerrits, 1992). In Dayan and Katz's terminology, this would constitute a "hijacking" of the event. Dayan and Katz, however, referred to public and physical hijackings—as in the case of the massacre of the Israeli team members in the Munich Olympics, or the assassination of Yizhak Rabin at the end of a peace rally—which use the event as an occasion to eliminate its heroes.

But there are also disruptions that are motivated by the wish to influence the event itself. Disruptions invade the event either by playing by the rules yet introducing oppositional voices, or by co-opting the event—from inside or from without, upfront or from behind the scenes. Such an invasion is not meant to stop the event but to change its meaning, either by opening up the debate beyond what the organizers have planned for, or by destroying altogether the option of an open debate. Thus, just as the message of the Archbishop of Canterbury's speech in Charles and Diana's wedding in 1981 had transformed the meaning of the event (Dayan and Katz, 1993), so did the speech of Earl Spencer, Diana's brother, insert an oppositional meaning into the ceremony of her funeral 16 years later.

Disruptions are particularly relevant in the case of "contests," the type of media event that comes closest to a democratic exchange. Useful examples for the co-optation of a seemingly open contest are the case of "managing" the most popular quiz show on television in 1957, or the behind-the-scenes takeover of the Congressional Committee hearings in the case of Judge Bork, President Reagan's nominee for the Supreme Court, in 1987 (Carey, 1998). In this case, the Democratic party, then in control of the Congress, cynically manipulated the event, turning an open hearing that was supposed to assist Congressmen in making up their minds about the professional qualifications of the candidate, into a public relations spectacle played out only for the benefit of the viewing public with the intention of bulldozing the candidacy. The experienced conservative judge was made to look like the enemy of the core American values. After it was over, Judge Bork himself described the hearings as "high-tech lynching," intended to turn public opinion against him. In this case, what may have looked on screen as a fair and open contest, was in fact a managed affair, which prevented the development of any genuine dialogue, demonstrating how a potentially meaningful public debate stands no chance when it is politically controlled.

Unlike the subversion of the rules from behind the scenes by the power in control, the marathonic broadcast of Anita Hill's testimony in front of the Congressional Committee, which interrupted the hearings on the nomination of Judge Clarence Thomas to the Supreme Court in 1991, demonstrates another way of hijacking a ceremonial hearing—upfront, by an outsider, and with the purpose of raising an issue that the committee would have otherwise ignored, had it remained in control. From the public's point of view, Hill's testimony—opening a public debate on live TV, which continued on everyday television, and in the press—made sexual harassment a legitimate issue for public discourse, placing it up front on the public agenda (in the United States and elsewhere).

Accidents, Scandals, Disruptions, and Public Debate. As argued earlier, crisis marathons often come about through an accident that reveals defects in the routine practices of various public institutions. Such were the cases of the Challenger's explosion in 1986 in the United States, and the helicopter disaster, and the Yarkon bridge in Tel Aviv in 1997. On other occasions, an accident, or a political enemy, or a chance camera, may point to a scandal, which reveals anti-normative practices in the government or the police force (Watergate, 1972; the Bar-On affair in Israel, 1997; Rodney King, 1991). But the question should be raised whether the distinction between accidents and scandals is as clear-cut as in Molotch and Lester's scheme. It could be argued that public debate over an accident consists of trying to establish whether the cause was only negligence, or was it rooted in a rabid violation of norms. Seen as such, a scandal is just a step beyond establishing that a violation has occurred.

Labeling loss of control as *disruption* signifies that the failure is not considered to originate from within, and that nobody can be held directly responsible. Here, the debate centers on indirect social and political responsibility, beyond a particular scandal. When an assassin is considered a lunatic operating on his own (Oswald, Yigal Amir in the initial reports from the murder scene), or when disruption is caused by known external enemies (the Moslem fundamentalists terrorists responsible for bombing New York's Twin Towers), or groups known to break the rules (the fringe extremist group responsible for the disaster in Oklahoma), the event does not become a cause for public debate, or, for that matter, for populist incitement. When, however, an assassin represents a radical political faction within the society (Yigal Amir in later stages of the investigation), or when a terrorist attack is considered the outcome of a weak government policy (the bus bombings in Israel, 1996), a fierce public debate would ensue. Here, as I argued earlier, the more devastating the collective trauma, the more the threat to the society is perceived as acute, the bigger the chance that the crisis would be used for political discreditation, that the ensuing public debate would be less rational, and that the affair would harm the resilience of the body politic.

Cultural Differences. The type of crisis that characterizes media marathons, and the frequency of the use of the genre itself, Fiske's (1994) list of major "media events" (in Scannell's sense of the term) in the United States consists of the Hill–Thomas Congressional hearings, the Rodney King Los Angeles riots, the OJ Simpson chase, and the Murphy Brown–Dan Quayle argument over "family values." Coverage of the first two started as media marathons on nationwide television channels; the third transgressed generic boundaries rather than interrupted the daily schedule. But it should be remembered that the criteria for deciding on a marathon, its length and its public impact, in a country like Israel, with its strong tradition of public broadcasting and political involvement, varies a great deal from the use of the genre in a country like the United States, with its tradition of commercial, entertainment-oriented television, and a less politically involved public.

Finally, the choice of marathon format reveals the type of issues with which society is preoccupied. As Fiske's list made evident, the American events that "spurred nationwide debates" are concerned with struggles over race, class, and gender politics, raising issues that belong in what Giddens (1994) called "life politics," that is, politics that presumes "emancipation from the fixities of tradition and from conditions of hierarchical domination . . . it is a politics of choice" (p. 214). Specifically, the events mentioned deal with individual and communal life and with self-identity, in the moral arenas of cooperation and personhood. Most of the marathons on Israeli television, however, belong to the more basic domain of existence, in the moral arena of national survival and being.

5

Constructing Scandal: Whistle Blowing, Entrapment, and Spotlighting

In the era of privatization, as chapter 4 argued, disaster marathons substituted media events as the high holidays of news. We turn now to daily news, the bread-and-butter genre that delivers to viewers an edited, sound-bite version of sensationalized, melodramatic stories. The major difference between the disaster marathons and daily news is that in the routine daily viewing of this controlled genre, viewers are free from the open-ended anxiety that accompanies disaster marathons. Nevertheless, rather than put out policy issues for public debate, news has become a series of tightly sealed vignettes, in which public and private affairs are wrapped up, packaged, and sealed as mini-dramas—visualized, personalized, and simplified. And news jingles or promos, now institutionalized on Israeli radio and TV, provide a useful way of finding out how editors define the genre, and/or sell this heretofore respectable genre to their clients.

Needless to say, the very resorting to promos or jingles redefines news in the new commercial, Americanized, media environment, as just another competitor for popularity among consumers, along with soap operas, quiz shows, and the like. This is yet another indication of the establishment of a free-for-all market, where prestige and dignity are no longer sufficient to secure the status of news. It has joined in the race.

As news and entertainment intermingle in the endless verbal and visual flow designed to capture and retain consumers, radio and TV advertise news in the best tradition of soaps, structuring sequences of best quotes of the latest season, reminding us of the melodramatic peaks, and inventing an instant virtual dialogue among characters that belong to different news plots. Are these promos meant to present last year's most important political events? Media reporters' greatest feats? The year's greatest dramas? The best remembered lines? The highlights in the fortunes of characters viewers love, or hate, or love to hate? The new ground rules under which any broadcasting institution operates mean that these jingles must have elements of all of the aforementioned. As jingles used to signal that we are in the realm of entertainment, news jingles relocate news and current affairs within this realm, metonymically encapsulating the characteristics of contemporary news, as a transformed genre.

This chapter argues that the increasing slavery to ratings has made scandal the dominant type of story on electronic news. It starts with a number of examples of Israeli news promos (an Americanized genre in its own right), in order to demonstrate that reminders of juicy scandals are used by news producers to promote their product and lure viewers. Having established scandal as the central news format, the chapter goes on to analyze the directions in which scandal has developed in the new media environment.

News Promos: American Form, Israeli Figures (Plus American Favorites). As in the sharing of a common history in families by evoking a fond memory, radio and TV promos cultivate a common ground with listeners by sharing punch lines of the greatest stories in recent collective memory. (Although in both family and society, favorite quotes remind us of who we are, the first typically invokes empathy, whereas the second often promotes cynicism toward our leaders.)

Jingles provide a unique opportunity for the electronic media to introduce a perspective that counteracts their daily glorifying of the hottest items of the moment. By making a checklist of "What do we (should we?) remember," they put us in the superior position of all-knowing listeners, capable of re-evaluating the various statements from the perspective of hindsight. This recapturing of the stock after the dust has settled makes news promos a good source for defining the genre from the perspective of its makers. What then can we regard as the essential news of the month/year/decade—the ones we are supposed to recognize in an instant? The ones that "made a difference"? The ones that media professionals can be proud of?

Let us look at the following cluster, broadcast on the Galatz (Galey Zahal = IDF Waves) channel of Israel's public radio. Advertising their popular morning news hour (3.8.2000), Galey Zahal plays four promo sequences alternately, all to a musical background, opening with the sentence "You never can tell what kind of news morning you'll wake into," and ending with "The news starts here. Good morning Israel with Micha Friedman, every day at 6 o'clock on Galey Zahal."

"We decided to convict Arieh Deri for taking bribes." (*District Judge Ya'akov Zemach*)

"All the things that have been hurled at me are not true." (*government minister Yizhak Mordechai*)

"I did not have sexual relations with that woman." (*President Clinton*)

"Ha beha talia" [in Aramaic—"one thing depends on another"] (*Foreign Minister David Levi*)

"Ha vetu lo ['Only that']. 'Read my lips' [*sic*–in English]. Ha vetu lo." (*Lawyer Ya'akov Weinrot*)

"When you say 'Damned be Hamman' say also 'Damned be Yossi Sarid.'" (Shas' spiritual leader *Rabbi Ovadia Yossef*)

What can we conclude from this example about what the constructors of news market to their (real and potential) audiences as the essential, or quintessential, genre of news? All six quotes are critical moments in stories that expose covert (or semi-covert) actions of major public figures, who have performed (or are suspected of performing) a major violation of social norms. The list of violations in the sequence goes as follows: bribe-taking by an ex-government minister and the leader of an ethnically based major party; sexual harassment by a government minister (and ex-candidate for the office of prime minister) and by President Clinton ("naturally" incorporated into the family of Israeli politicians); a threat for an "eye-for-an-eye" revenge addressed to Lebanon from the Knesset podium (in response to Hezbolla terrorist attacks); bribery charges against Israel's president at the time; and the incitement to the murder of a political foe delivered in synagogue by the spiritual leader of a major political party.

The first thing that arises (from this cluster of quotes as well as from a larger sample), then, is that the majority of jingles evoke a narrative of scandal, that is, the uncovering of illicit conduct that constitutes a deviation from acceptable, normative behavior. This chapter argues that in the new era of electronic press, scandal has become a routine component of news and, at the same time, decreased in status. What used to be considered the journalist's finest hour, associated with investigative work, and the exposure of substantiated and valuable information, has been transformed. The technological revolution, the commercialization and proliferation of media channels, and, with it, the routinization of live broadcasting, have trivialized scandal and made the role of reporters in its unraveling less important. This chapter then examines the genre of scandal in light of the Americanization of Israel's media environment.

Scandal as the Other Pole of Routine Reporting. Among the attempts to classify news stories, Molotch and Lester's (1974) classic fourfold typology is based on the relationship between event makers and news constructors, proposing scandal as one pole in the seesaw game between political sources and reporters over who controls the agenda (Schudson, 1992). Accordingly, scandals are juxtaposed with "routine news," the daily menu with which the political establishment feeds the press. While in routine events, such as press conferences (Boorstin, 1964, called them "pseudo-events"), the event perpetrators are in charge of making them publicly known (often creating the event for the sake of publicity), scandals tell the story of events that their perpetrators choose to initiate but would do all they could to keep away from the public eye. Such stories become public knowledge when revealed by sources other than their initiators, sometimes engaging journalists in an active search to unravel and substantiate them. As scandals are made public against the will of their perpetrators, they are also the moments in which, seemingly, reporters (rather than perpetrators) control the agenda, moments in which they demonstrate the power they have over public figures and institutions (Molotch and Lester's fourfold table is completed by two additional narrative forms: *accidents*—events whose perpetrators did not want to occur, and certainly would not make public if it were up to them—and *serendipitous* events that, although not deliberate, do constitute a lucky turn for politicians who co-opt them after the fact, making sure that they are made public). Within this model, then, *scandal* is the type of news story in which journalists, at the risk of shaking the delicate balance that they normally try to preserve with their sources, fulfill their watchdog role by tearing apart the managed image of public figures and unveiling the "true" face beneath the facade.

Conceived at the beginning of the 1970s, Molotch and Lester's definition of scandal as a subgenre of news is based on a reality of restricted and regulated media channels, of a society that shares basic norms, and of journalism that at its best is encouraged (or, at least, allowed) to invest time and energy in the hazardous job of investigative reporting. In the year 2000, electronic journalism, to a large extent, had taken over. Media everywhere had become segmented (making nationwide media less central), and the press, both printed and electronic, in its ever increasing chase after ratings, was working increasingly vis-à-vis professional image makers in promoting routine events, while at the same time was constantly on the lookout for exposing that image. Scandal seemed a more prevalent but perhaps less noble genre, as it became increasingly difficult to separate the economic dictates of the press from its professional ones; as violations of certain social norms, once made public, could no longer be ignored, whereas other norms had become disputed by multiculturalism, and as the dictates of political correctness made for an abundance of "discursive" scandals. How did these changes affect the genre of scandal?

Scandal as a Good Story. As stated previously, the sheer fact of "promoting" the news means that it is no more the pure journalistic format that speaks to listeners as concerned citizens (on their way, sooner or later, to the next election polls), but has instead become yet another dramatic genre, to be advertised by the station or the channel for the purpose of selling itself to sponsors. News, the jewel in the crown of public channel journalism, has been incorporated in the routine commercial battle over consumers and ratings. In this race it competes over capturing listeners against other stations and other genres.

The salience of the scandal as a subgenre of news in the new electronic marketplace may be explained by seeing scandal not necessarily, or not only, as an important story, but also as a good story. Luckily for scandal, by competing on this dimension, it stands a good chance. Peeping into the "bedrooms" of public figures (the office would do, and is often more practical) to learn about their sexual practices, or invading their backstage intimate circle to witness what they "really think," has always been a joy, and constitutes a major source of pleasure in less pretentious yet no less titillating dramatic genres with a voyeuristic appeal (all defined as "soft porn" by literary theorist Leslie Fiedler, 1982). Thus, it is not always easy to distinguish between *scandal* as journalism at its best, and at its yellowest.

Personalized Politics Legitimates Scandal. But then again, the increasing centrality of scandal, it may argued, is not only dictated by the need to sell the channel, but is also part of the increasing legitimacy given to journalism proper to invade a widening territory of what used to be considered private spaces, along with the changing definition of politics and of social norms. The right to invade politicians' private spaces has been granted to media by the personalization of politics, which has rather given up on ideological differences in favor of competing over the integrity, authenticity and compassion of elected, or would-be elected, leaders (see chap. 8). This desired image is enhanced by a huge public relations machine on the candidates' side—mobilizing spouses, children, and parents for campaigns, apologizing for committing adultery (even confessing entertaining lecherous thoughts)—making the private domain heretofore defined as out of bounds into a legitimate (and central) journalistic concern. The urgent need for creating the "right" pubic image is even reflected backward in the decisions taken by candidates concerning their relationship and their style of family life. This has made it all the more crucial to find out whether the person is "really" what he or she claims to be. The more politicians invest in managing their own "private" image publicly, the more legitimate it becomes for journalists to batter that image, and the doubt whether intimate behavior is at all relevant to the qualities needed for public leadership is pushed aside.

Stricter Norms Legitimate Scandal. Not only has the public's right to know expanded to the lives of its chosen leaders in and out of the office, norms of political conduct (regarding the appointing of cronies, distributing favors, or sexually harassing subordinates) have become stricter, as social movements fighting for class, ethnic, and gender equality and opportunity have made their mark. These changes mean that practices that journalists used to go along with, or took for granted as the privilege of the powerful (remember the U.S. press turning a blind eye on John F. Kennedy's philandering, the French press respecting Mitterand's private life, and the Israeli press keeping the juicy stories of Moshe Dayan's womanizing for inner circle entertainment), now constitute a legitimate ground for scandal.

Multiculturalism Enriches and Relativizes Scandal. And yet, paradoxically, at the same time as mainstream public norms became stricter since Molotch and Lester's definition of scandals (as exposure of covert antinormative acts), the explosion of multiculturalism also means that there is a new tolerance to particularistic group norms, and that the Molotch and Lester dichotomy of overt–covert conduct has become less absolute. In contemporary Western societies, what would constitute a routine event for a range of segmented media channels, normally broadcasting only to their own cultural enclave, may be told as a major scandal once broadcast nationally. Despite the fact that anybody can listen in, for the public at large what is talked about may be not known, or known partially, or marginally, in ways that make it easy to disregard "knowing."

A TYPOLOGY OF MEDIA SCANDALS

Taking into account the changes undergone by press, society, and politics, I suggest a scheme for the relationship between perpetrators and media in the generating of scandal. This new typology organizes scandals in terms of three kinds of short circuiting or subverting communication between reporters and sources:

1. *Whistle blowing* occurs when insiders, for idealistic or political or personal motives, cut themselves off from their environment by volunteering information about a carefully hidden dark secret, damaging to the perpetrator.
2. *Entrapment* occurs when a reporter, or a production team, for professional or political or personal motives, breaks a tacit or explicit agreement with a source, exposing the source as violating the norm.
3. *Spotlighting* or *mainstreaming* occurs when an insider, or a marginal viewer or listener, calls attention to a potential scandal on a marginal channel (one that may even be vaguely known) in order to put it on the nationwide agenda; or when an accident, or an attempt to enforce the law on a widespread violation, calls the attention of mainstream media that pushes to enforce the norm or to modify it.

The two first types had been there all along, but have changed their nature in the new media environment, and the third is a product of the new environment. Although the issues unraveled by the scandals often represent the difference between U.S. and Israeli societies, the interaction between sources and media reporters takes similar forms. Live broadcasting is a major feature in transforming patterns of whistle blowing and entrapment by disintermediating the reporter, and allowing for new kinds of entrapment. Multiple channels give rise to mainstreaming and spotlighting.

Table 5.1 shows the three types of short circuits that occur between reporters and sources.

The power over the release of the scandals in Column 1 lies in the hands of "perpetrators," in the form of an insider who decides to split (Wigand, Vanunu) and becomes a "deep throat" (Column 1). In the

TABLE 5.1. A Typology of Scandals

Type I Whistle Blowing	Type II Entrapment	Type III Spotlighting/Mainstreaming
Insider's Betrayal	**Reporter's Betrayal**	**Spotlighting Routine Violation**
Aim Expose or reinterpret	Expose or reinterpret	Break pluralistic ignorance
Source's motivation political/ideological, personal vendetta, politically manipulated	*Reporter's motivation* political/ideological, personal vendetta, politically manipulated	*Insider/outsider's motivation* political/ideological, personal vendetta, politically manipulated
Tactic a. Reporter coaxes hesitant/frightened source	a. Reporter coaxes naive or unaware source	a. Reporter uses routine event to spotlight (i.e., police search)
Dilemma Can reporter protect source? Convince editor?	Can reporter betray source for sake of honest reporting?	No clear-cut solution; not "our" problem
Examples Idealist (Wigand, Vanunu)	Joe Klein (*Primary Colors*) David Bar-Ilan (*The New Yorker*)	"Massage parlors" (foreign workers)
b. Reporter coaxed by source	b. Reporter manipulates the way in	b. Insider/reporter/outsider transfers info from side stage
Dilemma Can source be trusted?	Betray trust, legal risk vs. public interest	Multiculturalism vs. universalistic norms
Examples Linda Tripp (as source) Yova Yitzhak	*The Practice* (breaking prior agreement)	*Din Rodef* on Channel 7; Rabbi Ovadia Yossef on Satellite TV
c. Source incorporates "off-record," confidential, illegally obtained info	c. Reporter incorporates "off-record" information, takes info out of context	c. Insider/outsider takes information out of context
Dilemma Is colleague/friend expendable?	Is interviewee expendable?	Is source expendable?
Examples Linda Tripp (as Monica's confidant)	Ori Or	Ovadia Yossef

scandals listed in Column 2, the reporter (and editor) holds the power over the source by winning their confidence, only to betray it in the name of public interest (or a great scoop). The scandals in Column 3 erupt either due to an initiative of a stubborn reporter (or one with a "mission") determined to spotlight an endemic issue, or to a voice from a marginal or enclave channel who decides to transmit to the rest of the society on mainstream media. This last role can also be undertaken by an "incidental tourist" (listener/viewer/reporter) who draws the attention of mainstream media to an aberration in its marginal channels.

WHISTLE BLOWING: BETRAYAL BY AN INSIDER

This is the classical, "purest," form of scandal, closest to the Molotch and Lester model. Here, scandal erupts when a source, hostile to the perpetrator, "outs" an institution or a person for blatantly deviant practices, kept heretofore under cover. Although such an exposure is considered the journalists' "finest hour" (since they reveal information damaging to establishment figures or institutions), I argue that reporters are much less powerful in these cases than they seem to be. It may be obvious, but it is worth reiterating, that (unlike the impression given by Molotch and Lester) journalists need sources, no less for scandals than for routine news.

Can He or She be Trusted? Can He or She be Protected? Would My Editor Print It? In the interaction between a reporter and an insider about to blow up a scandal, both source and reporter are aware of the price they may have to pay. The source may risk his or her reputation or livelihood, or even the possibility of standing trial; and the greater the treachery and the resulting damage to heretofore employers/friends, the greater he or she has to be motivated in order to overcome it and come forward. The journalist must face the risk of destroying crucial links with major institutions and individual sources, of failing to protect the source's anonymity, of failing to make the story foolproof, and, now more than ever before, of failing to persuade the editor (or publisher) to run the story. The "hotter" the story, and the more powerful its object, the more doubtful the willingness of editors or owners to pursue it, and the greater the damage to the reporter if story collapses.

In the insider-type scandal, the reporter's dependence on the source is greatest. Take, for example, the case of the women's circumcision, regularly carried out in certain communities in Britain, which was generally avoided by national media until one of the victims dared to defy her community and speak out. Because the (justified) fear of people within closely knit hierarchical communities of being ostracized often overwhelms their wish to speak out, deviant practices can continue undisturbed within these groups.

But not all whistle blowers are equally trustworthy, or equally committed. Ironically, the ones who are most eager to tell all may be the least trustworthy. On the one hand, they may have nothing to lose by self-exposure, and may therefore anyway skip reporters altogether. On the other hand, the more trustworthy whistle blowers may also be more hesitant (or scared, or ambivalent), as they have the most to lose, making the journalist's role crucial yet placing serious responsibilities on their shoulders (Woodward and Bernstein worked hard to convince "deep throat," and managed to keep his identity under cover; Linda Tripp, eager to tell her story and receive publicity, was no journalistic feat).

The Idealist Insider. Although the reporter's motivation is to achieve professional success (without burning bridges) and to get along with his or her employer, the motivation of the whistle blower can be idealistic, political, self-serving, revengeful, or a combination of all of these characteristics. The idealist deep throat is easy to deal with, as the reporter can have real empathy, and a notion of shared motivation. Yet, idealist whistle blowers may have the most to lose from changing alliances, and may get cold feet in the process. Consider an insider like Daniel Ellsberg, who handed the Pentagon Papers over to *The New York Times* (*NYT*); or, more recently, Jeffrey Wigand, the scientist who had worked for cigarette manufacturers Brown and Williamson, and reported to Lowell Bergman, a producer for *60 Minutes*, about the practices used by the firm to create addiction. Both had signed confidentiality agreements—one with the state, the other with the company. In the struggle to solve the dissonance between their loyalty and formal commitment to their institutional role and their conscience, both ended up handing over the incriminating information. Ellsberg, who was fervently trying to influence the U.S. administration to withdraw from Vietnam (by approaching congressmen, government officials, right up to Kissinger himself), was eager to see the Papers in a major newspaper. It was the management of the *NYT* who needed long deliberations about whether and how to publish the Papers. In the *60 Minutes* case, producer Bergman had to maneuver between persuading Wigand, his source, to deliver, persuading his own bosses to air the story, and trying to protect Wigand from the ensuing revenge of his former employers. The worse scandals seem to their perpetrators, the more desperate they are for "damage control," and the greater the risk that a series of offshoots, or "side" scandals will surface, which may develop to overwhelm the original story. Remember the erasure of Watergate tapes, the attempts to blackmail and discredit the whistle blowers on how cigarettes are made and on how the Vietnam war was run—Wigand's pension was stopped (by the company), the office of Ellsberg's psychiatrist was broken into (by the government).

What complicates matters is that reporters (or editors, or producers) are put in a position where they make promises that they cannot keep. Although Bernstein and Woodward have managed to keep the identity of Watergate's deep throat in secret (it was easier 20 years ago), Lowell Bergman of *60 Minutes* (as the tale is told in the film *The Insider*), managed to convince Wigand that he would be protected by the nationwide publicity following his appearance on the most prestigious program and be given a hero's status. But once Bergman had managed this feat, he ran into the problem of the refusal of his editor (Don Hewitt) to broadcast the item. Although Bergman's professional mission put him in the same camp with the altruistically motivated whistle blower, the broadcasting institution, CBS, apparently had strong business interests against publishing, and they convinced Don Hewitt to go along. Had this policy prevailed, Bergman would have lost an important story in terms of public interest, betrayed the confidence of the source, who would not be able to complete his mission, and would have been destroyed by the company he betrayed. (It is easy to understand why, following this experience, Bergman left CBS to work for PBS.)

Not surprisingly, the most dramatic whistle-blowing stories in Israel emerge in the realm of national security, the most damaging of which is the case of Mordechai Vanunu, a technician in Israel's hush-hush atomic reactor, who sold his story to the *London Times*, and was caught, put on trial, and given a life sentence for handing out Israel's most precious secret. Unlike the Pentagon Papers, no Israeli paper would publish the story. During the 1990s, with the individualization of the society, and the opening to competition of print and electronic media, issues of security increasingly came up for public debate.

The Insider on a Personal Vendetta. Whistle blowers can also be overly enthusiastic to go public, making the reporter's part easier in terms of retrieving the information, but sometimes more complex in terms of judgment: Does the story fall under "public interest" or is it only of prurient interest to the public? And, even worse, the framing of such a story calls on the reporter for deciding if he or she believes the charges.

This dilemma has become particularly acute in the last decade for two reasons: First, there is the broadening of the definition of deviant practices with the increasing personalization of politics. As politicians shift from right and left into center, the emphasis on trust and credibility, rather than on differences in ideology or policy, remain the main campaign issue. Electing a candidate for "really caring" rather than for the policy he or she proposes legitimates disregarding the separation between the public and private realm, and focusing increasingly on the private mores and morals of politicians. Second, with multiculturalism and feminism taking root, there is a change in cultural norms, which makes unacceptable what used to be perceived as acceptable practice. For example, the seeping in of feminist ideas means that social norms concerned with gender relations have been transformed, bringing down public figures who failed to notice this change in time. And three trends—the personalization of politics, multiculturalism, and feminism—have been modeled after the United States.

Thus, the context that made Linda Tripp's venture "take" as a big scandal is one that engages both the personalization of politics and the changing boundaries in the relationships between employers and employees. A former White House employee, Tripp rode the high seas of the new political culture, feeding on her personal vendetta, to revenge herself on her former employers, as did General Amiram Levin, Israel's deputy head of the Mossad, who lost his head over being passed over for the top appointment. Both hurried to the media to expose the personal weaknesses of their former superiors. Such sources are gung ho to tell all, and are likely to enlist the support of the political enemies of their bosses and buddies. A particularly vulnerable whistle blower is the woman who exposes what she claims is sexual harassment. First, the victim may need to be coaxed, as it is most likely that the "outer" is fighting against superior powers, that it's often her word against his, and that even if she is proved truthful by the court and the press, her reputation may remain dubious, and her motives questioned (the question of Anita Hill's credibility has never been fully decided). Second, as the harasser is usually in a higher status position, typically exploiting a subordinate, and as the story has the potential of becoming a scandal only if the accused is a public figure, it could mean the end of the accused's public career (as in the case of the complaint filed in the police by an office worker of an Israeli Cabinet Minster, an ex-army general and one of the three candidates for prime minister in the 1999 elections). On the other hand, the whistle blower may belong to the category of informers acting out of hurt pride, out to revenge herself for having been abandoned, or just out to blackmail the man she accuses (Paula Jones seems a case in point).

Politically Motivated or Politically Exploited Whistle Blower. Just as in the United States, whistle blowers on Israeli media may be politically motivated or themselves exploited by politically interested parties. The timing of some seemingly bona fide incriminating information about public figures may be telling, especially if it involves digging out an old or half-baked story. It may be timed just at the right moment to prevent a politician from making a politically significant decision (or to cause him or her to take a popular but irresponsible decision aimed at lowering media and public attention to the scandal, *Wag the Dog* style). When the chances of signing a peace agreement between Israel and Syria started to look up (in January 2000), a self-defined free-lance journalist called a press conference to expose President Ezer Weitzman's acceptance of "presents" from a (non-Israeli) millionaire friend while he was in public office, years earlier (the affair alluded to in the cluster of news jingles presented earlier). Speculation in the Israeli press pointed to Israeli millionaire Ya'akov Nimrodi (who owns a newspaper that had formerly employed the reporter) as the initiator of the exposé, designed to discredit the president and impair his capacity for persuading Israelis to support the peace treaty. Yitzhak Mordechai, the Israeli minister exposed for sexual harassment (another character in that jingle), pointed to the same motivation in order to insinuate that his accuser was backed by political interests who would like to end his career because he positioned himself against a compromise with Syria; this time it sounded more like a conspiracy theory adopted in desperation.

It is worth noting that in many of these cases the reporters have become increasingly marginal. First, there is evidence to show that even in the good old days, the label *investigative reporting* could be just a euphemism, devised by a paper or a TV channel to give themselves primary credit for obtaining the scoop, which is what took place (after the fact) in the case of the Pentagon Papers (Ungar, 1972). Nevertheless, there are cases in which reporters do deserve the credit for taking up and pursuing the tough investigative work. But the radical transformation in the part reporters play for whistle blowers occurred in an era of a multiplicity of electronic channels, which has brought about new current affairs formats, and live broadcasting. The speed to beat the competitors to it, the range of options to choose from, and the will to control the broadcast all mean that both whistle blowers and public figures under attack often prefer to choose their own stage, and dictate their own conditions. Making a statement directly on TV, selecting an easy interviewer, and/or the highest remuneration, are favored options (recall Monica Lewinsky). The press is then left to write background stories, to interview "spokespersons" of the perpetrators and of the victims, and to do the follow-up. Thus, the reporter is not accountable, and potential scandals later turn out to be exaggerations or simply lies.

For editors, whistle blowers who are personally or politically motivated (or exploited) are problematic. First, there is the over zealousness of these sources. Such whistle blowers, acting when they they obviously bear a grudge, should be suspicious, and the information they carry (or claim to) is tainted. If not treated with caution, the story may boomerang on the reporter. Unfortunately, in today's media reality, these whistle blowers can choose to appear live on prime time, speaking their minds without assuming any accountability, yet getting the stage by virtue of their being "a good story." The truth will be fought out in the courts or in the political system. But the (often damaging) impact to the public figures targeted has already been done.

In their over-zealous adoption of technological innovations and commercial standards, Israeli media professionals have more than once caused themselves serious embarrassment. One major case in point is PM Netanyahu, who, during his term in office, demanded and received time on the evening news on both TV channels to speak to the public, following a decision not to put him on trial for conspiring to appoint a state prosecutor promoted by criminal elements. He demanded to deliver his statement uninterrupted by any questions from reporters, and used his airtime to launch a vicious attack on the police and the state prosecutor. The fact that the decision not to prosecute the prime minister was taken due to lack of sufficient evidence, and that the decision had been accompanied by a severe condemnation of the PM in an attached "public report," was naturally not addressed. The heads of the news departments on the two channels regretted their collaboration only after the fact.

ENTRAPMENT: BETRAYAL BY THE JOURNALIST

Going to Bed as Best Friends, and Waking Up? Betrayal is always lurking when journalists walk the thin line of befriending sources while remaining sufficiently free of personal commitment to do honest reporting. At least two U.S. presidents (Nixon and Clinton) had the experience of being followed on the campaign trail by a reporter, whom they believed (rightly to some extent) to be their fan, only to wake up to the criticism directed at them by their supposed buddy (Joe McGinniss' *The Selling of the President* and Joe Klein's *Primary Colors*, which was originally published anonymously). Presumably, one good reason for Klein's reluctance to reveal his identity was his embarrassment over betraying his subject (who, despite the unflattering stories, still comes out as a lovable and charismatic person). Incidently, the second time is supposed to be easier, and McGinniss did it again after he was hired by an army doctor on trial for killing his wife and two daughters. Employed to report on the trial from the perspective of the defendant, McGinniss accepted the job, liked the client, at least for a while, and then, following the doctor's acquittal, ended up writing a book proclaiming that he was guilty after all.

Among Israel's first generation of journalists, important editors and reporters had a symbiotic relationship with politicians, in which treachery was unthinkable (Liebes, 1997). The reason was simple: The government consisted of the same leaders that these journalists had served before the establishment of the state, in the newspapers and radio of the Zionist revolution. The problem of the press then (from a professional perspective) was its exaggerated loyalty to the political establishment. Ben Gurion, Israel's first prime minister, strengthened the editors' protective feeling toward the new state by establishing an "editors committee," in which he supplied editors with secret information on condition that they keep it to themselves. All this has changed with the rise of a new generation of reporters and editors, who did not regard themselves as journalists-cum-propagandists for the state. An early dramatic example of this change was the resignation of PM Yitzhak Rabin in 1977, after an ambitious reporter discovered that Rabin was still holding a bank account (in the amount of $20,000, received as lecture fees) in New York, which had been opened during his term as an ambassador to the United States. Although Rabin apparently was not aware of its existence (it was in his wife's name), he resigned from office immediately. With the growing competition, the laying down of scruples, and the growing hostility within the various groups in Israeli society, media professionals have increasingly resorted to all the techniques of entrapment laid out here.

Anything to Get a Foot in the Door. Whereas between politicians and reporters there is often a tacit understanding of mutual empathy (reinforced by the ongoing coverage by the "house" reporter during the campaign), there are cases in which reporters break an explicit agreement with their interviewees, who would otherwise not have talked to them or let them into their homes. Taking seriously the argument that prime-time best-selling TV series give expression to the prevailing climate of opinion, the following fictitious case in the U.S. media may indicate a growing suspicion toward the media, or at least a decreasing tolerance to techniques of journalistic entrapment. I refer to an episode of the best selling series *The Practice*, in which the owners of a reputed restaurant sue TV producers for manipulating their way into the restaurant by falsely promising to do a laudatory item about the quality of the food. Instead, the reporters chose to focus on the cockroaches the restaurant was infested with, thereby ruining the family business. Despite the fact that the owners did not claim the information was false, only that it had been obtained through a breach of trust, the jury found the TV producers guilty and recommended $18 million in compensation.

Exposing "Off-Record" Information. Another common type of entrapment is reporting information that was considered by the informant to have been told off the record. The more central the public figure involved, and the greater its scoop value (sensational, damaging, unexpected within an expected stereotype), the greater the reporter's temptation to break the (more or less) tacit agreement. And the more casual the understanding, the easier it is to ignore. Thus, David Bar Ilan, an ex-journalist himself and spokesperson for PM Netanyahu, who insinuated to the *New Yorker* that the PM's wife was not psychologically sound, must have either perceived his interviewer (colleague) as more "loyal" to him, or was sufficiently fed up with his boss, or thought the boss' wife was hurting her husband's image, and/or assumed that stories may have (or would be) leaked out anyway, and that doing it his way might limit the damage.

Encouraging Unsuspecting Sources to Dig Their Own Grave. A more damaging variation, or extension, of publishing what the source assumed to have been said off record, is egging the source on to further entanglement. Typically, such betrayal of faith takes place with a naive or inexperienced interviewee, who is cajoled to continue to express thoughts or opinions, which will get him or her into big trouble. Here the source may reveal information about him or herself that he or she does not perceive as damaging. But as a number of public figures have discovered too late—"the bastards have changed the rules."

In an interview by Daniel Ben Simon, of *Ha'aretz* (Israel's most distinguished daily newspaper; July 29, 1998), Ori Or, an ex-general and new Labor member of Knesset (MK), talked freely about what he thought of MK's from his own party, who are of (Jewish) Moroccan origin. "You cannot talk to them normally," he said. "The problem with Ben-Ami, Edri, Ra'anan Cohen and others is that they interpret any legitimate criticism as criticism motivated by ethnic prejudice." Tragically, in observing that his "Moroccan" colleagues suffer from an exaggerated sensitivity to their ethnic origin—which, he claimed, prevents them from relating to points of view that differ from their own—Or had fallen into the same trap he has pointed to, marking himself as a racist.

More seasoned politicians know that any generalizing about an ethnic group would cause an automatic knee-jerk reaction of "racism," thereby preventing any open discussion. But the role of the journalist in putting and end to Or's political career should not be belittled. As Ben-Simon (himself of Moroccan origin) recounted following the interview, he kept on egging Or to continue unraveling his insights about Moroccans. Although Ben-Simon could envisage the front-page box ("Ori Or: 'The Moroccans have no curiosity to look at what's going on around them'"), Or unknowingly rambled on. And Ben-Simon, knowingly, helped him to tie the noose around his neck. This type of entrapment is increasingly more common, as the politically correct dictum of multiculturalism, for better or worse, has set strict boundaries regarding which type of statements are allowed in public. The journalist, in this case, is skirting on the border of another problem—taking a story out of context.

"Taking Out Of Context." This is a broad and complex issue that underlies routine journalistic practices, and is the most common defense of sources who feel they have been wronged. In the case of damaging talk on a scale that can put an end to a person's public career, taking out of context becomes particularly damaging. In Or's case, however scandalous the revelation of what can be labeled racist beliefs, there is no doubt that his statements were stereotyped, simplified, and distorted by the journalist's reframing, which has taken it out of (his) context.

Ironically, the context in Or's case was his own role in the effort of Ehud Barak, Labor Party's chair at the time, to win over voters of Moroccan origin (most of whom traditionally vote for the right-wing Likud party, and the ultra-religious Shas). Barak had started his campaign 1 year before that interview, with a grand gesture of pleading for the forgiveness of Oriental Jews for the Israeli establishment's treatment of the mass Oriental immigration in the 1950s. Or, Barak's man (trusted from their time in the army, where both served as generals), had been a major actor in this operation, and expressed deep disappointment to Ben-Simon over the reactions he had encountered. Or first expressed himself publicly on the subject (as Ben-Simon discloses in the small print of the inside page with the complete interview) in responding to an attack (in a local paper) by Moroccan born, history professor and Labor Knesset Member Shlomo Ben-Ami (later a cabinet minister). Ben-Ami had accused the party's leadership of being cut off from the masses (meaning from Moroccan Jews). The frustrated Or, who was in the midst of campaigning for the party to change this sentiment, retaliated by telling the paper (shooting from the hip?) that Ben-Ami (an antithesis for everything that the stereotype of Oriental Jew stands for) should have been the subject of Heinrich Boll's novel *The Lost Honor of Katharina Blum*. "He constantly seeks to be caressed." Or, who had "discovered" the sensitivity of Moroccan Jews to criticism, was not smart enough to understand that by counteracting he opened himself exactly to this sensitivity.

There is no doubt that in the case of Or both the use of "off-record" information and taking his words out of context have played a part. That Or was convinced he was speaking off the record can be seen in his telling the reporter that he contemplated criticizing Rafi Edri, another (Moroccan) Labor MK, on what Or considered was a stupid initiative on his part. "But I did not tell him anything," he confided in Ben-Simon, "because I was afraid he would be hurt and take it as an ethnic offense. One cannot say anything to these people without it being regarded as scheming against them." This is exactly the kind of statement that could be made behind closed doors, among friends (remember the Watergate tapes). Had he been a little more perceptive to his interlocutor, Or would have realized that Ben Simon was serving as the voice of the repressed underclass in his paper, and that, just as in the case of Ben-Ami, academic learning and sophistication would not make him immune to ethnic generalization.

The larger context in which Or aired his thoughts, as he told it to Ben Simon, was his own disappointment over what he saw as Israel losing what had held it together. He hoped the second and third generation of the oriental immigrants of the 1950s would find the power to disconnect from the past and their sense of bitterness. But his hope was lost. He recounted that in meetings and conferences he kept hearing the same old poisoned slogans against the Labor party. He saw a lack of interest, an unwillingness to listen, to understand, to become acquainted with life in order to distinguish between good and bad. He thought this was damaging for the whole of the society. He suspected that old grudges were used to eternalize intergroup hatred and to make political fortunes at the expense of the poor classes. Or also mentioned a new film (*Shchur*) by a Moroccan director, "in which for the first time the Moroccan culture looks at itself critically." But these are the rules of the politically correct game. Observations by group members about themselves could end the public career of an outsider who dares to voice the same observations. Any true or useful insights are sacrificed for the opportunity to create this week's scandal and, perhaps, to end a good man's career. Ironically, it may be argued that the more flattering explanation to Ben-Simon's framing is that he, too, demonstrates the tendency of Israelis of Moroccan origin to take any criticism as an expression of ethnic prejudice, making it easy to ignore any substantive truth there may be to the argument. In this case it was the reporter's framing, not the substance, which might be questioned. "Taking out of (one) context" and into another is all that is needed.

Breaking an Agreement Not to Publish in the Name of a Higher Value. Another breach of faith is the publication, or broadcasting, of information that journalists agree not to make public, with the understanding that it would be damaging to a shared higher value. It is accepted that in war, reporters tend to act as citizens, not just as professionals. The risk to human lives is considered higher than that of freedom of expression or the watchdog role. A case in point is the (gradually eroding) willing cooperation of the Israeli press with the military censor in not making public any information about Israel's nuclear capability, and the pros and cons of having it. Secrecy about semi-official Jewish immigration from non-democratic countries was considered almost as crucial as the case of exposing military technology. It was based on the understanding that countries such as Poland, Russia, Yemen, and Ethiopia, which have allowed large numbers of Jews to leave their borders at certain points in time, could shut their gates in an instant if their (shut eye) policy was made public. This collaboration between journalists and authorities stemmed out of the dominant Zionist ideology, which sees the absorption in Israel of Jews who suffer in other countries as the ultimate mission of the Jewish state. Yet another case of such agreed-on discretion was the media's considerate attitude to the right to privacy, where the private tragedies of public figures are concerned.

Typically, the breach of an agreement not to publish occurs after it has started to wear thin at the edges. During the wave of immigration of Jews from Yemen in the mid-1990s, one paper began discussing the fight between secular and religious schools over the new immigrant youths; another described them as dark, thin, and long-bearded, and the rest of the media followed suit. Likewise, the consensus among media to respect the wish of Ophra Haza, a popular singer hospitalized in a critical condition, to refrain from exposing the exact nature of her illness, only made the topic more salient, and increasingly gave rise to rumors. Israel's most serious paper decided to publish the story (after the singer's death) arguing that it was the paper's duty to contribute to the fight against the notion that any illness should be regarded as stigma. This story demonstrated that in the age of the Internet and fierce competition, such agreements are becoming all but impossible.

SPOTLIGHTING AND MAINSTREAMING

Now more than ever, manufacturing scandal does not necessarily entail the exposure of information heretofore unknown. It can also consist of exposing violations that take place routinely, that may be (more of less vaguely) known, but which the authorities, the public and the media tacitly agree to ignore (Elisabeth Noelle-Neumann's pluralistic ignorance). *Spotlighting* is the phenomenon whereby an editor, or a reporter, sets out on a crusade against a transgression that has taken root (such as the issue of the treatment of foreign workers, which was put on the national agenda by journalist Eynat Fishbein in *Ha'aretz*). More often, reporters' attention is drawn to an accident or crime that the chronic violation brings about. Attention to a story on a marginal media channel, which causes its "mainstreaming," may similarly occur in the wake of an act of violence (such as Rabin's assassination) that proves to have roots in routine practices on marginal or intra-enclave radio or TV channels (sometimes by the casual listening-in from sidelines).

RUBBING YOUR NOSE IN A ROUTINE VIOLATION OF A NORM

Non-normative practices—such as the import and exploitation for prostitution of young women and the living conditions of illegal foreign workers—which cannot be eradicated because they fulfill a need, and/or seem better (morally or practically) than other alternatives—have no clear-cut solutions and are conceived as an ongoing condition, which is not "our" problem. In a similar manner, information that is written or broadcast on "small," or non-mainstream media, is considered not to concern "us," the mainstream public. When mainstream editors or reporters happen, for some reason, to spotlight processes that we would rather ignore, or cross over to pick up material from a channel of a "cultural enclave," this has a scandalous potential.

Consider the issue of illegal foreign workers in Israel. The numbers are mounting, and without a clear policy, Israel will soon be facing a grave social and political problem. Most people are somewhat aware of the phenomenon but would find it easier not to be concerned; some may employ a Rumanian or Ghanaian housemaid, or an agricultural worker, or know people who do. Normally the journalistic spotlight would not land on this kind of story. It is not as cruel as murder, there are no straightforward "bad guys" (or "good guys"), no clear and feasible policy that can be formed, and the problem has no particular relevance to most readers and viewers. To focus on this issue would take an editorial decision to cover the story of the sordid daily existence of these people, and of the inhuman ways in which they are treated. A press (or better, television) item can, however, put an end to this avoidance, putting pressure on the various ministries in charge to act, that is, to acknowledge both their responsibility for going by the book (arrest and eviction of illegal workers), and the need to either find a way to implement regulations, or make new ones, such as granting them legal status.

TRANSPORTING INFORMATION FROM A SIDE STAGE

The present proliferation of electronic channels—local and national radio and TV, cable, the Internet, as well as small media, such as audio and videocassettes and home video cameras—means that the distinction between public knowledge, what everyone knows, and private, or secret, knowledge, known to no one, has been relativized. Daily interaction may be carried out among radio listeners on a Chicago Black radio channel, or on the Rush Limbaugh program, in the United States, or on a pirate radio channel of Israeli West Bank settlers, which the mainstream public remains unaware of. Likewise, a videocassette may be a best seller within a particular community, and normally remain confined to its target audience; even a sermon broadcast by satellite to synagogues around the country is unknown information for the mainstream public. Ironically, the flooding of information, and the multiplicity of channels, while complicating the national networks' decision on what to put on the nation's (and/or the world's) agenda, makes such decisions, in terms of the public's right to know, more crucial than it had been before the disintegration of the common sphere.

Among the electronic channels targeted to specific audiences, the ones with the most potential for the production of scandals are channels of religious, cultural, and/or ideological minority groups, which offer their audiences alternative daily schedules. Such cultural enclaves do not necessarily accept dominant universalistic principles, and therefore what they broadcast to themselves may contain the kind of talk that the general public would deem a breach of norms.

Ordinarily, mainstream media tends to ignore these side stages (Goffman, 1974), not only because it considers what goes on in the wings as irrelevant enough for their audiences, but also because mainstream journalists have accepted the legitimacy awarded to multiculturalism, which, in its radical version, is interpreted as the right for speaking in one's own voice to one's own community, in a conversation that nonmembers cannot join (Gross, 1998). This tendency is reinforced by the dictates of political correctness, that is, the tendency to avoid stepping on controversial issues in which the media may find itself accused of supporting an elitist, antiminority line. Nationwide media thus rarely bring up practices such as women's circumcision, or killing women in the name of family honor, prevalent in particular religious communities. This reluctance to interfere in the internal debates may be overridden only by a very good story.

The Writing Was on Their Wall: Mainstreaming After the Fact. A good story, one that involves some form of violence, or threat of violence, or a blatant assault on social norms that threatens mainstream society has a chance to cross over (Galtung and Ruge's, 1970, rules for crossing over the threshold still hold). Consider the case of Israel's PM Rabin, assassinated by a national religious zealot, following the decrees of (more that 40) rabbis in the settlers community, who found the prime minister guilty of transgressing the biblical law prohibiting the giving away of parts of the Land of Israel. As we all knew after the fact, threats on Rabin's life were heard months before the assassination on the West Bank settlers' radio, and even on the religious program on one of Israel's public radio's four channels. But these voices, although aired in public, were not picked up by any mainstream media. In the aftermath of the crime, when these rabbinical deliberations were widely discussed, Israelis, mourning the death, could not comprehend how they had been left unaware of these currents while "the writing has been on the wall." The reason was that although it was there to see, nobody outside the settlers' community had looked that way. This story of the absolute belief in the supremacy of religious law over state law, the incitement against the "traitor PM" within the settlers' community, and the negligence of the Secret Service, became a scandal only after the assassination. Nationwide media was oblivious until tragedy struck.

Not all peripheral channels carry the same weight. C-Span is considered an important channel despite its small viewership. Similarly, in Israel, the weekly sermon given by Rabbi Ovadia Yossef, the spiritual leader of the Ultra-Orthodox, oriental Shas movement, which is transmitted via satellite to synagogues around the country, has become an important political arena. On the Saturday of the Purim holiday, 2000, Rabbi Ovadia made political use of "The Wicked Hamman," the evil character in *Megilat Esther* (read in synagogues in Purim), who, according to the traditional text, planned to eradicate the Jewish community. The rabbi called his followers to revenge themselves on Education Minister Yossi Sarid, in the same manner as the ancient Jews have revenged themselves on the Wicked Hamman. "When you say 'Cursed be Hamman' in *Megilat Esther*, say also, 'Cursed be Yossi Sarid,'" ordered Rabbi Ovadia, adding for good measure another major enemy of the ancient Israelites, the people of Amalek. "In the same manner that Amalek and Hamman were uprooted," he continued, "so should Sarid be uprooted." In an attempt to routinize what seemed (especially in the wake of the Rabin assassination) a major scandal, one of Shas ministers explained to *Ha'aretz* that nothing in this was new. This type of interweaving of curses directed at politicians (considered political enemies) with the *Megila*, in the community's synagogues, has been going on for a number of years. "It's folklore," he concluded. The sudden journalistic attention, and the ensuing scandal on mainstream media, was the result of Shas' rapid growth (becoming the second largest party in the Israeli government), and the continued pressure that this party exerts on the government. The threat it represents to the society's norms makes what is said within the community relevant, and makes it unacceptable to dismiss as folklore.

A Phone Call To The Newsroom. Before violence has actually ensued, the attention of broadcasters to deviance, and/or to a good story on a marginal channel, may be drawn by whistle blowers, motivated idealistically or personally to expose non-normative or threatening voices. Consider the case of an Israeli football fan who happened to watch the 3-hour-long revelry for the cup-winning team, in Jerusalem's main town square, broadcast live on a peripheral channel of public broadcasting (see chap. 3). When he saw PM Netanyahu waving from a balcony above the square, smiling broadly, while rhythmic "Death to the Arabs" cries were heard from the crowd, the fan decided this scene was evening news material, and notified the First Channel newsroom. The incident (not the first of its kind) appeared on the news, and became a developing scandal (Tuchman, 1978), in which the editors were accused of doing an unprofessional job in order to malign the PM. Note that while nobody from within the settlers' community ever informed the media in time about the rabbinical debates over Rabin's fate, it was a viewer from within the soccer fans' community who pointed to the scandal during the celebration for the team. Rabin's assassination emerged from the core beliefs of the assassin's community, whereas the football fans' community is not normatively homogenous, and racism is not part of its ethos.

Home Video Camera Exposes Routine as Scandal. In addition to peripheral channels, the infiltration of small media into nationwide channels has proved to play a major role in the eruption of scandal. Recall the home videocassette in the Rodney King scandal, which, by exposing the routine practices of the police in true colors, brought about a radical change, including the resignation of the chief of police (Alexander and Jacobs, 1998). Note that although police brutality was generally known, and the subject of many articles, the issue needed the evidence "in action" in order to gather momentum. And television's practice of recycling good stories has made it one of the most recognized clips in the last decade. Another example of the role of home camera in scandal comes from the Rabin assassination, taped by an amateur photographer, and sold to the highest bidder a month after the event, making heartbreakingly clear the negligence of the Israeli Security Service in guarding PM Rabin at the moment of his assassination. Mutatis mutandis, the Monica Lewinsky story was picked up from the semi-public Internet, and the tapes of her private conversations became a major attraction for mainstream TV viewers. Thus, community and home media provide mainstream media with an eery mixture of non-normative practices occurring regularly in segmented cultural communities, negligence or brutality in the practices of public institutions, and stories that appeal to voyeurism, with only a slim journalistic justification.

SCANDAL: WHO IS RESPONSIBLE?

Since Molotch and Lester charted their scheme, journalism, society and politics have been transformed, first in the United States, and soon after in Israel. What they saw as the journalists' finest hour seems no longer to be the case. In the case of whistle blowing, which seems to follow the pattern described by Molotch and Lester, the seesaw tilts in the direction of putting the reporter at the bottom and the source on top. Although some whistle blowers do seek the reporter's encouragement, it is typically the heroic, or tragic, or evil whistle blower who takes most risks. For the source, initiating contact means switching their loyalty from friend, employer, or country, to reporter. One's betrayal of former loyalties, undertaken either for a higher cause, calculated self-interest, or taking revenge, is carried out at the cost of exposing oneself to possible retaliation.

In the case of entrapment, it is the reporter who knowingly betrays his or her source by breaking a formal or tacit understanding for (what he or she considers) a higher cause, or for professional success. Unlike the source, the reporter does not usually have to worry about paying a price (since the responsibility is shared with editors and publishers, and the commitment to source is ambiguous).

Spotlighting and mainstreaming differ from the first two in the sense that they do not involve the uncovering of a *secret* violation but the mobilization of public attention to a phenomenon or a continuing condition that is generally known, but ignored. Paradoxically, spotlighting is the form that comes closest to the traditional notion of in-depth investigative reporting. Known but repressed issues are typically endemic (rather than a one-off personalized scandal). As such they are less than "hot," and putting them on the public agenda depends on the reporter's motivation, initiative, and dedication (although here, too, the exposure of an insider, with an interest to promote or damage the perpetrators, may be necessary).

It seems reasonable to assume that the rate of scandals should be decreasing in today's increasingly electronic press. Journalism's shift to TV (which allows politicians more opportunity to disintermediate journalists), the taken-for-granted mediation of spokespersons (whose function is of course to protect their clients), from whom reporters seems to be getting most news items ready-made, and the constraints of increasing commercialization and cutthroat competition, which redirect journalists from doing investigative work, all suggest the predominance of "routine news," in which sources, not reporters, are in control. Nevertheless, scandals have by no means disappeared; their number may even be on the rise. In Israel it seems that there are hardly any politicians left who are not under indictment.

Yet arguing that scandal is still going strong does not necessarily mean that it should be regarded as the journalists' finest hour. True, traditional wisdom sees scandal as the quintessence of professional journalism. Unlike the routine exchange between reporters and spokespersons, the argument goes, it is "investigative reporting" that digs out the sleeze from its hiding, with reporter and editor fully in control. The way to reconcile the notion of reporters-as victims-of-public-figures-and-their-PR-staff with journalists-as-investigators is to argue that investigative journalism is not the only explanation for the proliferation of scandal.

Today's scandals should probably be explained by the direct access of whistle blowers to the courts, the police, and the scramble of commercial, fiercely competitive newspapers and TV channels to cover everything everybody else is covering (according to the paradoxical rule that the more competing channels there are—the more homogenous their content). Whistle blowers can make use of the Internet's easy accessibility in order to make the print and broadcast press follow suit. Live broadcasting and an assortment of talk shows enable whistle blowers with a good story to be interviewed directly, and informally, on TV. If they prefer anonymity, they can have their voices changed and their faces shadowed.

Another reason for the increase of scandals is the normative change which western societies have undergone. Since Spiro Agnew's famous "the bastards have changed the rules," public figures caught on charges of corruption have lamented time and again that "everybody had done the same" (as did, most recently, Benyamin Netanyahu, Israel's PM in 1996-1999, when the police recommended that he be put on trial on bribery and gift-taking charges. For Netanyahu—"everybody" meant "all former PMs").

Normative change is also the byproduct of multiculturalism, with its enclaves of particularistic norms which, to some extent, have gained a tacit agreement to be left alone. Nevertheless, scandals do emerge as a result of the inevitable clash between mainstream society norms and those of ethnic fundamentalist and/or ideological groups. This may happen when an insider bolts, or in the interface between the way everybody acted "down home" (as was argued in the case of Clarence Thomas' conduct as described by Anita Hill) and the way the same people are expected to act in the workplace or in public office.

In what has become the media environment in the Western world, the constant flood of stories means that scandals have to compete harder in order to cross the threshold, and they need staying power to hang in there. Scandals that "take" may have endless screen hours, a success that may be self-defeating as it causes the erosion of public interest.

Thus, the technological ease of producing "evidence," and the easy access to the screen once you have it, has made the scandal game open for all. Within this global reality, cultural differences between the United States and Israel may be seen in the different agendas: sex, lies, and videotapes in the United States; spies, fake heroes, and failed military operations in Israel; corruption and its cover-up in both.

At the same time, multiculturalism, and, with it, the sensitivities to political correctness, have shaken the certainties regarding what constitutes normative versus antinormative action, and which private actions or community practices should be exposed to the public at large as deviations, while others are deemed nobody's business. All this has only contributed to the entrenchment of journalists in an attitude of keeping a low profile and sticking to the "strategic" level of stories (Hallin, 1994). Scandals used to be the exception to this rule of "objectivity," whereas the new type of scandal, based not on investigative reporting but on an external initiative without media-documented evidence, direct broadcast journalists to comply with the old practices.

6

The Americanization of Election Campaigns

In hindsight, the Israeli elections of 1996 could be regarded as a watershed of Americanization. Three major elements coincided at that point to transform the political culture in Israel from a European model to an American one. It was the first campaign in which direct election of the prime minister went into effect, the first in which a commercial television channel competed with the First (public) Channel, and, not unrelated, the first in which the prime ministerial debate played an important role. However, it should be stated at the outset that although these characteristics of Americanization were dramatically visible, they were responsible only in part for the outcome of these elections, or the 1999 elections.

Concurrently, with the forces of Americanization, there were other, no less powerful forces at work. These forces were not anticipated, and can be seen as external to the mainstream election campaign. One such force was the Hamas, fundamentalist Moslem terrorists who carried out a series of bus explosions 2 months before the elections in order to bring about a hard-line right-wing government that would stop the Oslo process. These terrorists were extremely successful in making Israeli TV work for them. In their efforts to influence Israeli public opinion, the terrorists could count on the newly adopted routines for Israeli television and radio, inspired by U.S. TV, to enhance the effect of the bus attacks. The second force were the small media operating within segmented cultural and linguistic communities in the country's increasingly multicultural society, that developed a mixture of old and new media technologies to reach their publics (and who regard Americanization as the symbol of the moral deterioration of Israeli society).

Thus, rather than tell a straightforward tale of the Americanization of the Israeli elections, this chapter burrows into a mixed bag of sophisticated media strategies, the substitution of image for ideology, the campaign's shift into entertainment genres, overshadowed by the intervention of violent events planned by external "participants," and bypassed by in-group community campaigns, on traditional and modern media. Lulled by the similar promises of the two candidates, unaware of the sectarian campaigns backstage, and battered by the chain of terrorist attacks, mainstream public opinion chose to look for shelter, that is, to do the safe thing rather than gamble on a vision. The dissonance between the "new Middle East" promised by Labor's candidate Shimor Peres, and the morbid reality of the old Middle East raging in the streets, was too overwhelming.

THE MEDIA, AND THE POLITICS, ARE AMERICAN

Media-Centered Campaigning. As argued in chapter 2 the first generation of Israeli politicians had a deep suspicion of the possible power of radio and television for demagogic appeal. In fact, the law prohibited interviewing (and showing) candidates onscreen in the period preceding Election Day, limiting appearances to the advertising time allocated to the parties. Prime ministers running for re-election could of course control the timing of acts that would produce favorable news. One example that comes to mind is that of PM Menachem Begin, who, at the end of the his first term in office, ordered the Israeli air force to bomb Saddam Hussein's yet unfinished nuclear reactor, in what was certainly a great news event at the time. The decision to carry out a preemptive attack was praised, the operation was successful, and it certainly played its part on Election Day. The timing was considered by some not disconnected with the elections, but allegations of *Wag the Dog*-style distraction were only marginal. However, when Begin met Anwar Sadat in Sharm-el Sheikh weeks prior to Election Day, television news reported on the meeting but did not show the two leaders. Instead, the camera excised Begin from the pictures, and made do with shots of Sadat.

Until this day, despite the growing Americanization of the culture and the political life, the regulations that prevent candidates from appearing on media on public affairs programs during the 3 weeks prior to Election Day, are still in place. The traditional allocation of free air-time to the political parties (based on their relative strength in the outgoing Knesset), allow political messages only in the time slots allocated to for political advertising. In 1996, Americanization could be sensed in the introduction of political spot advertising, in the televised debate between candidates for prime minister scheduled 2 days before the election, and in the usual flood of newspaper ads, bumper stickers, and window placards.

But as the campaign begins long before the official 3-week period, this hardly slows down the Americanization of the elections, primarily in the sense that it centers on the electronic media (Griffin and Kagan, 1996; Negrine and Papathanassopoulos, 1996; Swanson and Mancini, 1996). Gone are the days of mass rallies in the town square and group meetings with candidates in private homes. Television brings the candidates into your living room, or bedroom.

Second, politicians scramble to appear on the news and on political talk shows, assisted by professional, usually American, media consultants. And the kind of advice they get is all to do with reflecting the right image. Thus, for example, Netanyahu took to having an aid carry a pillow to put on the chair in the studio, so he would always look taller (and presumably, loom larger) than the other participants.

Third, politicians do not turn down invitations to appear on entertainment chat shows, with their usual mix of celebrities, and seem more than ready to exchange ideas with teenage models, stand-up comedians, and released murderers, to expose their private lives and dreams, even if at all possible to sing, play the flute or the piano.

The perception that television can make or break a person has become a major consideration for candidates. A rumor about a tape showing him in a compromising position with a woman who was not his wife, brought Netanyahu running to the studio. He confessed it all on prime time, Clinton-style, apologized for causing his wife pain, promised it was over, only to discover that such a tape did not exist. The advantages of producing prime-time chat shows for media owners and directors are obvious—they are cheap, popular with audiences, and "count" as part of the quota of domestic production demanded by the controlling bodies of both channels. The candidates like these shows because they provide opportunities for appearing on prime time, and, more important, allow them to campaign on their own terms. With the two nationwide channels, and a number of popular prime-time chat shows competing over the hosting of popular candidates, politicians are free to choose the most empathetic hosts and to set their own conditions. Gone is the worry about some over-zealous reporter who may insist on getting precise answers about policy issues. Journalists, who should be looking after the public interest, are almost out of the game, liberating the candidate of any need for accountability.

Direct Elections for Prime Minister. The introduction of direct elections for prime minister meanwhile superimposed a "president" on a parliamentary system, giving a major push to the creeping Americanization of Israeli politics. The vote was now split into two (one vote for prime minister, one for a political party), and voters' attention has shifted from choosing among ideological parties to choosing between the personalities of two (or more) individual leaders. The introduction of popular primaries within a number of political parties in order to choose the party's list of candidates for the Knesset, has created an additional need for party candidates to be personally recognized on the small screen. This process of personalization of politics, which was in itself influenced by TV, speeded up the process of making television the main arena of the race. Its largely emotional appeal, and its operating on a personal level, fitted the bill. The printed press, which used to be the site for public debate, was left behind (Jamieson, 1996; Meyrowitz, 1985). Indeed, television seemed more central than ever, with journalists mostly preoccupied with the tactics of the campaign, adopting horse-race images, and the practice of ad watches (Patterson, 1994, cited in Alger, 1994), and with the press, radio, and television devoting major amounts of space and time to the machinations of electioneering.

In their eagerness to appear on screen, politicians themselves clearly share the belief in television's effect on public opinion (Peri, 1995; Schudson, 1996). Indeed, a public opinion poll, at the beginning of the 1996 campaign, supported the notion of the public's faith in TV's credibility by reporting that only 9% believed what they read in the newspapers, whereas 55% believed in the credibility of television. Moreover, right-wing politicians continuously kept attacking journalists and broadcasters for their "leftist bias."

Competing TV Channels. Television too had a stake in presenting itself as the central forum for the elections. The 1996 elections were the first to be covered by the two competing national channels. The ratings race between channels was so salient that one newspaper described the broadcasts on election eve as the Super Bowl of their competing news shows. The need for constant breathtaking drama in the battle over ratings, promoting the framing of the elections as a horse race, contributed to the proliferation of hybrid, quasi-political entertainment shows, outdoing each other with sophisticated production gimmicks. As the best show in town, the political race dominated the screens from the announcement of early election in February to Election Day, and the closer the race, the better it was for television.

Blurring the Differences. As was the case in recent election campaigns in the United States and Britain, the two major parties were doing their best to blur the ideological differences between them (thereby weakening the effectiveness of the campaign). Trapped in a double bind, the two major competing parties ended up transmitting identical slogans in order to lure the fraction of undecided voters located in the middle, between the two, on a single-issue campaign agenda. The Labor Party adopted the Likud's promise of security, countering with "A Strong Israel with Peres." The Likud, realizing the depths of the voters' craving for peace, adopted the slogan "Netanyahu—for a Secure Peace." Instead of judging them by their messages, viewers had to remind themselves what the two parties were really about, underneath the election makeup, and despite their almost identical slogans.

Exposing Campaign Strategies. The increasing role of professional advertisers caused the press in return to follow the U.S. model by adopting a critical and derogatory approach (Jamieson, 1996; Sabato, 1992). This additional marker of Americanization provided a new role of extensive and critical coverage of the campaign for the printed and electronic press, diminishing its effectiveness in the process. The intense preoccupation of the press with exposing tactics, techniques of persuasion, and advertising gimmicks, undermined the campaign's importance. It lowered the status of the campaign to that of entertainment, and situated viewers into seeing themselves "not as voters but as spectators evaluating the performances of those bent on cynical manipulation" (Jamieson, 1992, p. 10).

As in the United States, press and television pundits criticized the manipulative character of the campaign, its preference for technique over substance, the lack of "real" election politics as it "used to be" (Arian, 1996). Ad Watcher columns were introduced for the first time. The image of a dove, chosen to express the Likud's longing for peace, became a symbol for the discrepancy between TV's image and reality. Exposure of the manner in which the jingle was filmed—with the white dove a fumbling prisoner tied to a stick, a far cry from the image of flying gently into the sky—caused embarrassment in Likud headquarters.

Thus, the focus on exposing the strategies behind the campaign was largely responsible for its low credibility in the eyes of the public. Unsurprisingly, with the exception of the candidates' debate, the television campaign ended up not causing any appreciable change. The public's indifference—almost two thirds thought that "the media devotes too much time to the election campaign"—is the best proof to demonstrate that the campaign has lost its relevance. Significantly, among the undecided, an even higher percentage of people thought that the media wasted time on the campaign.

The Significance of the Prime Ministerial Television Debate. The low credibility assigned to the political ad campaign most probably also contributed to the relatively low extent of viewing throughout the 3 weeks prior to Election Day. Despite the opportunity to view the campaign ads at two different time slots on the two television channels, viewership never rose above 20% for all or almost all the campaign broadcasts produced by the parties for TV (Wolfsfeld and Weimann, 2001), and was even lower among undecided voters. The debate between the two candidates, however, was an exception. Set up by reporters and pundits as a media event, and credited as influential in advance, the scheduled debate endowed Netanyahu with equal status to that of the incumbent Peres, smoothing over his relative lack of experience. In the two days separating the debate from Election Day, most commentators gave the lead to the younger, more telegenic Netanyahu (see chap. 7).

One possible reason for the ease with which Netanyahu handled the debate, and for his ensuing victory, was Labor's strategic decision to refrain from "negative campaigning." Considering the mutual exchange of personal accusations and insults that prevails in the American campaigns, this decision seemed quite un-American, and clearly did not draw on the American experience.

Labor's strategy was part of an attempt to keep the formal campaign sleepy, with the rationale of decreasing the chances of the Likud opposition to receive equal exposure. For Labor, this strategy meant starting the campaign as late as possible, and not bothering to counteract the negative campaign on which the Likud strategy was based. Labor's most extreme (and probably misconceived) decision in line with this strategy had been not to make use of the obvious weapon—Rabin's assassination. Although the assassination was generally attributed to the incitement against Rabin by the right-wing political camp, whose demonstrations marched after his symbolic coffin and called him "traitor" time and again (Wolfsfeld, 1998), the attack ads showing the evidence remained in the drawer, unused. The reason was Labor's strategists' fear that potential Peres supporters from the right would feel they were being assigned to the ideological camp that nurtured Rabin's murderer. Pushed into a defensive position, such undecided voters would be driven "back home" to the Likud. In hindsight, the lesson from the failure of this strategy may be that once the American form of debate is adopted, the candidate's arm should not be tied behind his back.

Israel's embrace, by and large, of the American model during the second half of the 1990s, due to legal changes in the election process and in the structure of media, did not mean that these changes alone carried the responsibility for the election results. Two other equally important factors had a major input on the result. The first was introduced for the first time in 1996, partly as an unforeseen result of the new election law with its introduction of a split vote (PM and party). I refer to the strengthening of the sectoral parties that ran in-group media campaigns far from the mainstream media, surprising all pundits by their transformation of Israel's political party map. Whereas the speedy development of multicultural communities has a parallel in the multicultural society of the United States, their methods of appealing to voters were a far shot from the Americanized ones of the mainstream campaign. The other influence on the elections was the harsh reality of the Arab–Israeli conflict, which played a major part in the 1996 race (and caused the downfall of Barak's government in 2001, bringing to power a notoriously hawkish candidate). When all is said and done, any violent act on the side of the Palestinians tends to push the electorate to the right, as it provokes and reinforces the despair of ever reaching an agreement.

THE MEDIA ARE AMERICAN, THE EVENTS MIDDLE EASTERN

Any discussion of effect, American or not, should take into account that Israeli society has been politically divided down the middle for two decades, and Netanyahu's victory in 1996 made hardly any change in the balance of power between the two major political blocs. This could be seen in the minute majority—14,729 voters—that made him prime minister of a nationalist coalition government, which replaced a moderate-dovish coalition headed by Peres.

However, a look at the polls in the year before the elections does show two dramatic shifts in public opinion. The first, following the assassination of PM Rabin, gave Labor a significant lead of about 30%; the second (mentioned in chap. 4) occurred following the series of suicide terrorist attacks (see Fig. 6.1), overturned this lead, bringing voters who had deserted the right-wing bloc back to their camp, with an almost tie continuing right until Election Day.

Initiating News Stories. The daily appearances of political figures on the small screen, the daily press reviews on how well each

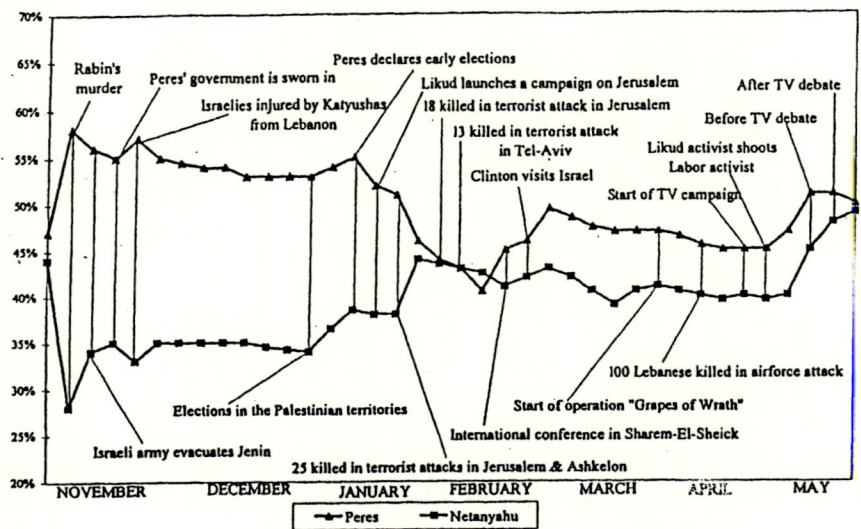

FIG. 6.1. The 1996 election race in Israel: Peres versus Netanyahu.

was doing, the tough negotiation over the rules of the prime ministerial debate, all created a frantic activity about and around the television campaign, giving the impression that "passing the screen test" was all that mattered. This turned out to be wrong. The contest among TV personas gave way to the inventiveness of political actors. Labor organized a news campaign to utilize its advantage of being in power and marginalize the advertising campaign. It consisted of sending PM Peres on trips to the United States and to a number of Arab states. A more tricky initiative was the international anti-terrorism conference in Sharm-el-Sheikh (with 29 heads of states taking part, 13 from Arab states) in the wake of the Hamas terrorist attacks. A brave act of damage control following the Hamas attacks, it was unfortunately (but rightly) perceived as such, thereby losing its effectiveness as a news event.

President Clinton's visit to Israel in the wake of the conference was particularly blatant because the U.S. president has done everything in his power to support PM Peres short of direct endorsement of his candidacy. Clinton's visit was somewhat reflected in the polls but may have backfired (against Labor) with the undecided voters, and in any case, could not compete with the bus bombings horror show on television.

The Hamas terrorists themselves, regardless of their lack of official standing in the race, also mobilized to influence the vote, and it seems likely that they made a difference. These unacknowledged participants carried out the suicide bus attacks that television covered in a live marathon, which turned out to be the most memorable show of the campaign. Getting TV coverage of the sort that no candidate could even dream of—longer, more intense, more melodramatic—Hamas' strategy to replace the government by a right-wing one most probably worked. It may have been insufficient for putting an end to the Oslo process altogether, but the process did receive a massive battering. On Labor's side, as mentioned previously, PM Peres mobilized U.S. President Clinton to put up their own media event, but it could not rub out the anxiety and hopelessness caused by the violence.

Evidence of the success of Hamas arises from public opinion research (Gallup for *Ma'ariv*, see Fig. 6.1), strongly suggesting that the decisive events that influenced the election campaign were the three bus bombings by Hamas terrorists in Jerusalem and Tel-Aviv (February–March, 1996) mentioned earlier, and, to a lesser extent, the Hezbollah attacks on Israeli soldiers in south Lebanon and on Israeli towns on the northern border, which brought about an Israeli retaliation in the form of massive air raids (Operation Grapes of Wrath, April 11–26, 1996). These were the turning points in terms of the support for the two candidates. However, it was television, with its Americanized conventions of disaster coverage, that made a massive contribution to the effect on public opinion planned by the Muslim fundamentalist group.

Live Broadcasting of Terrorism. Separating events from their coverage can only remain an analytic exercise. Nevertheless, there is evidence to show that television's handling of Rabin's assassination and funeral, and, later, of the Hamas terrorist attacks, had a major political impact. Moreover, there is evidence to support the claim that the familiar format of CNN's breaking news, chosen by the two channels for the coverage, was particularly effective from the perspective of the perpetrators.

Labor's diminished chances were primarily due to the horror of the arbitrary killings. But while the dubious credit for pushing public opinion to the right has to be given to the initiators of these events, it is also clear that the practices of TV coverage—in the form of live transmission of disaster marathons—had contributed to the dramatic shift in public opinion. Moreover, the initiators, acting in the context of the elections with the aim of stopping the Oslo process, were probably fully aware of the practices taken up by television whenever a "relevant" disaster strikes. Thus, the two (inadvertently, in the case of television) have reinforced each other.

Once the routine of live broadcast is adopted for what is considered a major disaster (for any event that has, say, more than 20 casualties), editors and reporters have to tow the line. Declaring a disaster marathon, as described in chapter 4, means interruption of the regular schedule for long hours, sometimes days. In the case of the Hamas attacks, this unplanned live broadcast lasted for 72 hours, featuring the endless recycling of the horrors—body parts in the streets, burned buses, victims in hospitals—interrupted only for interviews in which reporters kept looking for scapegoats on whom the tragedy could be blamed (the government), or asking for advice on government policy from relatives of the dead, speaking in the midst of the most privately emotional moments in their lives. The most politically extreme voices, and/or the people who suffered the greatest tragedy, were chosen as representatives of "public opinion." "The public's right to know" is a poor excuse for what was happening on screen.

Disaster marathons are often not about news, and often do not even attempt to include a serious debate on the issues they bring up. Instead, they often provide an opportunity for television professionals to cater to the neo-populist mood of an anxious, frustrated, revenge seeking public. What complicates matters even further is the fact that during these long hours in which viewers are captive audiences—afraid to leave the house, anxious about what might happen next—the practices of the professionals are influenced not only by their public duty, but also by the knowledge that winning the marathon is considered crucial in the race against the rival station.

The impact of disaster marathons on the 1996 elections may also be viewed in the context of the on-screen advantage of events over processes, and of simple messages over complex ones. The definition of TV news as something that happened between the previous night and the present night means that any dramatic action (which may seem trivial the next day) can easily eclipse small steps in an intricate, cumbersome, complex process (Edelman, 1988). This is one reason why the Oslo accords between Israel and the PLO, the greatest achievement of the Rabin–Peres government, fared poorly in the television campaign, whether in talk shows or in Labor Party broadcasts. Competing in television's virtual reality, the agreement suffered the fate of any slow and intricate process, strewn with problems and setbacks, as compared with a dramatic, one-time event (Wolfsfeld, 1998).

The advantages of Oslo are best seen as small but significant steps (such as developing cooperation with the Palestinians, furthering international trade, cultivating understandings with other Arab countries), but these remained mostly an off-screen reality. They could rarely count on making the news, which favors more dramatic, visually moving gestures. Too much time had elapsed since the Rabin-Arafat handshake in Washington and the signing of the agreement (Liebes, 1997). Although the Oslo process had already dissipated into the details of diplomatic negotiation over the nuances of various clauses in the agreement, the most newsworthy events, at the time of the elections, were the terrorist attacks.

Television's preference for events over processes relates to its preference for simple, catchy, immediately understandable messages over complex ideas that need time to explain. The television debate of 1996, for example, allowed only 90 seconds for each contestant to address each major policy question. Thus, the rules of the game did not allow for more than sound-bite slogans, as in the United States, where "Media prefers issues that . . . rest on principle and can be stated in simple terms . . . [preferably by] a shorthand label rather than complex details, or relationships" (Patterson, cited in Alger, 1994). The need for instant answers gave an advantage to the Likud, with its unidimensional ideology and unequivocal messages, in comparison with the more complex reality presented by Labor (Peri, 1988).

Disaster marathons are also a dramatic example of the journalistic principle according to which "objectivity" in reporting is maintained through balance between a government that "acts" or "is responsible" (for anything that goes wrong) and an opposition that "reacts." While government is celebrated for initiating events, the more dramatic the merrier, the opposition has its moment when events get out of control, the more disastrous the more advantageous. Even reporters with allegedly leftist ideologies, even those who believe that the government should not be automatically blamed for terrorist acts, did not act less aggressively when interviewing a government representative following these attacks. Professional conventions and structural constraints are far stronger than individual inclination. Not surprisingly, in the week following the bus bombings, in line with the practices of the disaster marathon genre, Netanyahu was interviewed more often than Peres on both channels.

In short, the Hamas bus bombings can be seen as proof that the Americanized campaign, with its focus on personalization of the race, and, with it, the increasing emphasis on the candidate's image, can become instantly marginalized by a nasty reminder of the Arab–Israeli conflict. Ironically, perhaps tragically, the Hamas, even if inadvertently, also carried out a television-focused campaign, with the advantage of not having to bargain with the competing channels over the allocation of airtime, or over exclusivity.

The second major influence on the election results, which first emerged in the 1996 elections and gathered momentum in the 1999 election, was the emergence of cultural, ethnic, and religious communities who (in varying degrees) turned their backs on mainstream television and its Americanized campaign, and, it could be added, on the Americanized values of Israeli society. These include the new Ultra-

Orthodox Shas movement of Jews of North African and Middle Eastern origins, the Ashkenazi Ultra-Orthodox, Israeli Arabs and Jewish immigrants from the former Soviet Union. These communities, regarded as "cultural enclaves" in the first part of the 1990s, gathered strength, and by the year 2000 constituted Israel's society as a multicultural entity, in which "mainstream" Israelis were well on the way to becoming no more than one (granted, the largest) sector. (This is reflected in the fact that by the beginning of the millennium, only 50% of 18-year-old Israelis entered compulsory army duty). This trend toward segmentation may have a parallel in the increasing multiculturalism in American society, but certainly works to counteract the trend of Americanization of Israeli politics and media systems.

CHALLENGING MAINSTREAM TELEVISION CAMPAIGN: SMALL MEDIA AND CULTURAL/ETHNIC/RELIGIOUS COMMUNITIES

The double ticket (separate votes for prime minister and party) introduced in 1996, led voters to turn away from the center and to vote for their sectoral interests, thus enhancing the power of small, community media, at the expense of national integrative ties including nationwide television (Just et al., 1996). Ironically, the American-style campaign, which was, to a large extent, the result of individualization and de-ideologization of the society, has reintroduced the collective, counterindividualized elements from the back door. The collective that was lost on the national level, re-emerged on the community level. This campaign was conducted in the segmented press, radio, and television channels, on audio- and videocassettes, and in the preaching in synagogues and in mosques, in three different languages. All of these were on their way to usurp the common meeting ground of Israeli society. From the perspective of these communities, television no longer served as a shared space for dialogue, in which each group sees and hears the others and represents itself to the rest. The new election law pushed the various minorities increasingly to talk to themselves, about themselves, on their own segmented channels, and to increasingly absent themselves from national television (Gitlin, 1998; Gross, 1998; Katz, 1996).

The result of these segmented campaigns was the surprising outcome of the election, which marked an unprecedented increase in the representation of four groups. They consisted of the religious bloc (rising from 18 seats to 23 seats in 1996, and to 30 in 1999), which includes the Shas Oriental, traditional party (rising from 6 to 10 seats in 1996, and to 17 in 1999), the Russian immigrants parties (which ran for the first time in 1996, receiving 7 seats, rising to 10 in 1999), and the Israeli Arab bloc (rising from 5 to 9 seats, and to 10 in 1999). There can be no doubt that the separate sphericules with their combination of old and new, "small" and mass media, unnoticed by the center, were instrumental in the rise of a coalition of minorities to victory at the polls (Shinar, 1987; Teheranian, 1979).

The victory of the cultural enclave communities raises the question of the role of these almost unnoticed, small, internal community media in the election. In this context, several questions should be considered: First, to what extent did these communities participate in the general public sphere, on national media, compared to their involvement in their own community media? The answer varies according to the types of communities. As shown in detail here, the ones who believe that they have a potentially larger circle of supporters (mainly Shas, but also other religious parties) operate on both fronts—closing the ranks in their own community media, and wooing new recruits on national television. Next, one should ask, whether the national media has a lesser role in these communities. The claim that it does may be defended on the grounds that in a collectivistic set up there is a smaller number of "undecided" (who may be influenced), and group identity is dominant enough, including sanctions against deviants, to marginalize individualistic effects.

For example, a voter's professed dislike for a candidate for prime minister, following his appearance on TV, would by no means prevent the individual from voting for that candidate if community leaders so decreed. In a TV documentary about the elections, an Ultra-Orthodox activist justified his community's rallying around a candidate with dubious morality by stating that "there are more important issues in these elections." The endorsement of a candidate by Rabbi Ovadia Yossef, the spiritual leader of Shas, became a major issue in the campaign.

The task of the community media was well defined. They were assigned to fight fiercely against the tendency of mass media-centered campaigns to strengthen the two large, catch-all, parties. What the Ultra-Orthodox community, the traditional Oriental community, new immigrants from Russia and Israeli Arabs, all have in common, is that, in varying degrees, they do not participate in "mainstream" Israeli culture. While in the case of the Russians, isolation may be explained as the transitional phase of immigrants' adjustment to a new society, the other groups nurture suspicion, hostility, and alienation from the liberal, secular, modern center.

For the segmented media, in charge as they are of enhancing internal solidarity, the strategy of stressing the immorality of external society is central. Mainstream society is regarded as a threat that must be fought (Sivan, 1994). American films and television series have become a symbol for the corrupting influence of the materialistic, hedonist, secular society. Although membership in these communities is voluntary, internal sanctions exist to various degrees. The degree of flexibility may be demonstrated by the degree of exclusivity of the community media.

Social control is strongest among members of the strictest, Ultra-Orthodox community, where even the owning of a TV set is prohibited. Radio is in a different position as it is used to inform the public in emergencies. Thus, for example, the Ultra-Orthodox community was granted special permission by its Rabbis to acquire radio sets during the Gulf War of 1991, following which the instruments were publicly burned. In the less internally cohesive community of Shas voters, control is far less strict. National radio offers ethnic music programs and talk shows targeted to this group, but they may choose to listen to their own *Kol Haemet* ("The Voice of Truth"), or to one of Shas' other radio channels, rather than tune into most of the programs on national radio, presented by Yuppie broadcasters whom they distrust.

The suspicion of Israeli mass media harbored by these peripheral communities and largely unnoticed by the elites, is not unlike the alienation felt by the Iranian masses in the pre-Khomeini era toward the Shah's television. As Tehranian (1979) demonstrated in his classic article, the Iranian people, culturally disconnected from the Shah, resented the attempt to cut them off from Islamic tradition. Thus, Iranian television had no influence on the people in spite of the dictatorial regime's total control over television. In the years preceding the Shah's downfall, Iranians had more faith in the voice of the Ayatulla Khomeini, which they listened to on audiocassettes smuggled in from his exile in Paris, and in the preaching of the Mullahs in the mosques.

Unlike Iran, Israel is a democracy, and community channels do not operate underground. Nevertheless, prior to the 1996 elections, their existence went largely unnoticed by the secular majority of Israelis. Within the religious-cultural communities, however, modern-secular television has been a suspect, as a threat to traditional Jewish or Moslem values. Paradoxically, Shas, the fastest growing group, had no hesitations in using American technology to disseminate its messages—starting with popular audiotapes with the preaching of its spiritual leader, moving on to incorporate these in the network of local radio channels, and to live broadcasts of religious preaching on satellite TV. If the medium ends up being the message, could this adoption of the technology eventually carry with it its own winds of change? As the Shas movement is by far the most successful sector in terms of increasing its political power, and the most adept in the utilization of mass media technologies, we take a closer look at the manner in which it usurped new media technologies, incorporating them in the specific context of reception and, in the process, transforming them into community media.

The Shas Campaign: Diffusion and Reinforcement Via New and Old Media.

The Jewish-Oriental traditionalist movement is

the success story of recent Israeli politics. The fastest rising party in the Knesset, it has become the third largest by the 1999 elections. It is also the most dynamic (the most Americanized?) in its use of media. Shas was the first Ultra-Orthodox party to break the taboo, entering the election campaign on TV in 1984 after having received a special permission from their chief rabbinical authority, as means of widening the circle of voters. This proved an effective strategy when an increasing number of Oriental voters, who were not Ultra-Orthodox, joined in. The sophisticated use of electronic media, in diffusing the aura and prestige of traditional interpersonal influence, has also played a major part in the creation of community identity.

Before the 1996 elections, political jingles and personal addresses of pop stars "born again" to the Jewish faith, were added to the traditional, widely revered, religious preaching in the audiocassettes. Shas has thus managed to address a larger public of potential recruits. Through the accelerated process whereby an "older" medium becomes the content of a newer medium, audiocassettes have become the content of the Shas pirate radio—the latest medium to enter the community (Blondheim and Kaplan, 1993). "The Voice of Truth," used at first strictly as means for the diffusion of audiocassettes with religious teachings, now operates as a live radio channel, with a schedule, with programs interposing religious teachings and religious chants with interviews of rabbis, Psalms readings, and live transmissions of weekly religious lessons, featuring Rabbi Ovadia Yossef, the spiritual leader of Shas.

At election time, the movement's pirate radio channels are used for publicizing the party's mass rallies and open meetings in stadiums, and for transmitting them live. The weekly lessons of Rabbi Yossef are also transmitted via satellite to a cable television channel, from his Yeshiva in Jerusalem to 300 reception points in synagogues, community centers and public halls throughout the country, with a weekly attendance of 50,000 to 60,000 participants, turning Bible lessons into overt political speeches.

By creating a set up in which members of a community are physically sitting together, in a public hall, in the traditional manner in which they are used to study and pray, Shas leaders have transformed the context of television reception from the typical situation of isolated individuals, to a warm, supportive social setting. Newcomers, often secular, who are contemplating a return to tradition, are encouraged to join and are brought in to listen in the company of the worshippers. Shas has transformed the weakness of mass media—the fact that it transmits directly to isolated individuals. The transmission of live satellite broadcasts to a hall jam-packed with worshippers and potential joiners, reinforces solidarity among the spiritual leader's worshippers, endowing participants with a sense of power derived from their increasing numbers and the knowledge that all over the country there are simultaneous gatherings of people who are going through the same experience. Mass media bring the leader into the room, and the interpersonal dynamics reinforces the message.

The viewing context transforms television from a mass medium to a small community medium. Although anybody can tune in, only those who belong to the community make the effort. Whereas alternative media in dictatorial regimes such as Iran or the Soviet Union had to operate underground, and were therefore restricted to small interpersonal means like fax machines and audiocassettes, an open society allows for the use of mass media itself for community purposes. This domestication of media within cultural enclaves has become part of the general process of the segmentation of media into multiple channels for specific target audiences (Katz, 1996).

In addition to engineering the reception of mass media in the social context of community, Shas also made massive use of traditional and interpersonal forms of interaction during election time. The most individually targeted form of campaigning, in 1996, was an "election kit," distributed in public gatherings and circulated daily by Shas volunteers going from door to door. The kit—containing a silver amulet with the portrait of Rabbi Kaduri, a 102-year-old Kabbalist saint, a series of written blessings, and a "soul candle"—was offered to ensure that the receiver would be "blessed, protected and successful." This package was distributed free to all who committed themselves—under oath and by adding their signature—to vote for Shas. The effectiveness of these tactics should be seen in the context of the forces assigned to the word within communities with a strong oral tradition such as Shas, characterized by the power to bless and curse. A number of tactics were challenged in court as a democratically unacceptable means for persuading voters. Questions such as "Does a promise of going to heaven in return for the vote (or a curse in the case of failing to vote) constitute a legitimate form of campaigning?" were raised. After the amulets were declared by the courts as inappropriate means for campaigning, Shas did not lack for substitutes in the 1999 campaign, distributing blessings printed on cardboard and bottles with healing oil, and mobilized its radio channels for bringing the followers to its mass rallies.

Whether motivated by their own ideology or barred by language or ethnicity, the boundaries of the three remaining cultural communities are clearly defined. Membership in these communities is more total, and contact with the rest of society is more restricted. Although these groups vary in their access to national media, they all have in common vital networks of internal community media (for a detailed account of campaigning within the cultural enclaves, see Liebes and Peri, 1998).

THE RISKS OF ADOPTING THE AMERICAN MODEL IN ISRAELI ELECTIONS

To sum up, Americanization of the Israeli election is blatantly apparent since the 1996 campaign, with the introduction of the direct election for prime minister, and the coming of age of a second, nationwide, commercial channel. The competition between the two nationwide channels makes for the salience of television in the campaign.

The commercialization of Israeli TV also meant that it was covering the campaign under two hats. As professionals, reporters and editors were committed to lay before the voters the issues on the agenda, and the policies proposed by the candidates. At the same time, they were committed to ensure viewership, in order to supply skulls for advertisers. These conflicting commitments can be seen in the adoption of the two Americanized forms of campaign coverage. TV's commitment to professional journalism is carried out by the deconstruction of political advertising and campaign strategies, in order to facilitate viewers' ability to critically decode political rhetoric. Its battle over ratings leads to abandoning the debate on issues, focusing on good stories and allowing itself too easily to be carried away from rational discourse to high melodrama, whenever events with a prurient potential come its way. This tendency is exacerbated by the new technological capacity of live transmission, from multiple points, which makes professional editing of breaking news all but impossible.

Yet the existence of two undercover participants in the elections undermines the mainstream media campaign. One major force is the intense campaigning that goes on within Israel's cultural enclaves—on small media and, in the case of the Russian Jews and Israeli Arabs, in different languages. Direct elections for the MP have significantly strengthened these groups politically, turning the Knesset into a site of intercultural (international, in the case of the Israeli Arabs) conflict. Although campaigning here does focus on ideology, it is concerned with identity politics, that is, with the interests of the group rather than with those of the collective (Ram, 1997). As such, it aims at strengthening the existing commitment for the group's ideology/culture/religion/nationality, for increasing support in the fringes, and for the mobilization on Election Day. It addresses listeners and viewers as committed to the cause, often attacking mainstream media as marginalizing or biased against the group. The Ultra-Orthodox groups point to the corruption of nationwide media by American hedonistic values.

The mainstream television campaign is not only weakened by competing community media but also by a third, unrecognized group of potential participants in the elections. This is the collective body of

Moslem terrorists, free to exploit the breaking news format adopted by Israeli TV for their own purposes. Ironically, they make use of one aspect of Americanization that does not lie within the realm formally defined as "the Americanization of election campaigns," but has nevertheless far reaching consequences for the campaign.

In the United States, the live broadcast of real-life melodramas as they evolve—OJ, Monica, Princess Diana—is often carried out for its entertainment value, using the involvement built into watching live events for the titillation of viewers. In Israel, however, a series of buses exploding (as a result of Hamas attacks) unleashes existential anxiety. Television's marathonic live broadcasts, filled with endless gory details and speculations about further developments, cash in on the vulnerability of viewers, glued to their TV screens, enhancing the terrorists' message and radicalizing people's attitudes to the conflict. Thus, the attacks were exacerbated by the broadcast, and had potentially far-reaching consequences for the elections. Superimposing the American format on an unstable situation became an irresponsible act of the kind that the U.S. media did not have to grapple with in the 1990s.

One result of these developments was that the effectiveness of conventional campaigning is on the decrease, and the impact of news coverage, especially those stories that are treated as disaster marathons, is much increased. The prioritization of hot news events makes journalists captives of any individuals or groups who are out to produce such events for the sole purpose of destroying one of the candidates. Television journalism by 2002 in the United States also has yet to find a way in which to defend itself and the public against such manipulative acts.

Second, mainstream politicians, journalists and media scholars were slow to realize that large segments do not take part in nationwide TV. Some never did, others are moving away to their own particularistic sphericules. These are now talking to themselves, in competition with national television.

In contradiction with the idea that modernization implies a media-dominated democracy, or that the effectiveness of alternative and complementary media systems is limited to the early stages of nation-building (Mancini and Swanson, 1996; Shinar, 1987), the Israeli case leads to a different conclusion. Although the continued existence of cultural enclaves and their community media has been ignored by researchers, they nevertheless went on existing and were given new vitality in the era of cultural politics. Thus, instead of a linear development of societies and media, from one stage (characterized by traditional society and small media) to another (modern society, mass media), we see the ideal of a unified nation, with its national broadcasting, splintering into a plurality of cultural communities who define their own identity within segregated spheres.

Interpersonal communication within these communities (Caspi, 1996) is reinforced by small media as well as by mass media channels and advanced communication technologies, which are now accessible thanks to deregulation and technological advances. Although the proliferation of channels is accessible to all, only members of specific cultural identities tune into "their own" channels, thus giving a new twist to the image of community media as "small," sometimes even clandestine.

Nationwide and community media are assumed to differ not only by their target audiences, but by their value orientations. Nationwide television claims to act according to universal and rational norms, whereas community media draws legitimacy from particularistic and emotional bases. However, a closer look makes clear that the supposedly rational discourse of television journalism does not always live up to the task, and what seems to be nonrational, alternative media, may often be the site of issue-oriented, analytic discourse.

In both cases, the type of discourse is influenced by the broadcasters' perception of their audience. The producers of nationwide TV see viewers mostly as depoliticized, individualistic, entertainment seekers. In the case of exposing advertisers' manipulations, sophisticated analysis happens to be entertaining and, at the same time, is important for public interest. On the other hand, competing over large audiences for the viewing of news melodramas dictates the most extreme emotional titillation.

The alternative media primarily address their viewers as members of a cultural community, with a deep, unquestioned commitment to the group. This means mobilization to the common cause by evoking shared symbols, and introducing authority figures, such as cultural heroes or religious leaders. On the other hand, because most of these groups are highly involved politically, constantly working out their ideological positions, serious debates over political issues are more likely to be held on some of the community media than on nationwide TV (Alexander, 1981). But, rational as the debate may be on the particularistic channels, it passes up the interaction with the other groups. For that, the metaphor of a shared public space should be resurrected and invigorated with these voices, to create a real debate. We seem to be left with the choice of an "Americanized" campaign with mainstream, commercialized, depoliticized television in its midst, or with issue-oriented separate campaigns, busy promoting their own agenda, safe in their trust that the center would somehow look after itself.

7

Netanyahu Defeats Peres: The Victory of Style Over Substance

At 10 p.m. on May 29, 1996, as election ballots closed, the news anchors on Israeli television announced: "According to the television sample polling, Shimon Peres has won the election for prime minister by a 2% margin." However, during the long night that followed, as the real results from the various ballots accumulated, this tiny lead gradually shrank. By next morning, it became clear that victory had changed hands, making Netanyahu the winner by a 14,900 votes lead over Peres. This virtual tie between the two candidates has been established on May 27, two days prior to the election, following the only television debate between the two candidates for prime minister on May 26. On the eve of that debate, the polls still showed the small but steady lead that Shimon Peres had over Netanyahu in the polls. Two days later, on May 27, the most popular tabloid (read by 70% of Israelis) came up with the verdict: "BB was more convincing." The next morning, with 24 hours to go, Netanyahu closed the gap in the polls, equalizing the two camps. Shimon Peres, aged 72, an experienced political leader, the incumbent prime minister, and the architect of the Oslo peace accords, who took over the premiership following the assassination of Prime Minister Yitzhak Rabin, lost to Benjamin Netanyahu, aged 47, an inexperienced politician, known for his telegenic qualities alone.

In hindsight, this debate was emblematic of the Israeli elections of 1996, which, as chapter 6 argued, may be regarded as a watershed campaign in terms of Americanization. To what extent can Netanyahu's last moment victory be ascribed to the debate? I do not argue that the elections were won entirely by the victory in the debate. I do, however, believe that the close race in the polls, the proximity of the debate to Election Day, and BB's endorsement as winner by the press, make the debate into a major landmark in the campaign, equal only to the terrorist bus bombings 2 months earlier.

PERES VERSUS NETANYAHU: TELEVISION WINS

Although the public had been indifferent to the parties' advertising campaign, the debate between Shimon Peres and Benjamin Netanyahu was an exception. Viewership was high, commentators overall gave Netanyahu the victory, with the public following suit, and political analysts regarded the debate crucial in the last-minute shrinkage of the (tiny) gap between the two.

The debate was constructed in advance as a media event (i.e., an important broadcast) carefully planned by the politicians who initiated it, and by the media that promoted it. It conferred an equal status on Netanyahu, who until then had been rated as an inexperienced novice, "not suitable for the job." The close battle in the ratings between the two candidates created a sense of a last resort, which could have a decisive last-minute impact on the enigmatic "undecided," or, at least, send them to vote. Two days away from Election Day, any impact would be meaningful as there would be no time for it to wane. Labor's ambivalence about whether to hold a debate had increased the notion of its importance. And a confrontation moderated by a journalist conveyed the message that the contestants would not be in control, and would have to be accountable, something they had managed to avoid in the 3-week TV propaganda campaign, during which it is illegal to interview them. Underlying all of this may have been the naive belief that the truth would emerge in the clash among different opinions.

NEGOTIATING THE FORMAT

The underlying assumption about the value of debating is that it ensures that a true argument would be more persuasive than a false one. A precondition for that is a format that offers participants equal opportunity to present their case. Auer (1962) argued that the format of modern public debates between political candidates fails to meet the criteria of a true debate, as it does not meet all the necessary criteria. These stipulate that a debate has to be played out as a confrontation, between opponents of equal status, concerning a declared proposition, aimed at winning over the audience, and with sufficient and equal time allotted to both participants.

The Israeli case, similar to most U.S.presidential debates, is characterized by a strong tendency to suppress the first condition. None of the six televised debates between candidates for prime minister in Israel was ever set up as a direct confrontation between the two candidates. The preferred format took the form of a three-way interview, in which the moderator posed questions to each candidate in turn. Only in the first debate, in 1977, was a rebuttal format used, according to which, following a question and a response by one candidate, the opponent was allowed to respond to the response, and the first responder was allowed the last word (an A-B-A response structure).

In the 1996 campaign, it was clear that a debate could only serve Netanyahu. As the incumbent prime minister, Peres could win the election by showing leadership. BB was no match. He had no relevant experience, but was known for his great performances on television to explain Israel's cause to American audiences. Appearing on television opposite Peres would not only put him on equal standing but would also bring to the foreground the fact that he was a generation younger, and could appeal to viewers for whom Peres could seem too sophisticated, too "heavy", not "realistic," or too much of a dreamer.

BB's advisers were thus keen on conducting a number of debates (they suggested four debates, each on a different topic), on timing the debates as close to Election Day as possible, and on an interactive format, ideally with no moderator. Peres' advisers were aware that this would be the first time in which an older candidate confronts a younger one. Weighing the damage of the debate versus the damage of shying away from it, they decided Peres should not be perceived as absconding. Their strategy (as explained by Haim Ramon, Labor's negotiator) was to continue the line taken in the campaign by showing that "BB is not in the same league, so that even supporters of the right cannot vote for him." This meant no direct interaction, a signal that there was nothing that BB could tell Peres. The most that Labor's advisers hoped for, was that the debate would make no difference. The format agreed on was a stricter and more formalized variety of former debates:

- Opening statement by moderator.
- Opening statement by the two candidates: Peres first, Netanyahu second.

- First question to Peres (Peres responds, 90 seconds).
- Follow-up question to Peres (Peres responds, 60 seconds).
- First question to Netanyahu (Netanyahu responds, 90 seconds).
- Follow-up question to Netanyahu (Netanyahu responds, 60 seconds).
- Three additional questions to each of the candidates in turn, with 90 seconds to respond, with no follow-up questions.
- Each candidate addresses one question to the other.
- Closing statement by Peres.
- Closing statement by Netanyahu.

This format, favored by Labor, constructed the debate as a ceremonial media event, elevated from the normal genre of political debates.

MODES OF ADDRESS: TO WHOM DO THE CONTESTANTS TALK, AND WHAT DOES IT CONVEY

The format agreed on was carefully adhered to by the moderator and the director. Thus, throughout the debate's 30 minutes, except for one opening shot and one closing shot, in which all three participants were captured by a wide angle shot, the camera focused at each moment on the speaking candidate only. When discussion time was allowed following answers to the moderator's questions, candidates did engage in direct confrontation, simultaneously occupying the screen (Bilmes, 1995; Carlin and Bicak, 1993). In our case, at any given moment only one participant appeared on the front stage (Goffman, 1974). Although the audience is of course aware of the opponent's presence backstage, the discursive acknowledgment of the presence of the other remains open for negotiation.

Peres strictly adhered to the interview format. By fixing his gaze on Dan Margalit, the moderator, most of the time (except for his closing statement when he looked directly at the camera, namely at the audience) he set Margalit up as his only partner in the conversation. Targeting Margalit as direct addressee ("Look, before we began Oslo . . . Look, you are not talking about . . . Dan, I am not new in this business") stands in sharp contrast to the glaring absence of direct address to Netanyahu.

Not once during the 30 minutes, and, as is seen here, withstanding repeated attempts by Netanyahu to invite direct address, did Peres ever acknowledge Netanyahu's physical presence in the studio. Except for answering Netanyahu's direct question at the end, Peres never referred to anything he said, framing the debate as a one-on-one interview (of the type David Dimbleby held separately with the two candidates, Tony Blair and John Major, prior to the 1997 elections in Britain). Had Netanyahu's sound track been erased from the tape, the "debate" would still make sense as an interview with Shimon Peres.

A count of the two candidates' modes of address illustrates the point (see Table 7.1).

TABLE 7.1. Candidates' Modes of Address

	Peres	Netanyahu
Address the moderator	9	15
Address the audience	5	10
Address the other	0	34
Refer to the other	11	44

Even indirect references to Netanyahu are scarce in Peres' discourse, and relate only to events taking place prior to the debate, avoiding mention of anything said during the debate, and are put in the third person. As in his opening statement, when Peres defended his position on Jerusalem:

> In the last 3 weeks Mr. Netanyahu has organized a terrible negative campaign, as if I wished to divide Jerusalem. He brought damage to Israel. He brought damage to Jerusalem. As if some of the people wished to divide it .

It seems as if even in mentioning Netanyahu by name, Peres endowed Netanyahu with more recognition than he was willing to grant him. Counteracting the Likud's attacks on the government over its presumed failure to prevent terrorist attacks, Peres backed away from the third person to indirect innuendo:

> We are a people experienced in war. We won all wars, we shall also win the war against terror. . . . There are those with little faith that . . .

In the last round of questions, when the two candidates were supposed to address each other, Peres was careful to answer Netanyahu's question but not to Netanyahu: "The answer is. . . ." When it was his turn to ask, he bluntly stated his refusal to address a direct question to Netanyahu: "I do not have a question for Mr. Netanyahu. I have a wish for him."

Peres was only following the (many would claim ill) strategy, mentioned earlier, of ignoring BB to manifest his contempt for the very idea of BB's candidacy, implying that if BB was not worthy of acknowledgment by his opponent, he was not worthy of being taken seriously at all, as a contender.

But on the interpersonal level, such treatment is the gravest of affronts. Recall Geertz' (1983) initial experience in Bali, when the Balinese treated him and his wife with studied indifference, acting "as if we did not exist . . . [as a way of] informing us, we did not, or anyway, not yet." As the Balinese made Geertz and his wife feel invisible, vaguely disembodied, non-persons (p. 413), so did Peres treat Netanyahu as "a cloud or a gust of wind," as somebody who has not yet "crossed some moral or metaphysical shadow line" (p. 413), or passed the test to be regarded as a political being.

The underlying motivation is the same: Non-address was used as a magical rite to deny or minimize acknowledgment of the other. Gusts of wind blow away, they need not be taken seriously. Yet for the television audience, the true target of this behavior, the effect is one of a deliberate, grave, threat to face. The undecided viewers, typically Likud voters who worry that "BB is not suitable," vacillating between the two, might find this lack of acknowledgment highly offensive, deeply undemocratic in a sense. These viewers, over whom the battle was fought, may return "home."

And indeed, this strategy of avoidance, criticized by the press on the next day, seemed to have badly backfired. All the more so as it contrasted with Netanyahu's deliberate and consistent attempts to resist denial by direct address. Belittling the formal, ceremonial aspect of the debate, Netanyahu did everything possible within its ritual constraints to turn it into a direct confrontation. To continue the Geertz (1973) analogy, he went for the Balinese model of cockfight, where "the cocks fly immediately at one another in a wing-beating, head thrusting, leg-kicking explosion of animal fury" (p. 422). Netanyahu addressed Peres directly 34 (!) times, and referred to him in the third person 44 times, relying on a wide range of rhetorical strategies designed (but failing) to draw Peres out and create a direct confrontation.

Demonstrating his proficiency in the uses of address in his opening statement, Netanyahu, in contrast with Peres, who only acknowledged the audience at home briefly, in words but not gazes, opened by fixing his gaze directly on the camera, looking the audience in the eye. This was a violation of the convention of the three-way interview format, introducing from the outset the mode of direct political appeal, typical of political speeches.

In his opening statement, Netanyahu managed to interpollate the audience (Tolson, 1996), stress the personalized angle of the election ("my way"), package the key concepts of the Likud election campaign slogan ("peace" and "security"), and launch an attack on Peres on the sensitive issue of terror.

> Good evening. I am pleased to have the opportunity to present before you tonight my way for leading the country. In three days, you'll have to choose which of two ways can bring Israel true peace with true security. The way offered by Mr. Peres brings no peace and no security. It brings us fear . . .

Netanyahu's direct address to Peres throughout the debate was spatially and temporally anchored in the here-and-now of the debate itself ("Mr. Peres, it does not matter what you say here tonight"), systematically highly accusatory and challenging in tone and content ("You are dividing Jerusalem. You refuse to close down the Orient House. You refuse to chase Gibril Rajub's people out of Jerusalem. You have. . . . So it does not matter what you say here because in fact you are dividing Jerusalem. Why should we believe you?") and related to what Peres had said and done in the past to expose him as a liar during the debate.

Netanyahu's persistent attacks on Peres tended to be contrastively framed: "He did X (with bad consequences), but I'll do Y (with good consequences)." Thus, for example: "I want to tell you, Mr. Peres, it's not enough to get photographed with the children, one should defend the children. That's what I intend to do, that's the peace that I intend to bring."

This frame of "He did X, but I'll do Y" covers up the inherent asymmetry between the two candidates. Peres, as a seasoned politician with a rich track record, which, by definition, must contain both successes and failures, was facing a young contender with virtually no political record, who was free to make any promises. Thus, Peres could be challenged on his personality, and on what he did, as well as on what he said, while Netanyahu could only be challenged on his little known personality, and mainly on what he said.

In this imbalanced situation, Peres chose to ignore Netanyahu; Netanyahu, in turn, chose to exploit all possible angles for direct challenge. Curiously, the uneven styles of address seemed to work to balance the initial imbalance between the two candidates: by framing Netanyahu as a "noncontender," Peres has violated the expectation for democratic fair play. Netanyahu was thus endowed with the aura of the underdog, thereby inadvertently justified in his fierce and accusatory mode of challenge.

CONSTRUCTING POLITICAL PERSONAE

The construction of public "personae" in the media, and through the public relations industry, are becoming a basic feature of modern consumer societies (Ewen, 1988). The personae of politicians in our culture are constructed out of diverse public appearances and of what is known of their private life. This public self is cultivated, and enhanced, through practices of salesmanship and image management (Tolson, 1996). The newly split vote in the 1996 elections, mentioned earlier, shifted the focus of the campaign from ideologies to personalities, and has thus shifted attention to the debate itself. In the debate, this shift is noticeable in the moderator's questions, and in the contestants' tactics of public self-construction, both in responses to personal questions, and in the use of such tactics through uninvited references to self.

Personal Questions. Personalization was apparent already on the moderator's side, in the choice of questions. One of the two first double questions to each of the opponents (question + response + follow-up question) concerned personal issues. The moderator did acknowledge in his opening statement that because this was the first debate in the era of personal elections, "this [personal matters] will be given some weight in the debate." Nevertheless, he and Peres exhibited certain unease in dealing with personal issues. After posing one policy question to each of the contenders, the moderator labeled the next question "personal," and, at the same time, announced his reluctance to ask it: "As I said, the elections this time in Israel are personal, and hence, as difficult as it is, there is no escaping from personal questions."

The first personal question was addressed to Peres, raising the issue of his age (73) as a possible liability for the job in terms of health, and as a possible motivation for hasty decisions. After challenging the question ("If these elections were for a fashion model, age would have been an issue"), Peres responded with atypical directness for a politician ("The state of my health is excellent, I have a full working capacity and my head is young").

In the personal question addressed to Netanyahu, the moderator challenged him on strength of character and behavior under stress, evoking his "frightened behavior" when he hastened to announce an extramarital affair on television, attacking unnamed opponents in the Likud for spreading rumors about a videotape documenting it.

In response, Netanyahu gave every sign of having found the question highly face-threatening. He vouched for his own strength of character by evoking his military service as combat officer, circumvented the issue of his appearance on TV, focusing instead on his regret about the extramarital affair ("It gave me pain, it gave pain to my wife. It was a mistake"), only to shift the topic to launching a fierce attack on Peres. The topic shift is realized most awkwardly—through lexical cohesion, with no attempt at establishing a logical connection. "It was a mistake," said Netanyahu, "but the mistake Mr. Peres is making . . ." when the reference to Peres relates to the political direction he had taken. Netanyahu's evasiveness on this issue was considered a major blunder by the journalists who evaluated the debate.

Netanyahu's Tactics of Self-Aggrandizement. A simple count of references to self shows Netanyahu as the major player on the arena of public self-construction: Netanyahu refers to himself in the singular "I" three times as much as Peres (66, including both invited and uninvited references to Peres' 22). This shows that it was Netanyahu, who invested by far the most effort into image building, exploiting the debate for blatant personal salesmanship. Peres' first choice was to talk about past achievements and future plans, in self-inclusive terms ("we"), incorporating himself in the political body he represented. Even when the question was framed as highly personal, coming as a follow-up on the question of age, Peres framed his response as a collective issue of policy, with reference to both past, present, and future:

> Margalit: Mr. Peres, still, there is a question here: weren't you too hasty in announcing that the Golan Heights are Syrian land because you wanted to round up [negotiations] quickly?
> Peres: Look, you are not talking about announcements, you are talking about citations from the press, and the two are not the same. With the Syrians we have conducted negotiations for four years and have reached agreement on one issue but not on others. The issue we have reached an agreement on was that the negotiations with Syria and Lebanon will be about ending the conflict in the Middle East as a whole. We have not reached an agreement on the parameters with Syria because we insist on security arrangements for the borders, on securing the issue of water supply, on full normalization. We shall conduct the negotiations stubbornly and with patience until we reach an agreement . . .

Peres referred to himself in specific cases only: (a) emphatically, to reaffirm his personal commitment to specific policies ("I feel with total confidence/I am positive/I feel deep in my heart"); (b) when directly called for, as in response to the question of how he is going to go about establishing the coalition government, if elected, (c) once, when faced with the proposition that he might be willing to relinquish the Israeli nuclear option, a highly sensitive issue which Peres considers his "baby" from its inception, he reacts angrily with "You are insulting me. I built the nuclear reactor"; and (d) as a statement of his credentials: "I know where I am going and I have behind me unusual experience."

In contrast, Netanyahu prefers "I" to "we" in most contexts. His opening statement framed the debate as a personal contest between two personalities, and he continued throughout the debate to use direct attack on Peres as the basis for image building, presenting himself as the better-suited persona for the job of prime minister.

As in the case of the other major elements of the strategy used throughout the debate, this too appeared right in the opening statement. Netanyahu began by talking about "my way," continued by attacking Peres on the issue of security, and continued to list, in the well-known macro format of a "list of three," inviting applause so typical of political oratory (Atkinson, 1984), to detail his plans:

> First, I will retrieve the responsibility for security [from Arafat to ourselves]. Second, I will propose to the Palestinians a fair arrangement for self-government but not a Palestinian state that risks our existence. Thirdly, I shall conduct negotiations with all our neighbors with caution, responsibility, and patience, while safeguarding security, the Golan Heights and above all, the united Jerusalem.

Netanyahu continued along this line in what follows. For him it was "I believe/I will/I want/I do not plan to," on both personal and policy matters. "We" was used sporadically, mainly in connection with his future plans on economic policies.

In addition to the personalization of the debate through the rhetoric of "I" versus "we," Netanyahu engaged in cultivating his public persona through inserted sequences that presented his personal credentials regardless of their relevance to the questions asked (see the section on response to questions). Thus, for example, he used allusions to his experience as Israel's spokesman in the UN and as deputy foreign minister, to assure the public of his ideological origins: "I come from a Zionist family," and to claim expertise in the domain of economics: "I know about [economics]. That's my professional training."

The difference in style of personae construction between the candidates may be seen in terms of two major advertising strategies: the "personalized" format, in which the product is associated with personal qualities and the appeal to the public is made by direct address, and the "product-information" format, in which experts present argumentative reasons to convince us to purchase the product (Leiss, Kline and Jhally, 1990, cited in Tolson, 1996).

RESPONDING TO QUESTIONS

Do audiences judge candidates on the specificity of their responses to questions during the debate? Do they receive good marks for answering the question? On one hand, political discourse in general is well known for its high level of equivocation. As Bavelas, Black, Chovil, and Mullett (1990) found, politicians themselves readily describe their communication as "ambiguous," "vague," and "wishy-washy," justifying it by claiming that the situation usually does not allow for simple, direct communication. This means that politicians asking to be elected avoid conflicts of many kinds on principle, and that leads to vagueness and ambiguity.

On the other hand, a study assessing the 1992 presidential and vice-presidential debates in the United States, showed that specificity of response to posed questions was the second most frequently mentioned reason for determining winners and losers in the debate. The five most frequently mentioned reasons (by respondents to an open-ended questionnaire) were confidence/presence, specificity of response to posed questions, honesty/trustworthiness, use of an attack strategy, and connectedness to people's issues, in that order (Winkler and Black, 1993). Thus, there seem to be limits to the level of equivocation allowed to politicians, especially in a debate situation.

The four questions posed during the 1996 debate to each of the Israeli candidates were all face-threatening. Each question contained an element (usually packaged in a complex way through its presuppositions and implications), that if found true might undermine the justification for the candidate's claim to power. Generally, in political interviews (Blum-Kulka, 1983; Jucker, 1986), interviewers can signal, through follow-up questions, whether, in their judgment, the response was satisfactory. Blum-Kulka showed that such judgments are based on a built-in requirement for interviewees to relate not only to the stated topic of the question, but also to its covert implications.

The discourse of the debate is no exception. Through the two allowed follow-up questions and through several meta-comments (e.g., "the candidates responded with the degree of specificity they chose to"), the moderator signals to the audience that his questions were not responded to in a fully satisfactory manner, even hinting that the two candidates differ in this regard. In summing up, Margalit said, "whoever did answer—did, and whoever didn't—didn't." Indeed, a closer examination reveals a dramatic difference between Peres and Netanyahu in their attitude to answering questions.

Answering Questions, Peres Style. Despite the advice given by his team to say what he considered important, regardless of the questions, Peres basically conformed to the convention that questions need to be answered. His responses did not always relate to all levels of implicature, but as a rule they related to the topic raised, and occasionally also to the challenging implications of the question posed. Moreover, as a rule, he never used the floor for raising completely new topics of his own.

For example, the first question challenged Peres on his position on Jerusalem, implying that it was not a viable position. Specifically, he was asked to explain the discrepancy between his statements that Jerusalem will remain united under Israeli rule, and the reality of the complete rejection of such a possibility by the Palestinians. Peres responded by evoking the success Labor government had in excluding the issue of Jerusalem from the negotiation about Palestinian autonomy, and by an emphatic reassertion of his personal commitment to Jerusalem.

On the whole, despite the equivocal character expressed in leaving several logical gaps in his response, it did remain within the conventional boundaries of "giving a response to a question" in the genre of political communication.

But in addition to cooperating with the moderator's questions in terms of content, candidates also had to comply with the pace and timing of the debate as TV quiz show. The main requirement here is the need to package one's response in the allotted 90 seconds, preferably in a way that will build up to a memorable closing statement that sums up the main argument. Peres, who, as his advisers told us, rebelled against the need to "practice" for the debate, did not always keep in sync. In the first and fourth question, he did sum up on time, with clear closing statements (e.g., on Jerusalem: "I am convinced deep in my heart that the occasion has been created now to bring peace while Jerusalem remains the united capital of Israel"). But his response to the second and third round had to be cut off by the moderator ("Your time is up, Mr. Peres. I am sorry," and an interruptive "thank you very much, Mr. Peres").

To appear timely and elegant within the interview format is only one of the constraints of the debate. An equally important consideration stems from the overall goal of the debate as persuasive discourse in the service of the campaign. The issues raised by the moderator might not be the ones the politician judges most pertinent to the campaign. Hence, inevitably, tension is created between messages the candidate can fit into his responses to questions, and other messages that he considers important, which do not fit. Peres was highly skilled in walking this tight rope of balancing the two agendas. Consider his response to the question as to which political bloc (the Left and the Arab parties, versus the Right and religious parties) he would prefer when forming his future coalition:

Why should I choose? Anyone who wants peace will be invited to join. I do not rule out anybody. I am not basing myself on frameworks, (?) I am basing myself on substance. Mr. Netanyahu's efforts to scare and disseminate fear are in vain. We are a people experienced in war, we won all the wars. We shall also win the war against terror to clear the way for peace. In the next four years, an opportunity has been created to reach a comprehensive peace in the Middle East . . . and I am telling you, I'll call in all the parties that want to move towards peace, towards an economic boom. We shall defeat the terror despite all these fears, and the country will look different in four years. It looks extraordinarily good now, since the government established by Yitzhak Rabin, and it will look even better, and I am full of faith and confidence and experience, and I have no doubt as to where we are going.

Rejecting the presupposition that he would have to choose between parties, Peres talked instead about the choice that the parties (and by implication, all his viewers) would need to make. This shift in focus, while keeping the question in the background, allowed him to emphasize the major theme of his campaign, namely, the hope for peace created with the Oslo agreements, presented here in contrast to Netanyahu's message of fear from terror. Thus, in this case, the moderator's and interviewee's agendas are successfully merged.

Answering Questions, Netanyahu Style. Netanyahu seemed to treat his time allotment to answer questions mainly as floor space for getting his message across. This need by far superseded the requirement to appear cooperative with the moderator. The result was an extreme fluctuation in the degree of specificity with which he related to the issues raised by the questions. On three (out of six) occasions, he opened the response slot with a lengthy confrontational digression attacking Peres.

Question 1: "Thank you for the question, but before I respond I must relate to what Mr. Peres said about Jerusalem. Mr. Peres, you . . ."
Question 3: "I'll answer in a minute, but first I must relate to what Mr. Peres had said."
Question 4: "First I have to respond, to correct Mr. Peres."

The digressions served to continue and amplify the main theme of Netanyahu's negative campaign—to attack Peres personally as responsible for Oslo, and therefore for terror. In most cases, the responses that follow such digressions tend to be only superficially related to the questions, adhering to the stated topic but ignoring the implication and challenge of the questions. Two extreme examples deserve closer scrutiny. The first case, already mentioned, appeared in Netanyahu's response to the highly face-threatening personal question that required his acknowledgment that the action he took following his extramarital affair was demeaning, and cast a severe doubt on his capacity for decision making under stress. Netanyahu changed the topic—"I made a mistake but the mistake Mr. Peres is making . . ."—thereby blatantly violating the conversational norms that require relevance between question and answer.

The second case shows Netanyahu's skill at stretching the limits of equivocal communication. Consider his response to the follow-up question to Question 1. In order to catch the flavor of this response, here is the text of the original question as well as the follow-up.

1. Interviewer: Thank you, Mr. Peres, and the next question now is for Mr. Netanyahu. You are willing to invest in the settlements less than 1.3 billion shekel, but this is still a considerable sum. At the same time, you say that you are aware of the reality and you accept the Oslo agreement. You say that you accept the Oslo agreement but you will not retreat now from Hebron or redeploy the army there. You say that despite your refusal to redeploy immediately in Hebron, under certain conditions you will be willing to meet with Yassar Arafat. You are willing to meet with Arafat but you are committed to closing down the Orient House [Palestinian political headquarters in East Jerusalem], something that even Shamir's [right-wing Likud] government did not do. I am asking you, in this mixture, what is policy and what is election smoke screen?
2. Netanyahu: [answer, 90 seconds].
3. Interviewer (camera focused on interviewer): Mr. Netanyahu, here we'll stop your answer and I would like to ask you a follow up question, and the question is, and I have asked this before and the answer was as it was. And if, as a result of your policies, the *Intifada* [Palestinian uprising] is renewed, will you then, against your will, return IDF soldiers to the Cassba of Nablus, to the alleys of Gaza and its refugee camps?
4. Netanyahu: (turning to interviewer): I must tell you that from my experience with the Arabs, with Arab representatives and generally, both at the UN and at the foreign office, the office of the Prime Minister and during public contacts, the Arabs are much more realistic than generally depicted. When they see a weak government like Mr. Peres's government, they demand

everything, get everything and demand more. Mr. Peres has promised them half of Jerusalem, now they are demanding forty percent of West Jerusalem as well. But when they come up against a government that knows how to take a firm stand [literally: insist on the red lines], and we know how to do that, then they eventually calm down. When we entered the Madrid talks, the Intifada was already behind us. I mean to conduct peace talks. I intend to lead Israel in security and I am convinced that all the Arab leaders, with no exception—the Palestinians, the Syrians, the Jordanians, the Saudis—will conduct peace talks with me and it will be a lasting peace. A secure peace.

The question ostensibly asked about a hypothetical course of events, and interrogated Netanyahu's response to those events, implying that they were bound to happen. In a way, it can be read as a yes or no challenging question: "I am putting it to you that this is what will happen, and asking you to confirm or contest my proposition."

Netanyahu did not answer directly to the challenge. On first glance, his response seems completely unrelated: There is no reference to entities mentioned in the question, such as the IDF, there is no reference to the stated topic, namely the possibility of an outbreak of the *Intifada* in the future.

One reading can be that Netanyahu chose to ignore the question completely in order to say whatever he wanted to say. But this is a simplistic interpretation.

A more accurate account would present this as a classic example of what Grice (1975) called "maxim exploitation." Deviating manifestly from the maxim requiring one to connect one's current move with the previous one in an informative, clear, coherent, and relevant way, the speaker "invites" the listener to understand what he or she has meant by the deviation. In other words, an implicature is invited, and it remains the task of the listener to decipher its exact nature. Netanyahu was clearly exploiting the maxim of relevance. Instead of relating to the scenario proposed by the host, he sketched an alternative scenario, one in which the Arabs "relax" and there was a "secure peace." Assuming that he is still cooperative in a general sense, his response to this question should be read as deliberately designed to generate an implicature.

The response is a blunt rejection of one aspect of the proposition implied by the question. The question implied that Y (Netanyahu's policies) are to be condemned because they will lead to X (the renewal of the Intifada). The response indirectly answers the challenge that such policies are to be condemned, by painting a rosy picture of the future under these policies ("secure peace"), thereby eliminating the need to respond. It is no longer necessary to relate to what could happen if the policies were indeed to be condemned.

If responding to the content of the questions does not seem to be a first priority on Netanyahu's agenda for the debate—timing and "packaging" his responses certainly were. He was a fast speaker (much faster than Peres), and in most cases managed to time his responses exactly to the time slots provided, and close with a slogan. Thus, the first response ended with "a secure peace," and "peace" appeared in several other slogans like closing statements: "One can not separate peace from security," "a broad government will bring good peace to Israel," "I believe we shall revive the hope for real peace for the people of Israel." Netanyahu may have been aware of marketing research that shows that rapid speech (regardless of pitch, inflection or intensity) makes speakers more persuasive), and was definitely aware of the importance of slogans. As was seen, Peres had difficulties fitting his responses to the time slots provided, and did not always manage to round up the response with a sound-bite. These two "packaging" features, which characterize Netanyahu's performance, probably played a role in creating the impression that Netanyahu was more persuasive.

The analysis makes clear that the strategies employed by the candidates for prime minister in the television debate, 72 hours prior to Election Day, were a direct continuation of the strategies adopted by the two camps during the campaign. But unlike the daily spot-ad campaign on television, which failed to get much notice, the debate was a major public event, carefully watched by political analysts and journalists, and by the public at large, as an indication, and a cause, for the direction in which the tie between the two candidates would be broken.

By encapsulating the strategies of the two large parties, and testing them through a confrontation, the debate demonstrated the asymmetry created by Labor's decision to refrain from attacking the right-wing camp for systematically inciting against PM Rabin during his last year, thereby creating a climate that led to his assassination. This meant that Labor has given up on using the strongest card at its disposal. The rationale behind this most crucial strategy was the wish not to antagonize potential voters from the right who may this time vote for Peres. As the right has a majority among Jewish voters (whereas Israel's Arab citizens, who constitute 20% of the voters, can generally be counted on to support the left), the debate's target audience was not evenly divided between the camps. Peres was supposed to convince Likud supporters to vote Likud for the Knesset, and Peres for PM. These voters, so the theory goes, would take offense if the representative of "their" camp would be charged with the grave allegation of leading (perhaps even orchestrating) the rhetoric that fueled Rabin's assassination, and may "return home." This strategy led to the paradoxical situation in which Yitzhak Rabin, whose figure loomed large after his death and who remained the most relevant personal leader in that election, was left out of the race.

Whether flawed or not to begin with, this strategy meant that Peres (known to be a great orator when he gets really angry) was prevented from attacking Netanyahu at his Achilles' heel. The condemning fact, that Netanyahu had spoken at a mass rally under a picture of Rabin dressed as Arafat only a year earlier, was not even mentioned. This left Netanyahu free to attack Peres without having to worry about being reminded of his own embarrassing role in the incitement against Rabin. Peres himself, on the other hand, was pushed into a defensive position, fending off Netanyahu's accusation of his intention to "divide Jerusalem."

The other side of Labor's line of "appeasement" was to emphasize that Netanyahu was no match for Peres, by instructing Peres to ignore him during the debate. This tactic boomeranged for several reasons. It made Netanyahu the underdog, it seemed to violate the rules of a democratic contest, and it left the field wide open for Netanyahu to attack Peres without worrying about a direct counterattack. The effect of ignoring Netanyahu was particularly unfortunate considering the identity of the "undecided" voters, who may have felt the opposition candidate was snubbed.

This asymmetry between the two candidates, in which one is prohibited from acting outraged or lashing back, and the other focuses on doing just that, was exacerbated by the old-fashioned manner in which Peres presented himself, one which belongs to the era when politicians presented themselves as part of an ideological camp, or a political movement, not as individual heroes. Thus, Peres talked about what "we"—the Labor party, the government—had achieved, allowing BB to freely concentrate on selling himself.

The inequality of the candidates in the debate may be summed up in terms of their compatibility with the medium, the rules of the genre, and the different strategies each had to follow. Television was the environment in which Netanyahu flourished. He may have been tense and nervous before going on screen (as indeed he was, as witnesses reported, before the debate) but recovered instantly once he was on. He appeared youthful, energetic, and self-assured. Skillful at packaging his responses in accordance with the requirements of the show, he also had the confidence, derived from rigorous practicing, that he did it right. Moreover, his strategy of attack makes him sound tough and determined. Within the virtual bubble, Netanyahu exercised his compatibility with the medium and the rules of the genre, and his advisers' line "demonstrated" the truth of his claims.

Peres, on the other hand, demonstrated a lack of compatibility with all three. To begin with, he had certain distaste toward the very idea of practicing for the show. He believed that his long history of achievement and the power of his vision should do the trick. His responses tended to be too dense, did not wind up with a slogan, and at times spilled over the time allotted. But worst of all, Peres was constrained by his own advisers. At his best and most eloquent when getting angry in the Knesset, lashing out against his critics, Peres was now acutely uncomfortable with being prevented from fighting back. In a real confrontational debate, he would have stood a good chance. In this watered-down version, encumbered by his instructions to pretend it was a one-to-one interview, Peres was a lame duck.

8

The Political Discourse of Authenticity: American and Israeli Style

Analysis of the crucial television debate in which Benjamin Netanyahu won (chap. 7) demonstrates that the candidate's ability to convey a confident, trustworthy, folksy image on TV is more important than his capacity to elaborate on his policies. In the situation of a (permanent) draw in the Israeli electorate, BB's televisual skills may very well have given him the tiny advantage he needed. As policy issues become increasingly complex, ideological differences between parties shrink, and politicians disintermediate the political institutions by appealing to would-be voters directly via the media, we voters are often called on to put our trust in a politician because he or she is genuine, sincere, and means what he or she says. Pleas to "Read my lips," or to "Look me straight in the eye" display attempts to connect verbal claims to other, more physical (and therefore supposedly less cerebrally controlled) clues to whether the claim is "real." Such tactics of "performing" authenticity, as in the shedding of a tear in empathy for human suffering, can also be used more generally to attest to the speaker's personality, serving as it were as unmediated evidence to genuine caring. The political salience of this kind of (verbal and nonverbal) rhetoric, designed to provoke viewers' emotional trust, has gained power as TV goes increasingly live, editing is marginalized, and the blurring of news and entertainment seeks out these moments for countless recycling.

This chapter analyzes two case studies, one in the United States, the other in Israel, in order to examine media's contribution to a new type of neo-populist politics, and to see how the need to project authentic concern plays out in the United States and in Israel, perhaps indicating something about the differences among the two political cultures.

Two dialogues, taken from two genres, are presented here. One is intimate and confessional, the other is intimate and adversarial, but both are highly personal, intensely emotional, and performed for the benefit of unacknowledged over-hearers. In both the U.S. and the Israeli cases, a candidate for the highest office, in real time, in a highly emotionally charged confrontation, creates an intimate alliance with TV viewers by performing the role of someone who really cares—genuine, sincere, spontaneous. The real thing. Someone you can trust. Not your everyday politician. Authenticity is performed live, on stage, and may be watched, in action, so that everyone can see and judge for themselves (or so it seems) if the candidate is for real or just faking. I present the two in light of the expectations of theorists of press and democracy about the place of media in producing enlightened voters.

A CLOSE LOOK AT THE POLITICAL STRATEGY OF AUTHENTIC CARING, U.S. STYLE

The U.S. case features a fictionalized Bill Clinton, named Jack Stanton, launching his first election campaign as described in the book and the docudrama, *Primary Colors* (published anonymously, it was later discovered as the work of Joe Klein, a *Newsweek* reporter who closely followed the Clinton campaign trail). I use a fictionalized example, as I see it as an interpretative observation of a close, critical, somewhat empathetic witness, written in the quasi-journalistic genre of McGinnis' *The Selling of the President* (see chap. 5, which also discussed fictional elements in press reports). Also, it should not be forgotten, that any tape of the "real" edited event (carefully predesigned for the taping) would frame reality to tell a story (remember the editing of the Safra Square incident). And the advantage of Klein's description over viewing the "real" taping of the event, or reading that day's press report, lies in his broader perspective as participant observer, who, in hindsight, can fit the scene as one link in the candidate's tactical chain.

The event in question was designed to convince a new recruit—an African-American from a classy family, a Yuppie graduate of an ivy-league university—to work for Stanton, the governor of a small southern state, seeking the highest public office. The yet undecided young man is invited to join the candidate in a meeting, at a center for adult education. On his arrival, Stanton/Clinton is introduced to the Black and Hispanic students gathered around a table. He joins the circle, and, with the others, listens to Dwaine, an African-American man in his 30s describing how, in his childhood as a dyslectic, he was transferred from one school to another, but never managed to learn to read and write.

"They just kept passing me up—third grade, fourth grade, and I just sit in the back sticking to my own self and it was like no one notices. . . . They could have sent me to the Bronx Zoo, I mean no one ever told me nothing, no one ever say, 'Dwaine you can't read, what you gonna do with your sorry ass?'" At the graduation ceremony in high school, "Mama come she taking the day off from the laundry where she work at. So we are there and Doctor Delambrety is calling out the names on the diploma and what each kid done, and you know, like, 'Sharona Harris—honors, Tyron Kirby—[?] diploma, and then, then he comes to my name and he say that everyone hear, he says, 'Dwaine Smith receives certificate of attendance.' You hear people buzzing, a couple of folks is laughing. I got to go up there and get this, I got to stand up there, just dying trying not to look at anyone, trying not to look too stupid, you know. And Mama sitting in front, she got her hat on, and she got her purse in her lap, and tears coming down from behind her glasses, like someone died."

Everyone around the table wipes away a tear. Stanton/Clinton blows his nose with his handkerchief and says: "I want to thank you for sharing this with us, Dwaine. I want to thank you all for having real courage." And he continues: "My uncle Charlie was a war hero. He was sent to Iwo Jima, you know, where they raise the flag. . . ." Uncle Charlie, Stanton/Clinton tells them, took out four machine guns that had pinned down a squad of his buddies. "He had one grenade, and his rifle, and his bare hands, and he took them out. Shit. They gave him the Medal of Honor, President Truman did. And when he came home to Grace Junction they had a parade for him, and the town's finest came to my parents' house and they say to him: 'Charlie, what do you got in mind for yourself now?' And Charlie said he didn't know. Well, the Mayor said, 'maybe you like a full scholarship to the State's University?' And the banker said, 'maybe Charlie didn't want to go back to school after all he's been through. He'd like a management job, a big future in the bank. Come manage my crew.' And you know what? Damn this. Charlie turned them all down." "What did he do?" asks a Black woman. "He just lie on the couch and smoke his 'Luckies', we couldn't get him off that couch."

"Cause he was messed up from the war?" suggests an older man. "No," answers the candidate. "It was just that he couldn't read. He couldn't read and he was embarrassed, he didn't want to tell anyone."

Here the candidate delivers the punch line: "He had the courage to win the Congressional Medal of Honor but he didn't have the courage to do what each and everyone of you is doing down here. He didn't have courage to admit that he needed help and get it. So I want you to know I understand what you are doing, and appreciate it and honor your commitment." And he closes with, "people say to me, 'Jack Stanton, why do you spend so much time and effort on adult literacy?' and I say to them, 'because it gives me a chance to see courage.' I want to thank you ... for allowing me to come visit you today."

What clinched it for the would-be aide, supplying the final proof that all he had seen was not just a phony performance, was watching Stanton/Clinton continuing his chat with the people at the center after the formal meeting was over, and having to be practically torn away. (The young aide was too naive to figure out that despite his situation of watching from the wings, he himself—whose acquisition was marked as number one priority—had been targeted as the prime audience, making the scenes "behind the stage" the most crucial part of the performance.)

When our hero tells his activist African-American girlfriend that he is joining Stanton's team, she reminds him that as governor, Stanton did nothing for the Blacks in his state, and that his only interest in acquiring him is to have a young prestigious Black on his team to assist in bringing in more Black votes. But our hero, having been hooked, answers, "I want to work for someone who really cares," following which he adds, by way of explanation, "Since Kennedy, nobody has used words such as *history* or *mission*."

This conquest proves the effectiveness of the candidate's tactics at the multipurpose meeting, scheduled as it were for TV's campaign coverage, and for the candidate's ads.

Specifically, this case provides an answer to the question why the candidate, in his effort to convince Americans that he is the right choice for running the country (and the world), does not bother to provide any clues to demonstrate that he has ideas about the policies needed to address social ills, let alone ways of implementing them. The informal, intimate chat that the electorate later witnessed has nothing to do with the specifics of marking social targets, or with policy plans and strategies. With one exception, a most general, but, at the same time, a most deeply felt statement: the candidate's expression of his intense concern for adult education. Yet although the subject was at the heart of the exchange, it was not deliberated as a policy issue. There was no attempt to discuss problems of implementation, or to consider strategies to insure success where others failed. Instead, the symbolic support for overcoming illiteracy was substituted for a program of conquering literacy.

The secret of winning, then, is to convince people that one "really"—sincerely, authentically—cares. How did Stanton/Clinton convey his caring in this case? First, there was the form of interchange that he chose. Rather than a longwinded delivery by the candidate, or a question/answer exchange, the campaign meeting was constructed as an equal dialogue between Dwaine and Stanton (with the others listening in), each telling an intimately personal story (Dwaine from his own experience, Clinton from his uncle's), each exposing a vulnerability, an embarrassing weakness. But within the equalizing exchange of stories, Clinton also grants Dwaine an advantage, as the point of his own story is his uncle's failure to overcome his disability, versus Dwaine's success in overcoming his own. Acknowledging Dwaine as the real hero, Clinton incorporates the listeners in the room and, ultimately, the overhearers at home, in his circle of people who really care.

THE IMAGINED PUBLIC THAT CALLS FOR THE STRATEGY OF "AUTHENTIC CARING"

Politicians opting for this kind of strategy implicitly assume a particular image of their public. First, this imagined public is not interested in listening to a political debate. This may be due to a number of reasons. One tallies with Schudson's (1997) perception that real political conversation creates embarrassment. The public is threatened by expressions of conflict, of clash of opinion, and the need to adopt an opinion, preferring to join a pleasant and sociable, sometimes an emotionally moving, conversation. (Eliasoph, 1998, went even further by arguing that people might be prepared to talk politics in private but not in public.)

Another assumption, in the spirit of Walter Lippman (1924), regards the issues on the public agenda as too complex for nonexperts. In this view, most people are not capable of following the logic of the argument and are therefore not interested in listening to information in these areas.

A third assumption, leading to similar conclusions, points to the public cynicism toward politicians. Accordingly, even if people were tolerant of political debates, most of them would not trust politicians and remain skeptical about their real motivations for supporting a particular policy or action. The general assumption underlying this perception of the public is that politicians' attitudes are perceived as decided by personal interest. Moreover, media practices of horse race reporting, which relate to tactics and the odds of winning, only work to strengthen that cynicism, socializing the public to suspicion. Instead of debating the nitty-gritty of issues and policies, politicians thus have to revert to a strategy demonstrating that they can be trusted. The question remains why have the experts come to the conclusion that the public do not want to hear about policy issues and instead look for someone whom they can trust.

CONVERSATION OF "TRUST" AND THE CREATION OF *PSEUDO-GEMEINSCHAFT*

Whether true or not, politicians' image of the public as incapable of, uninterested in, or suspicious of political debate, calls for the avoidance of genuine political conversation in public. *Pseudo-gemeinschaft* is introduced instead. The term *pseudo-gemeinschaft* ("a false sense of community"), used by Merton half a century earlier to describe singer Kate Smith's victorious bond-selling campaign, was defined then as "a feigning of personal concern with the other fellow in order to manipulate him the better" (Merton, 1946, cited in Benniger, 1987). By creating this kind of bond, Merton tells us, Smith "satisfied a craving for reassurance, an acute need to believe." And politicians are just another type of salespeople, trying to persuade their public to buy the goods they offer. Then as now, we may witness the paradox concerning public opinion: it is the fear of being manipulated by politicians, perceived as motivated by their own private interests, that makes people crave for "sincerity," through (phony) interpersonal communication within a community of values. It is no coincidence that the success of politicians depends on skills identical to those of a star singer. For both persuaders, connecting with the public in the age of cynicism and personalized interaction via media means performing as "idols of consumption," not as "idols of production" (Lowenthal, cited in Benniger, 1987).

The creation of a pseudo-community by conveying an impression of spontaneity, authenticity, and genuine caring, becomes crucial for the transmission of the one message which may appeal to voters—"you can trust that man." Paradoxically, however, the demonstration of qualities such as spontaneity and authenticity—which are supposed to reflect an uncalculating and incalculable personality—must be carefully worked out and rehearsed in advance (and is inconceivable without help from professional image-makers). Such planning and preparation, however, means doing something that contradicts the very nature of the quality that one is attempting to emulate, since to be "genuine" is to be "left in its natural state, not worked over and complicated by reflection" (Richards, cited in Merton, 1946).

To be judged as authentic or as fake means that the aura itself remains the sole content, the essence of what one is imitating Reproducing this type of conversation is a contradiction in terms. And yet it works. Because everyone is aware of the rules (and assumes that any show of sincerity or spontaneity is phony to begin with), and because the politicians know that everyone knows, the challenge is to persuade the public against their better judgment because they want to believe (or, rather, to suspend disbelief).

As real or as fictional as the Stanton/Clinton case may be, the dialogue between politicians and their constituencies plays a major role in the process of electing politicians and of keeping them in office. Masquerading in a number of forms, this phenomenon of candidates interacting with the mass public via media has infiltrated the heart of the political process. In this way, the rhetoric of *pseudo-gemeinschaft* infiltrates an increasingly large number of conversations in which politicians are seemingly talking to colleagues, in Parliament and in the studio, but at the same time creating intimacy with viewers and listeners. Participants address this overhearing public no less than they do the other participants in the room. This blurring of the boundaries between campaign rhetoric and political debate carries significant implications for the process of decision making in contemporary democracies.

Of course, such conversations between political figures and laypersons have always existed, especially during election campaigns. In the current political reality, however, the ever present media puts politicians under the pressure of virtual re-election every day anew, and the results are available next morning, to be checked in the latest poll.

FORMS OF BONDING: THE SUBGENRES OF TALKING TO THE PUBLIC

On-screen conversation between politicians and their constituencies takes a number of forms. First, there is the classic form, brought over from the *town square*. This genre has become less popular ever since TV brought politicians directly into the home. Moreover, the space and the rhetoric of enthusiasm it requires are not compatible with the advantages of the video camera (television's first attempt at live coverage of a mass demonstration, in the case General McArthur's parade in Chicago, showed only the people next to him, and left the rather indifferent multitudes out of frame) and with the context of viewing.

On the small screen, street rallies have given way to the less chaotic *"town hall" meetings*, carefully planned for televising and consisting of question and answer sessions, or to the more intimate, more casual meetings (such as the one we have presented) between candidates and "authentic" representatives of various groups of citizens, who represent us viewers. Because the intimacy and style of this kind of encounter looks good on the small screen, and because television presents these encounters to millions of viewers as observers in the wings, the traditional format remains seemingly untouched. Unlike town hall meetings (in which dialogue between politician and individual people is restricted to a formal question and answer exchange), in the meeting analyzed here we connect with the speaker through the admiring eyes of the candidate's interlocutors (an analysis of such identification is developed in cinema theory).

Another form, that Horton and Wohl (1956) termed *para-social interaction*, is designed for directly engaging viewers with the speaker. This format was introduced by President Roosevelt in his "Fireside Chat," in which he sat in his own living room, and situated his listeners as "my friends" (Ryfe, 1999). A variant of this form would be the grand confessions of Nixon and Clinton in the United States (and Netanyahu in Israel), who used direct address to admit that they had done wrong, asking viewers for their forgiveness. Clinton, of course, had his share of intimate interviews alone and together with his wife, Hillary.

A fourth form of engaging audiences is through granting *interviews to professional journalists*, who are thought to represent viewers' interests and/or curiosity. Naturally, with the "trust-me" politics taking over, candidates may easily prefer Larry King or MTV over more classic journalistic formats. Speaking to other politicians, usually via the mediation of journalists, constitutes a further variation of talking to viewers. This last type can take the (more casual) form of a *talk show*, or the more formal form of a *debate*.

ALLYING WITH VIEWERS TO EXPOSE AN OPPONENT AS INAUTHENTIC, ISRAELI STYLE

The Israeli case is taken from a televised debate of candidates for prime minister, which marked the watershed of the Israeli 1999 elections. Initiated by Israel's (commercial) Channel Two, and featuring Netanyahu and the incumbent prime minister, and one of the two viable contenders for the job, Itzhak Mordechai, then an ex-general, of (Jewish) Kurdish origin, who punctured a fatal hole in Netanyahu's credibility. Unlike the almost confessional mode via which Clinton so successfully created a *pseudo-gemeinschaft* with his audiences, this confrontation took an adversarial form. Rather then chatting warmly and informally, Mordechai here created an alliance with the anchor and the viewers by an adversarial exposing of his rival's lack of sincerity. Constructing his own authenticity was achieved in the act of destroying his opponent's.

"LOOK ME STRAIGHT IN THE EYE"

Traditionally, prime ministerial debates in Israeli elections were initiated by the two largest parties, and aired within the time slots allocated by law to the parties for election advertising on media, with the rules of questioning and the choice of anchor negotiated and agreed on in advance (see chap. 7). In the 1999 elections, however, the only prime ministerial debate had been initiated by the producers of *Mish'al Ham*, a sensation-oriented political talk show (see chap. 9). Ehud Barak, the Labor Party's candidate, decided to stay away, excusing himself as "not being good at it" and reinforcing the widespread belief (not least based on BB's victory in the 1996 debate with Peres) that Netanyahu was a "media wizard." This time, Netanyahu was left to face Itzhak Mordechai, his former defense minister, who had joined Netanyahu's government as a hero of the Sephardic community and was now the leader of a new party, the Center Party.

Whereas in Clinton's case, the role of media was hidden from view, limited as it was to the future transmission of the encounter, here the media took the lead, announcing the rules ("we will not stand with a stopper in our hand"), exposing to the public the two opponents' frantic preparations for the show, and framing the debate at the outset as "a personal—not only political—confrontation, touching on deep emotional depths." This introduction led viewers to expect a high degree of spontaneity, while, at the same time, informing them that the two men had spent many hours with their spin doctors (Netanyahu with his American consultant Arthur Finkelstein and his team, Mordechai with an Israeli consultant who had deserted Netanyahu).

The show opened with a short history of the relations between the two rivals—from their honeymoon in the 1996 elections, when they were seen campaigning side by side in the open vegetable market, to Netanyahu's firing of Mordechai from the post of defense minister some weeks before the show. From the beginning, it appeared that the anchor-producer and Mordechai shared an interest in putting Netanyahu's personality on trial by provoking him to expose that (to use Mordechai's words) "he doesn't deserve my trust and the people's trust."

Whereas Clinton acts out his empathy on screen by responding to Dwaine, Mordechai acted out his outrage over Netanyahu's betrayal of his own and everybody else's trust by frontally scolding him for his bluffing: "no truth, no honesty, no integrity." Ironically, in this case it was Netanyahu, ostensibly trying to serve the public's right to know, who tried repeatedly to redirect the debate away from Mordechai's "personally motivated accusations" to "really serious" issues of policy. The anchor ignored Netanyahu's efforts and did all he could to inflate the personal feud between the two, never letting Netanyahu get away with, or escape into, "ideology." The interviewer accepted Mordechai's framing, that insistence on ideological differences was "phony," whereas personality was the "real" issue. (It may of course be argued that there is something to this argument since both contenders came from the same ideological camp.)

For a foreign viewer who did not know Netanyahu, and watched the debate "cold," out of the context of the elections, Netanyahu would seem the genuine politician, concerned with the big political questions on the Israeli agenda, rather than with picking petty personal fights. For the Israeli voter, however, the issue was indeed Netanyahu's "unreliable" personality, perceived by many as nothing less than pathological. It is definitely a case in point for demonstrating the public's distrust of issue-oriented talk, because the candidate is considered to have only self-survival at heart. This means they do not know whether he would hold to his declared ideology (or even whether he has one), and cannot be trusted with any commitment, even if he is willing to commit himself.

The following exchange demonstrates Mordechai's winning tactic of reprimanding Netanyahu, taking on a superior stance, at times seeming to play the role of a father who attempts to shame his son into admitting his lies.

> Netanyahu (on the negotiation with Syria and the wish to withdraw from Lebanon): I am not ready to exchange one strategic problem, in Lebanon, for another strategic problem on the northern border (i.e., confrontation with the Syrian army).
> [Mordechai grins throughout]
> Anchor: Thank you, thank you . . . I would like to move on to the Palestinian problem.
> Mordechai: [continues to grin, with the camera on him] Look me in the eye, BB.
> Anchor: Just a moment, what does it mean "look me in the eye?"
> Mordechai: He knows.
> Anchor: No, but I don't know.
> Mordechai: OK, that's enough, ask a question.
> Anchor: I don't know, the public doesn't know.
> Mordechai: Ask, ask, ask, ask.
> Anchor: I'm asking—so?
> Mordechai: No, ask questions and I'll tell you.
> Anchor: Are you hinting that an opportunity to make peace with President Assad was missed?

Mordechai: Ask, I didn't say anything.
Anchor: I'm asking.
Mordechai: I hope that the negotiation . . .
Anchor: No, don't escape. Did the Netanyahu government miss an opportunity to make peace with Syria?
Mordechai: I didn't say that. I said that when I am elected, I will open negotiations with Syria and I tell you that Assad . . .
Anchor: You told him to look you in the eye.
Mordechai: . . . that Assad knows who he can make peace with.
Anchor: Sorry, sorry, When you told him "look me in the eye," what does that mean? Was there something in the negotiation with the Syrians that was missed?
Netanyahu: Nothing was missed because of the Syrians demand that we stick to the shores of the Kinneret. Barak is ready for it, I am not.

Missing in the written account is Mordechai's sardonic grin of disbelief, as if to say "BB-don't-try-to-sell-me this-(bullshit)-I know-you-all-too-well" (Margalit, 1999). By challenging BB to "look me in the eye," Mordechai implied that BB knew he was lying, and knew that Mordechai knew. Furthermore, Mordecai was hinting that this public show of shaming Netanyahu into blinking first was the only way of publicly demonstrating Netanyahu's duplicity without disclosing any state secrets. Mordechai himself benefitted twice from this insinuation, by juxtaposing his own sincerity and responsibility with his rival's evasiveness and frivolity. Note how the anchor picked up Mordechai's challenge, playing the game of insisting on uncovering the secret that Netanyahu and Mordechai supposedly shared, with Mordechai nobly maneuvering between (supposedly) exposing Netanyahu's lies and protecting national interests.

That Netanyahu lost his cool became evident toward the end of the debate, when he revealed himself as a paper-tiger, obstinately, childishly refusing to abide by the rules, and giving Mordechai a golden opportunity to demonstrate his superior, paternalistic stance. Mordechai's biggest moment came when he gallantly volunteered to assist the anchor when the latter called the prime minister to order, threatening to end the program if Netanyahu did not abide by the rules.

MORDECHAI, CLINTON, AND THEIR RESPECTIVE COMMUNITIES

The two examples presented here show how an American and an Israeli candidate bond with their audience. Mordechai did it by playing the game of discrediting the prime minister, winning the anchor over to accept his cues, relentlessly pursuing his adversary, signaling the audience that the issue at stake was Netanyahu's not-to-be-trusted personality, and gradually causing him to lose his cool and behave the part (i.e., to look scolded on TV for the first, and crucial, time).

But even as Mordechai administered a knockout to Netanyahu's credibility in the eyes of TV audiences, he failed to replace him in their favor. Clinton, on his part, managed to imprint his own credibility on viewers by praising one poor man's personal victory, achieved against all odds, and making it into a great opportunity to display his empathetic feelings, as they emerged in the spontaneous interchange. By invoking his own family history, he managed to convey that he came from the people, understood their pain, and therefore could be trusted to look after them.

The bond that Clinton created with the people around the table succeeded in enlisting the sophisticated, idealistic young man who, genuinely motivated to improve the lot of his people, opted to suspend disbelief and dedicate himself to the candidate's race in the months ahead. It carried over further to viewers like us, suspicious of sleek, seemingly efficient, professional politicians, who talk too fast, know all the answers, and hide their true self-interested motives. (All that was needed to transform the success into a fiasco would be the inside story of the careful targeting and planning of this spontaneous scene by Clinton's team of experts.) Incidentally, the answer to the question whether Clinton's story was fabricated or real was established some months later, when the young recruit came to Clinton's hometown, got introduced to his uncle, identified him as the hero of the story and addressed him with "Oh, so you are the heroic uncle." "I am the uncle," came the weary answer, "never mind hero." It took a few moments to clarify that the story was concocted. By then it was just another punch in the face concerning the credibility, and authenticity, of his boss—authenticity, mind you, being his most important asset.

WHY IS PSEUDO-SOCIABLE CONVERSATION DANGEROUS?

Regarding both the U.S. and the Israeli dialogues as cultural variants of the discourse of authenticity, it is interesting to note that despite the salience of this kind of conversation, it is often segregated in the slot of "campaign rhetoric." Therefore, it has not been given the significance it deserves in the democratic process, and was left out in a number of efforts to define and characterize political conversation in the context of the workings of democracy, that is, when considering the debate in terms of which decisions were made or policies undertaken. I refer in particular to Schudson's (1997) definition of political conversation, based on his juxtaposition of sociable conversation and political conversation. The first type he described as relaxed, friendly, intimate, conducted among equals, ever flowing, and never striving toward an instrumental aim, whereas the latter is depicted as a debate carried out among politicians, accompanied by structural unease, or embarrassment. In contrast with sociable chat, political conversation is bound to lead to conflict and disagreement, is based on inherent inequality (or rather on achieved rather than natural equality), and typically ends with a written document. As such, it remains the privilege and duty of professional politicians, and is guided by strict formal rules.

These two types of conversation—the "genuine" one, in which laypersons talk only to others who are like them, and the regulated political talk, which is typically carried in Parliament—leave out the talks, mostly electronically mediated, between politicians and the people. These are often disguised as conversations among politicians, or between politicians and journalists, but the journalists only act as the public's representatives in the studio. The problem is that the clear distinction between conversations among professional politicians and sociable conversations (which are not suited for deliberating political issues) is gradually eroding. With the ever increasing exposure of politicians, forced by the instant democracy of polls to keep their constituencies happy, and with Parliamentary sessions broadcast live on C-Span and its like in other countries, it is the over-hearers (or, in question/answer sessions, the direct addressees) who dominate the style and content of the interaction, their wishes and tastes carefully evaluated and catered to.

I suggest that this type of conversation is a third, hybrid model, which may be the crucial form of political talk, if only for its impact on the democratic process. Whereas Schudson's view of political conversation is desirable for the interests of a healthily functioning democracy, it seems to be corrupted by the ever increasing contamination in situations where politicians are playing this double game, one in which the qualities Dewey (1927) sees as facilitating genuine conversation become the desired achievement and sole aim.

Rather than representing one type of conversation as "political" and the other as "sociable," politics in the light of video cameras has created a third, hybrid type, which is political in the sense that it occurs in public, often among politicians, and includes the absent-but-present voters; and sociable in the sense that it often avoids political issues, often regulated less by the norms Schudson prescribed for political conversation and more by the norms dictated by media, and is aimed at projecting an informal, easy, intimate relationship with the mass of invisible public.

The fact that the conversation between politicians and public does not follow Schudson's model, represents a genuine, and major, problem of democratic life. It is the discrepancy between what it takes to be elected, and what it takes to do your job once you are there. Political conversation of the first kind marks the para-social interaction between the leaders and the public in an era in which ideology has been substituted by personality, impersonating what Dewy sees as the heart of democracy—amiable, authentic, free flowing, uncommitted. It calls for seductive skills of the kind that can warm people's hearts, and carry a politician into office.

Political conversation, as Schudson defined it, demands different skills—such as the ability to carry a sustained argument, the integrity not to give up on one's principles, and the knowledge when and to what degree to compromise in the margins in order not to lose the essence. These skills are crucial for doing a good job once in public office, but they do not necessarily assist political candidates in getting elected. Given that pre-election interactions between the candidates and the public affect election results, this means that candidates are voted-in on demonstrating skills which may have little to do with carrying out the task once in office.

Although the ability to charm voters has always played a part in political life, and perhaps a number of would-be great leaders were lost to the public because of the discrepancy between their ability to do the job and their "making conversation" skills, I argue that contemporary mass-mediated, image-oriented politics, with its constant and unrelenting exposure to "everybody," and the perceived need to be popular not only once in 4 years but in the daily opinion polls, have turned the contrived copy of the first model of "genuine" conversation into the only engine at election time and the focus of political survival. Returning to the score of our two heroes, it may be concluded that it is an easier job to call a rival's bluff than to convince the public of one's own caring.

The next chapter addresses some other aspects of the nascent political culture as it manifests itself in the semi-entertainment genres of commercialized television. Just as the debate is a strange brew of issues, personalities and body language, constrained by the strict rules of a "winner-takes-all" style contest, so do the new prime-time political-cum-game show-cum exposé shows, designed to parade their guests' talents from playing the flute to trivia mastery, delineate this new postmodern cultural environment in which the relevant and the trivial are equal partners. Although Israel has wholeheartedly adopted the American format, politics at this recieving end of globalized culture is still primetime material rather than food for late-night political connoisseurs, and the fighting style is far from the laid-back manner that any rookie politician in the United States must master.

9

Political Talk Shows: American and Israeli Style*

The introduction of American-style television in the 1990s went well with the cravings of Israelis for "normalization." With the Oslo peace process under way, and following the signing of a peace treaty with Jordan, it was perhaps time for settling down in the evening to watch something more fun than the news. Tired of the pompous presentation and the threatening undercurrents (e.g., a general forecasting the possibility of another war, a new deal to sells arms to a neighboring country), Israelis were relieved to have the news moved out of prime time.

When the dust settled, it became apparent that the substitute for news in the midst of prime time was the political talk show. This new genre caught on like a bush fire. Israelis still received their fix—politics once again—only this time rather than watching the respectable, "objective," disciplined news, we were watching an informal, entertaining chat, touching lightly on current affairs, with journalists, pundits, and politicians in the studio.

---

*This chapter, co-authored with Bruce Williams, is an early version of a more extended paper in progress.

Unlike the U.S. version, it soon turned into two Israeli subgenres: heated political debates on the public First Channel, and congenial, low-key, mostly nonpolitical interviews on the commercial Channel Two. Talk shows turned out to be addictive. And because, unlike drama series, they are inexpensive to produce, do not require special skills, and yet count as part of the channel's mandatory quota of local production, they dominated TV's prime time in the 1990s. This chapter compares the way in which the same format, born in the wake of similar economic and technological changes in the media, plays out in two societies characterized by distinctly different political cultures.

We have asked how talk shows reformulate the role of journalists and what sort of model of political debate they create. With this in mind, we looked at the ways in which these shows construct and engage their audiences; how they conceptualize politics; the ways in which they play out the relationship among politicians, media and public; and the way they mix forms and formats borrowed from genres of journalism and entertainment.

THE EMERGENCE AND SIGNIFICANCE OF POLITICAL TALK TELEVISION

Concurrent with the technological and institutional changes in Israel that resulted in the introduction of new "quasi-news" formats, the U.S. media underwent similar changes that also resulted in the proliferation of political talk shows (Delli Carpini and Williams, 2000). In the United States, four more 24-hour news channels (CNN, CNBC, MSNBC, and the new FNN), and constantly updated Internet news sites, augmented the news broadcast on the three national networks. This resulted in a dramatically segmented audience, and in changing journalistic practices. In both countries, news programs ceased being an integrative, shared space, but with a major difference. First, the Israeli shows are broadcast on prime time, and may still attract ratings of 18% to 25%, whereas U.S. shows are broadcast out of prime time, becoming a series of tiny enclaves for a small self-selected elite and/or "news junkies." (Although the combined cable ratings now often surpass the combined ratings for the networks, the rating for any particular show is quite low. For example, the highest rating *The Larry King Show* ever achieved, during the Monica Lewinsky scandal, was 5.3 points.)

The shows we studied all share some form of "political" or "semi-political" conversation (and/or debate, and/or confrontation) in the studio, and were broadcast live, with the host (or hosts) employing various combinations of the roles of reporter/entertainer/participant. Informal, sometimes funny, sometimes intensely emotional, sometimes malicious—these shows are the focus of this chapter. Of particular interest were the strategies used by the producers of these shows to construct audiences in the two countries, as manifestations of how this television genre both reflects and reinforces differences in the two political cultures.

The U.S. audience for political talk exists in a society where there is an underlying consensus about the legitimacy of the political system, the parties are nonideological, prior to the 9/11 terrorist attacks there was no external threat, and the problems that do confront the system are complex in terms of causes and solutions, and difficult to connect directly to the lives of individual citizens. As a result, TV talk shows took it for granted that society is largely apathetic, with only a small, informed and attentive audience of either dutiful citizens, the ideologically committed, or those who would like to see themselves as insiders. The latter group, in particular, view this type of programming as their preferred form of entertainment—they simply like politics more than they like sports, professional wrestling, or *Ally McBeal*.

In contrast, prime-time news in Israel has always been "the best show in town," and the evening news tended to downplay internal strife. As argued in chapter 2, the political talk show has replaced the news as the tribal campfire in a politicized society where ideological, ethnic, religious, and identity chasms play out in varying ways, influenced by a succession of ongoing waves of immigration and shifting external threats, which constantly redraw the political map. In the second half of the 1990s, these internal chasms no longer stopped at the level of struggle over policies and fighting for group rights, but increasingly challenged the very legitimacy of democratic institutions (Kimmerling, 1998). These culture wars, charged with real-life tensions and a threatening potential for exploding into violence, continued to make politics an inherently dramatic story.

Thus, the two trends—the establishment of a commercially motivated multichannel media, and the contesting of basic democratic norms by religious fundamentalist groups—fed on and reinforced each other, with the structure and content of media reflecting and exacerbating the social and cultural schisms.

Within this broader context, talk shows are interesting because they have the potential to overcome some of the limits of more traditional forms of news presentations. First, the more open, interactive form, actively solicits viewer engagement, which is what traditional news often fails to do. Second, although traditional news programs compress even the most complex issue into a brief period and then move on, talk shows allow for the extended discussion of a single issue. Third, unlike the news, the format potentially allows contending parties to make their own case to the audience, rather than be reduced to brief sound-bites or journalistic summaries.

Moreover, talk shows cast the professional journalist in a role quite different from that assumed in traditional news broadcasts. The personal presence of political antagonists on many talk shows reduces the journalist's responsibility for summarizing and balancing stories. At the same time, many talk shows exacerbate the already growing tendency of journalists to become celebrities and for celebrities from other arenas of public life to assume the roles formerly occupied by journalists. As competitive pressures increase, the criteria used by talk show producers to select their guests are increasingly based on celebrity itself and not necessarily knowledge of the issue under consideration. This means that the greater the celebrity appeal of the political figure, the greater the ability to influence the structure of the show (e.g., who will appear with the celebrity) or even restrict the questions to be addressed to the individual.

These changes create interesting challenges for journalists as they are forced to choose between professional ethics and the opportunities for increasing their personal popularity and income. In Israel, for instance, one of the most popular television talk show hosts has become the producer of his own show, and his weekly income is pegged to the show's ratings. The selection of participants and his style of interviewing cannot but reflect the contradictions between his role as journalist and his economic stake in the show's profitability (Fallows, 1996).

A TYPOLOGY AND ANALYSIS OF POLITICAL TALK TELEVISION

For this analysis, we chose only regularly scheduled television shows that deal with overtly political issues and/or feature prominent political figures and are structured around a relatively unrehearsed conversation. Included in this analysis are traditional public affairs talk shows such as *Meet the Press* in both Israel and the United States, newer styles of cable talk shows like *Hardball, Crossfire* (in the United States), and *Popolitica* and *Politica* (in Israel), as well as nontraditional, genre-stretching talk shows like *Politically Incorrect* and *Dan Shilon Live*.

Political talk shows are not, of course, a new format. The American *Meet the Press*, for example, is almost as old as television itself, and *Moked* (Focus) is one of the oldest shows on Israeli television. However, talk shows have broken out of their traditional place and have developed a bewildering array of new formats.

In order to make sense of the plethora of styles of political talk shows, we developed a simple typology based on the role of the host/journalist, the structuring of the conversation, and the positioning of the audience (both in the studio and at home). Differences in time span (U.S. programs usually last 30 minutes, Israeli shows are typically 90 or 120 minutes long), broadcasting niche (most Israeli shows are broadcast on one of the two major channels during prime time, whereas U.S. shows tend to be on cable stations or late at night), and, hence, the appeal to different sizes of audiences (Israeli shows could draw up to 25% or 30% of the audience, whereas U.S. shows seldom break 1%), all mean that our categories apply somewhat differently in the two countries. In the United States (and sometimes in Israel, especially on shows out of prime time), the categories usually describe a specific show in its entirety, whereas in Israel (and sometimes in the United States, especially for network shows), they may apply only to certain segments of a specific show (see Table 9.1).

CLASSIC JOURNALISTS AND CLASSIC CITIZENS

The first type of show positions the journalist/host in his or her traditional role as a mediator between opposing ideological positions. In such shows, there is a single host who typically interviews representatives of competing political positions, as well as drawing on various experts. The classic example of such a show is *Meet the Press* in both its Israeli and U.S. versions (also *Moked* in Israel and *Face the Nation* in the United States). These shows are aired in traditional public affairs time slots—Sunday morning in the United States, Saturday lunch and evening times in Israel (and prime time in the case of *Moked* and *Razi Barkai*).

The show takes the form of a debate between contending parties with the host probing and leading the debate (in some cases, where there is only a single guest, the journalist takes on the adversarial role). His or her role is that of the "socially responsible" journalist in a nonpartisan press. He or she is "our" representative (where "we" are an audience of interested citizens), whose job is to hold politicians accountable. Therefore, these shows posit a dichotomous model of the press and the political, the former representing the public and the latter accountable to it (Protess et al., 1991). To represent us properly, the host must do his or her homework on the issues discussed, synthesize the opposing positions, interrogate competing claims and counterclaims, while remaining balanced, neutral, and fair. These shows present a model for political debate, which narrows the audience to those who are already interested (because these shows do very little to engage the audience through

TABLE 9.1. Typology of Political Talk Shows

Genre	Subject Discussed	Underlying Ideology	Journalist/Anchor's Role	Audience Construction	Format
1. **Classic Journalism/Classic Citizens** (*Meet the Press*: U.S., Israel)	Issues	Social responsibility	Nonpartisan, adversarial	Attentive citizens	One interviewer interviewee/s
2. **Insider Journalism/Cynical Public** (*Hardball with Chris Matthews*, U.S., *The Saturday Game*, Israel)	Strategies, motives	"It's all politics"	Take us behind the scenes	Cynical insiders	One or more hosts, one or more guests/pundits
3. **Therapeutic Journalism/Voyeuristic Public** (*Larry King*, U.S.; *Mish'al Ham, Dan Shilon Live, Popolitica*, Israel)	Personality	Authenticity	Take us behind the image	Intimate insiders	Interviewer/celebrity

4. **Ideological Journalism/Sports fan Public** (*Crossfire*, in both U.S. and Israel)	Issues	Truth and/or entertainment	Adversarial, op-ed	Partisan	Two journalists, one or more guests
5. **Confrontational Panel Shows** (*The McLaughlin Group*, U.S.; *Popolitica*, Israel)	Issues/strategy	Truth and/or entertainment	Adversarial	Sports fan	Panel and guests
6. **Harmonious Panel Shows** (*Politically Incorrect*, U.S.; *Dan Shilon Live*, (Israel)	Issues (U.S.) Personalities (Israel)	Social, nonpolitical integration	Guests/hosts	Civic equality (U.S.) Populism (Israel)	Panel of celebrities, lay people, and moderator

recourse to the conventions of more entertainment-oriented shows), who can follow the arguments, and are open-minded enough to absorb arguments that contradict previously held beliefs or positions, regardless of who makes such arguments. In this way, these shows assume an enlightened citizenry endowed with civic virtue.

We watched the October 17, 1999 edition of the U.S. *Meet the Press* the Sunday after the Senate defeat of the Nuclear Test Ban Treaty submitted by President Clinton. Hosted by journalist Tim Russert, the show's first segment was an interview with Republican Senator Mitch McConnell and Democratic Senator Robert Torcelli. Russert began by showing a brief clip of Clinton's angry and inflammatory response to the defeat of the treaty. Russert said that these were "harsh words" and it appeared that the president was "practically accusing the Republicans of treason." McConnell was given the first chance to respond:

> I don't know where the president was. We asked him to do two things: withdraw the treaty and agree to not resubmit it until after the election. He didn't meet these modest demands. He knew he didn't have the votes and the only reason we voted was because he wanted to vote.

Playing the role of the classical journalist, who has done his homework, Russert aired a clip from the Senate debate, wherein Democratic senators demanded that there be a vote on the treaty. In response, Democrat Torcelli said: "I concede the point," and then turned to an attempt to discuss the merits of the treaty.

The second example comes from a viewing of the Israeli version of *Meet the Press*. The following interchange between a panel of three journalists (Dan Margalit, Amnon Dankner, and Yael Dan) and Ehud Barak, the Labor Party's candidate for PM, took place on the show's Saturday March 1, 1999 edition, aired on Channel Two. The subject under discussion was Barak's promise that he would "bring back the sons from Lebanon" (referring to the "security zone" in which the Israeli Army remained after the Lebanon War of 1983).

> Barak: I will treat the issue from its roots and bring the army home without damaging the security of the northern settlements.
> Margalit (a journalist): Just like that?
> Dankner (a journalist): How do you do this hocus-pocus?
> Barak: Action via all channels in negotiations we will carry out will give negotiations over Lebanon a very high priority and we will get there.
> Margalit: What will you do?

> Barak: We will bring back the sons without damage.
> Dankner: How? This is really just another slogan.
> Barak: Yael, these are not just slogans. There's no way to carry out such a sensitive security debate on television. Renewal of the negotiations with Syria, a change in parameters with Lebanon.
> Dankner: In what way are you different from Netanyahu?
> Barak: Let me finish and I'll answer every question. We have to renew negotiations with Syria. We have to change our mode of behavior in Lebanon.
> Margalit: You ask us to let you speak, but we would also like to understand what you are saying. What can change the patterns of action? They were decided by you as chief of staff.

These examples illustrate some of the fundamental differences in the political culture of the two societies. Although both examples deal with issues of national security, for Americans such issues are global, abstract matters far removed from their day-to-day concerns. For many Israelis, getting troops out of Lebanon is an issue that kept them awake at night and truly did raise basic concerns about personal and national security.

At the same time, both examples demonstrate the traditional form of journalistic interviewing, which attempts to hold public figures accountable by doing one's homework and by forcefully probing and interrogating what policymakers say. Russert started with the highly charged rhetoric exchanged between Republicans and Democrats, and wound up distinguishing between strategy and issue in the treaty vote. He even managed to get one side to concede that its strategy was flawed and at least partly to blame. In the Israeli case, journalists aggressively tried to get a candidate to move past campaign slogans to explain how he would manage to achieve the result he was promising voters. By not letting Barak slide by, Margalit reminded viewers that Barak himself had a role in continuing those current policies in Lebanon that he was now criticizing. At the same time, Barak was able to both make it clear that he stood behind his promise to voters and make the reasonable point that there were limits on what he could say in advance of negotiations, and that such negotiations could not be carried out on television.

INSIDER JOURNALISM AND CYNICAL PUBLIC

A newer version of this type of talk show alters the roles of host, participants, audience, and model of debate, while maintaining the same overall format. Here, the host/journalist is "our" representative, where "we" are an audience of actual or aspiring "insiders." We expect the host to take us behind the scenes, to show us how the political game is "really" played. This show assumes that what goes on behind the scenes is what is truly important, whereas the more "front-stage" statements of politicians are simply for effect. The host's task is to expose the strategies and motivations of the same political representatives who might be seen on *Meet the Press*. But unlike *Meet the Press*, ideology always plays second fiddle to strategy—what works and what doesn't work. The show thus positions us as connoisseurs of effective political strategy, rather than as concerned citizens interested in the substance of issues. The meaningful distinction is less between left and right, and more between insiders who understand how the game is played, and outsiders who don't. Whereas *Meet the Press* positions its audience as enlightened citizens who take part in the democratic process, this new type of show positions us as observers who can appreciate better or worse maneuvering, but who are unlikely to actually participate in the substance of politics. In focusing exclusively on the behind-the-scenes strategies of political leaders, these shows cannot help but feed cynicism by denying the sincerity of the front stage statements of political leaders. Examples of this show in the United States are *Hardball with Chris Matthews* and in Israel *The Saturday Game* and segments of *Popolitica* and *Hakol Politi* (*Everything is Political*), depending on the issue under discussion.

Underlying this style of talk television is the idea that politics is a game, much like a sporting event, or, in the extreme, like a war. Indeed, we coded one episode of *Hardball* for references to war or sports, and came up with the following list of terms, all in a single 30-minute program:

Game (8 references)	Punch (1)
Dugout (1)	Death (1)
Baseball (1)	Intramaurals (1)
Football (1)	Feud (2)
Ball (1)	Disarmament (1)
Strike (1)	Weapon (1)
War (10)	Surrender (1)
Golf (1)	Street fighting (1)
Play (4)	Knife (2)
Points (1)	Gun (2)
Win (17)	Peace (2)
Champ (2)	Protect (2)
Shots (1)	Treaty (7)
Gamesmanship (1)	Defense (1)

Hero (4)　　　　　　　　Blow up (2)
Battle (1)　　　　　　　Nuclear (only in the sense
Beat (5)　　　　　　　　of politicians behaving as
POW (1)　　　　　　　　if they were in such a
Fight (13)　　　　　　　war—4)
Race (6)　　　　　　　　Blocking (1)
Strategy (3)　　　　　　Tackling (1)
Run (2)　　　　　　　　 Hardball (2)
　　　　　　　　　　　　Gunslinger (2)
　　　　　　　　　　　　Grenade (1)

The conversation of the actual show reflects the conception of politics implied by this list. Matthews starts each show by saying, "I'm Chris Matthews, let's play hardball." In one of the shows we watched, he started off his guest, Democratic political consultant (and consummate insider) James Carville with what he called "a gopher pitch." There is something fundamentally misleading about such glib analogies between discussing sports and politics in terms of strategy because they inevitably gloss the differences between the two. In sports, discussing strategy is tightly linked to the essence of what a sporting event is about: winning and losing, and excellence in athletic performance. In contrast, focusing on strategy in politics means separating two inextricably related dimensions of politics: instrumental considerations connected to winning, and substantive debate over the very worth of a candidate's policies and approaches to societal problems. Focusing on strategy in this case reduces politics to the realm of techniques for achieving popularity with voters.

In the show we just described, Carville tried to connect strategy and issues by making clear his criticism of the White House for provisions of welfare reform they had accepted and, later in the show, arguing that the problem with the Republican repudiation of the president's Nuclear Treaty was that it was, "just raw politics, no principles were involved." However, Matthews was having none of this attempt to connect strategy and substance, or to discuss the ethics of the two. He immediately diverted the conversation to a discussion of how both the treaty vote and the budget showdown between the president and Congress were simply, "for the benefit of the campaign." Later in the same show, Matthews interviewed author Scott Turow, who had just published a novel about judicial corruption in Chicago. When Matthews asked Turow about the levels of corruption that still exist in the Windy City, Turow replied that today "the most common way you get to be a judge is by doing a good job as a prosecutor." Matthews replied, dismissively, "Let's get back to the dirty parts."

In Israel, on the *Mish'al Cham* show, journalist Nissim Mish'al uses his own pollster to conduct various opinion surveys, including polls done during the program, to guide his interviews of political guests and to test how they are doing on the show. This format cannot help but focus on the strategic elements of the political process, as the polling becomes a kind of substitute for scoring in a sporting event. The use of such polls became particularly significant during the 1999 election campaign, in which the overriding goal for many voters was the replacement of incumbent PM Netanyahu; the question of who was best qualified to be prime minister was secondary. Consequently, the most frequently discussed topic on the *Mish'al Cham* show and similar talk shows was whether or not Yitzhak Mordecai, the third-place candidate for prime minister, heading a newly formed centrist party (with Ehud Barak on the left and Netanyahu on the right) should run separately or should join Barak before Election Day. The underlying strategic issue was that a three-way race on the first round might require a second round. Paradoxically, the polls indicated that although Mordecai had no chance of winning in the first round, he did have a chance of defeating Netanyahu in a second round. The show's exclusive focus on strategic considerations, reinforced by the use of polling during the show, helped to exacerbate an already obsessive focus on voting strategically to the exclusion of any consideration regarding who the voter really favored. This turned the show's polls from an abstract exercise into a potentially self-fulfilling prophecy.

Aside from the use of instant polling, Mish'al also invited the candidates with the goal of provoking the most vicious onscreen fight possible. In the following example, Mish'al hosted PM Netanyahu and Yitzhak Mordecai (Barak declined to participate):

Netanyahu [accuses Mordecai]: Everything with you is personal ambition, but a direction? You have no direction.

At this point Mish'al interrupts and asks Netanyahu to address a question to Mordecai. So, Netanyahu says: "The public does not deserve to be led around by the nose and we hear a lot about a secret deal between you and Barak in which you abandon your candidacy before the first round. If that's true, this means that we are conducting a useless debate."

Mish'al: Is that true?

Mordecai smiles confidently and waves it off with his hand.

Netanyahu hits back: Let me ask the question. There is here a make-believe candidacy. Now it's like this. If it's true, you should resign and leave the race tonight. If it's not true, I'd like you to answer the following question: Are you ready to make a commitment now in front of the Israeli public that you will run until the end and that your candidacy will be decided in the polls? And I want an answer because the people want a unilateral answer: yes or no?

Unlike the *Meet the Press* format, where the journalist works to damp heated political conflict, here the focus on strategy, polling, and politics as sports or war, led the host to seek out conflict and avoid distracting discussions of substantive issues (e.g., Matthews' desire to "get back to the dirt"). Indeed, in the morning following the exchange between Netanyahu and Mordecai, Nissim Mish'al was interviewed on radio, and proudly declared that Channel Two had managed to get rid of the traditional rules of interviewing and there would be no more "sanitized" guidelines. He concluded that "television has won" the debate, demonstrating that his transition from journalism to entertainment was now complete.

THERAPEUTIC JOURNALISM AND VOYEURISTIC AUDIENCE

Another type of show that positions the journalist/host as our guide behind the scenes involves intimate one-on-one interviews with celebrities from all walks of life, politics included. We are promised against all odds that such a show will provide a glimpse of the real person behind the image. As with the strategy-oriented shows, these talk shows feed our hunger to see the reality behind the artifice of political figures. This model is ontologically distinct, however, because the "authentic" resides not in a sociological analysis of strategy, but rather in revealing the psychological core of the person under scrutiny (see chap. 8).

The techniques these shows employ to increase the likelihood of peeling away the images of celebrities include the live format, confronting guests with people from their past, and call-in questions, all of which increase the likelihood of unrehearsed, revealing comments or answers. These shows reflect both our desire to know what celebrities are "really like" (as a byproduct of the fact that we see them all the time) and the increasing centrality of personal character and morality in politics, as issue-based ideology becomes less significant. Examples of this sort of show include *The Larry King Show* in the United States. In Israel, this format is a major component of many prime-time shows.

The following Israeli example concerns Aryeh Deri, a rising star in the political firmament, the leader of Shas, a new political party representing Ultra-Orthodox Jews of Sephardic origin that in just 10 years became one of the three major parties in Israel. Having risen to power at a very young age and a quick study of *realpolitik,* Deri has outdone most veteran politicians in the questionable use of public money, bribes, and witness tampering. Having been prosecuted by the state, he made use of the best lawyers in the country and managed to drag the proceedings out for almost a decade. In the meantime, Shas has prospered tremendously in the shadow of the trial, which has been interpreted by its followers as an instance of persecution of Sephardic believers by the secular Ashkenazi elite establishment. Twelve hours before the (guilty) verdict was announced in court, *Mish'al Ham* brought together many supporters and critics of Deri, devoting the program to the question, "Who Is The Real Aryeh Deri?" The teaser for the program featured Deri dancing on the graves of Ashkenazi *Tzadikim* (righteous leaders) in eastern Europe, bowling, socializing with Labor politicians, studying the Talmud, and visiting supporters at various religious events. The experts mobilized to unravel the secret of Deri's personality included the program's producer (his claim to expertise was his Ultra-Orthodox family background), the reporter covering the Shas beat for the First Channel, a number of Shas Knesset members and Deri cronies, Knesset members from the left (including one who was born in Iraq), the leader of the National Religious Party (from a Moroccan family), and an ex-football player who became a "born-again" Shasnik.

Mish'al posed the focal question for the debate: "Deri: *Tzadik* or Crook?" The debate swirled around the relationship between Deri's spiritual and mystical nature, on the one hand, and the more secular aspects of his role as political leader, on the other. Supporters described him as a saintly person who had to suffer for his people because he had become a scapegoat for the Sephardic rebellion. The government prosecution, in this view, was entirely politically motivated and his followers rejected the legitimacy of the courts to stand in judgment of their leader. His critics saw him as a cynically manipulative politician who has created this saintly image to counteract the image of a corrupt, self-serving leader, which emerged out of the judicial proceedings.

For our purposes, the ultimate moment of this heated debate came after a protracted psychological analysis of the mixed motives and complexity of Deri's inner life and the conflicting struggle in his personality between his spiritual and secular sides. In response, a highly fed up journalist for *Ha'Aretz* (a specialist on Ultra-Orthodox matters) protested, saying: "How can you say we don't know Deri? He's always on television, we see him everyday. He's a politician and there's no more to him than what we see."

Just as the sports analogy of strategy shows has severe limitations, so too does the search for the "authentic" person implied in celebrity interview formats. First, it assumes that the hidden and intimate parts of a public figure's personality are relevant for judging the qualities of his or her leadership, a questionable assumption at best. The search for the real Deri here is analogous to U.S. viewers of the search for the real Bill Clinton, conducted by shows like Larry King's, or of the idea that in 1992 George Bush's glance at his watch during a debate revealed his true inner attitudes.

Second, there are fundamental problems with the basic model of "authenticity" that such shows assume. For instance, Erving Goffman's (1975) distinction between the presentation of self in various contexts assumes no such core, but instead suggests that we project ourselves according to our understanding of the demands of a particular social setting, thus no presentation is more real or authentic than any other, they simply reflect our performances in different roles. From this perspective, the attempts to trip someone up through unexpected confrontation may violate a person's own self-understanding of a role, hamper his or her ability to play a role as it was defined by both interviewee and interviewer, and hence obscure rather than reveal something essential about that person.

IDEOLOGICAL JOURNALISTS AND PARTISAN AUDIENCE

Another major category of political talk television has journalists themselves cast in the role of ideological combatants. Here the conversation is between journalists representing different ideological points of view, often joined by various guests. In these shows, the model of journalism implied is the op-ed page in the printed press, with the journalist acting as an ideologically committed political analyst, rather than a neutral observer. In a sense, this resurrects an older model of an ideological press that preceded the social responsibility theory of the press. This format goes the ideological press one better by placing both left and right on the same show in conversation with each other. At the same time, these shows eliminate the role of journalist as neutral fact checker for the audience because the hosts do not attempt a synthesis for a unified audience, but rather seek to score points for their side of the debate.

Such shows position the viewer according to his/her own ideological predispositions, as a member of one journalist's team, much like a fan in a sporting event. In both countries there are shows called *Crossfire* that are structured in this form. In the Israeli show *Popolitica* (later moved to Channel Two and renamed *Hakol Politi* and replaced by a more "serious" show called *Politica* on the First Channel), a regular team of journalists represents various ideological positions, studio guests are invited in for particular issues, and a neutral host presides over the large group of participants and an occasionally raucous studio audience. On the regular team there was a permanent member from the left and from the right, the third seat was filled in rotation by an Arab, an Ultra-Orthodox, or a woman journalist.

Our first example, from the U.S. *Crossfire*, illustrates what happens when the only role journalists assume is representative of partisan positions. *Crossfire* begins with the introduction of Robert Novak "on the right" and Bill Press "on the left," and there is no neutral moderator to direct the debate or to fulfill the traditional journalist's role of fact-finder and synthesizer. In effect, the viewer is positioned as a fan of one of the two competitors—Novak or Press. There is no viewing position or representative for the enlightened citizen assumed by *Meet the Press*. The result is that selective "facts" are used to further the arguments of the contending sides, but there is no way to check their accuracy or relevance.

We watched one edition of *Crossfire*, aired on October 19, 1999, and focused on the attempts by Al Gore to distance himself from Bill Clinton. The guests were Peter Fenn, a Gore adviser, and Charlie Black, a Bush adviser. At one point in the show, a heated debate ensued over Bush's environmental legacy as governor of Texas. A number of claims and counterclaims were made about whether the Texas environment has gotten worse during Bush's watch and whether or not Gore really proposed banning internal combustion engines. When the hosts intervened, it was not to probe the accuracy and relevance of these claims, but rather to return to the job of scoring points for their side. So, Bob Novak broke in by saying, "I'd much rather talk about political pollution," and went on to continue his critique of Gore's campaign.

Although the role of journalists on such shows is loosely modeled on the idea of a politicized press, more important is the desire to present an entertaining argument. The point is to disagree and develop good punch lines that improve the score for your side, rather than treat the issues seriously. As with the insider journalism/cynical public shows, the hosts of these shows focus on strategy to the virtual exclusion of issues.

In one edition of Israeli *Hakol Politi*, the members of the journalist team discussed the issue of sexual harassment allegations made by a young woman during her compulsory military service against her commanding general (25 years her senior). The journalist team played their expected role by taking opposing sides of the issue. Interestingly, because sexual politics in the workplace is a secondary concern in Israeli politics, the argument was played in ways quite similar to U.S. talk shows. Unlike many Israeli shows where politics becomes a war, here, as in most U.S. shows, politics was a game. At one point, for example, the two antagonist journalists suddenly switched roles and vigorously defended positions contrary to the ones they originally argued. This represented no sort of concession (as occasionally occurs in other formats), but rather the centrality of argument and disagreement as opposed to commitment to principle.

A spoof of *Crossfire* on *The Jon Stewart Show*, a Comedy Network variant on the entertainment talk show genre (like *Tonight* or *Letterman*), jokes about the dependence of these shows upon entertaining argument rather than deeply held political convictions. Here, in a feature called "Even Steven" (both hosts are named Steven), two comedians ape the Novak–Press confrontational style of *Crossfire*. After several back and forth rounds, the right-wing Steven turns to his left-wing counterpart and says, "You know, I never thought of that. I think you're right." At this point, there is dead silence and whispers from the shocked left-wing Steven asking the other Steven, "What do you think you're doing? We're being paid to argue." Still the right-winger continues to carefully weigh the arguments of his opponent, and often concedes the point. The left-wing Steven is distraught and finally breaks down crying, saying the show is his main source of income and if this goes on he will lose his house and car. He is only mollified when the right-wing Steven finally relents and calls him an asshole.

CONFRONTATIONAL PANEL SHOWS

Two final types of talk television involve a group of participants sitting around a table discussing a variety of issues. We divided this type of show into two general categories depending on the tenor of the conversation. One type involves open conflict and intense argument. In these shows, virtually every discussion winds up in a shouting match with participants talking over each other and fighting for air time. In the United States, we watched *The McLaughlin Group*, and in Israel we viewed *Popolitica*.

The McLaughlin Group, which airs on PBS, was one of the first new-style political talk shows. It consists of four or five journalists sitting in a circle, led by their opinionated and right-wing host John McLaughlin. More than most other shows, the point here is not to listen, but to talk, shout, and argue. It is, in many ways, a combination of *Crossfire* and *Hardball*. The audience is positioned as generally cynical insiders looking for the behind-the-scenes strategic reality of politics, but the journalists are also ideologically aligned, adding the argumentative feel of *Crossfire*. Indeed, *McLaughlin's* much parodied tendency to speak in brief sound bites, pose questions so oversimplified as to be inadvertently comical, and allow only the briefest time for anyone to speak, make it all but impossible for panelists to do anything but make the shortest of comments and try to score points with witty retorts.

In the episode we watched, the first issue addressed by the panel was framed by McLaughlin when he presented a brief sound-bite of Senator Tom Dashel criticizing Senate Republicans for blocking the nomination of Ronnie White, an African American, for a federal judge. McLaughlin introduced the clip by saying, "We give you Johnny Cochran Dashel, playing the dreaded race card." He then asked the panel, "Question: Why is Dashel playing the race card so shamelessly?" As in other shows, some of the panelists tried to give answers that addressed the complicated relationship between political substance and political strategy, but both the host and the format rule out such an approach. While the liberal Eleanor Clift of *Newsweek*, the only woman on the panel (indeed, the only woman we ever encountered in any of the U.S. shows we taped, save *Politically Incorrect*), tried to cite statistics on the number of women and minority nominations stalled by the Republican led Senate, she was largely shouted down and her approach was decidedly less effective than the cryptic but brief and strategy-oriented Michael Barone of *US News and World Report* ("War room stuff John. Cheap shot politics. Cheap politics.") or Tony Blankly, a syndicated columnist and former Reagan employee ("Look, this has nothing to do with racism and everything to do with Bush being ahead in the polls."). Our point is not that liberals are necessarily more issue-oriented than conservatives, just that the format of these sorts of shows rules out any sort of serious discussion of issues, preferring instead brief comments on strategy and witty one-liners.

At the end of the show, McLaughlin posed a series of brief questions, all cast in hideously simplistic either–or win–lose terms, calling on the panelists to counter in a few seconds. In our episode, for example, the challenge was: "Prediction: Gore–Bradley Debate: Who's going to win?," to which Jim Warren, a liberal journalist from *The Chicago Tribune* answered: "Pro-wrestling, they'll both put us to sleep." Once again, poltics is a game, and not a very serious one at that. One's cynicism, triggered by the show's approach to public affairs, is reinforced by the revelation by political columnist Christopher Hitchins, based on his own appearance on the show, that despite its unrehearsed look, the panelists are made aware of the issues that McLaughlin will raise, and hence are able to carefully prepare their witty and supposedly ad-libbed rejoinders.

As we have noted, Israeli talk shows are aired almost every evening between 9 and 11 on one or both channels, and divide into two types: those that focus on political, social, and cultural issues, tend to be conflictual; others, that mix politicians and other types of celebrities in a harmonious and relaxed sociable chat, aim to, among other things, expose the "authentic" personality of the guests. *Popolitica*, described earlier, belongs to the politically focused and conflictual shows. In the context of discussing confrontational formats, it provides a useful demonstration of the ways in which the conflictual format reflects and reinforces Israeli political culture.

On *Popolitica* on October 4, 1994, a discussion was held about the large-scale immigration of Jews from Russia in the 1990s (which added 1 million people to Israel's population). The show constructed the discussion as a conflict between two groups of guests, representing the Russian immigrants and the immigration of North African Jews in the 1950s, whose members still feel alienated from the center of Israeli society. Charlie Bitton, a Knesset Member whose tiny party's platform articulates the resentments of Moroccan Jewish immigrants, called the Russian immigration "prostitution," referring, in a narrow sense, to the negative stereotypes about young Russian women entering the country and, in a broader sense, to the immigrants as exploiters of a generous Israeli social welfare system. Yossef (Tommy) Lapid, the rightist member of the journalist team (himself an immigrant from Hungary), asked: "How can you call an entire population 'prostitutes'?" Bitton replied: "Didn't you [Ashkenazi old timers] say about the Moroccans that they were prostitutes?" Lapid retorted that if it were up to him, he would have stopped that immigration the day before Bitton arrived. He then walked out of the studio, followed by a large number of panelists. In the studio, the show's host threatened to throw Bitton out if he did not apologize. Bitton refused. Another guest rose to Bitton's defense; this was Ephraim Kishon, a world-famous satirical writer, who has immigrated to Israel from Hungary and shares the sentiments of rejection by the Israeli establishment. Kishon took the role of mediator, and produced a "compromise" that cleared the way for the return of the rest of the guests. This easy in/out traffic is an extreme form of protest, but one that often occurs in the show. It indicates the society's growing radicalization of "identity politics," the difficulty of conducting any type of dialogue (let alone a civilized dialogue) among the diverse ethnic/religious/ideological groups, and how close the tension is to exploding. For Yisrael Eichler, the Ultra-Orthodox member of the journalist team, "walking out" is already institutionalized by the host, who lets Eichler leave whenever a topic unacceptable to his community is discussed. The regularity with which communication breaks down on the show and one party withdraws is an indicator of how important it is to keep channels among groups open, in an increasingly fractious society. There can be no doubt that the show is "authentic" in the sense that it reflects actual intergroup tensions, and the degree to which these tensions threaten to undermine the rules of democratic politics. Another illustration of the "real" intensity of such shows and the fragility of the rules of conversation across disagreement, is the host's frequent recourse to either shouting down people who talk out of turn, and/or getting up from his seat and physically restraining them.

Another indication of the differences between U.S. and Israeli shows, despite the similarity of genre, reveals the significance of the latter in mobilizing massive political support. A dramatic instance of this occurs when politicians organize their own fans (sometimes even paying them) to pack the studio as audience, giving the impression to the home audience that they are winning the argument. Again, the stylized conflict inherent in the structure of the genre, when mapped onto Israeli political culture, heightens political conflict and tension rather than toning it down.

In many cases, the rules of the game that regulate sporting events or talk shows are expected to provide a safe vent that restricts and dampens wider social conflicts. In the Israeli example, however, the conflict cannot always be contained within the stylized presentation, but rather breaks out in ways that intensify and widen social conflicts, undermining the rules of civic engagement. The most blatant example of this occurred on the show *Politica*, which interviewed PM Netanyahu first, and then the head of the opposition at that time, Ehud Barak. The studio had been crammed with Netanyahu fans recruited by the PM's office, and the overzealous recruits would not let Barak speak, leading him to remark at the end that in this form, these shows can threaten democracy and freedom of speech. The show's host, helpless and frightened, confessed the next morning that he expected that next time there would be bullets whistling through the studio.

Whereas in the United States this genre maps onto the political culture in ways that produce a conceptualization of politics as a game, sometimes serious sometimes not, in Israel the genre represents politics as an all-out war.

HARMONIOUS PANEL SHOWS

A second type of panel show involves more harmonious and intimate conversation. Here there is little conflict, and the aim is to have a pleasant conversation among the panelists. The talk is informal, mixing politicians with other celebrities and sometimes "ordinary" folks. In the United States we watched *Politically Incorrect* and in Israel *Dan Shilon Live*. As with conflictual shows, despite the similarities of the genres, these shows mapped onto the two political cultures very differently. In the U.S. case, the show provided one of the most interesting and open substantive political debates we saw. In the Israeli examples, the only way to have a harmonious conversation was to rule out any political debate.

In many ways, *Politically Incorrect* was the most interesting U.S. political talk show we watched. The show originated on the Comedy Network, but was purchased by ABC and now runs nationally after *Nightline*. The host, Bill Maher, is a stand-up comedian who delivers a politically focused monologue at the beginning of each show. Following the monologue, there is a panel discussion of various public issues of the day. The panel consists of celebrities (and the occasional "ordinary" person) drawn from a wide variety of entertainment, sports, political, and even academic realms (the occasional television professor, who has achieved celebrity by appearing on other talk or news shows). They discuss two or three subjects selected by the host (panelists are told what they will be discussing and are provided with a package of background materials before the show, although the degree to which they actually seem prepared varies widely). There is a live studio audience (the only U.S. case, although quite common practice on Israeli shows) that participates by applauding, cheering, and laughing at the comments made by the panelists. Despite its light and humorous tenor, the show positions its audience not only as entertainment seeking, but also as interested citizens (a less elitist version of *Meet the Press*), because the panelists, although celebrities, are not usually political insiders, but rather approach the topics as witty, but reasonably sincere citizens.

The episode we watched was aired on October 19, 1999, and the panel consisted of Sheena Easton, a singer; Chuck D, a rapper; Jay Thomas, a comedian; and Donnie Kennedy, the author of several books defending the south (*Was Jefferson Davis Right?* and *The South Was Right*). The first topic discussed was the same as the first topic on *The McLaughlin Report* discussed previously: the attempt by Senate Republicans to block Clinton's judicial nominations of African Americans (*Politically Incorrect* was the only show we watched with African-American participants, in this case two members were Black). However, the tenor of the discussion was decidedly different from that of the earlier show. First, the conversation was generally civil, despite rather heated disagreement; there was little shouting or talking over one another, by either host or panelists. Moreover, there was no discussion of political strategy, but rather the conversation focused on the substance of the issue and even moved onto a discussion of the legacy of the Civil War. We are not claiming that this discussion was on par with the Lincoln–Douglas debates. Most comments were indeed designed to elicit a laugh from the audience, but the participants seemed to enjoy the discussion and were engaged by it. The second issue dealt with was the question of whether the mentally ill should be allowed to vote. Now this issue was inevitably played for laughs by several of the panelists, but again there were important and subtle issues raised. Sheena Easton, for example, asked: "What constitutes being too mentally ill to vote?" She noted that there were times when she and probably everyone felt "crazy," but at what point did one deserve to lose one's rights as a citizen? This led to a discussion of Prozac (which Easton admitted taking) and the reasons why certain anti-depressants were legal and others were not.

In many ways, this show seemed a model way for presenting pressing issues to a mass audience. The participants, although well known, were not all drawn from any particular public realm and so their interactions were more open and spontaneous than seemed the case in any of the other U.S. shows we had watched. The use of humor kept the audience engaged, whereas the format allowed for a relatively extended discussion of any particular issue (albeit constantly interrupted by commercials). Unlike the more "serious" talk shows, the use of humor, the absence of an exclusive focus on strategy, and the diversity of the guests (which cast them as generalists, rather than the political experts of the other shows), made the discussions seem as if they were being conducted by and for interested citizens, rather than either cynical insiders or committed ideologues.

For the Israeli case, we focused on *Dan Shilon Live*, broadcast for 2 hours twice a week on prime time, and the most popular talk show on Israeli television. The host, a sort of Israeli Roone Arledge, started as head of the sports division of the First Channel, and then headed the news division, before moving onto the commercial Channel Two. The show combines elements of many different television genres: there is a large studio audience, there is a studio band, and the show features musical performers. The show invites a carefully balanced panel of politicians, military figures, entertainers, beautiful women, and sometimes "freaks" and human interest stories. As they sit around the same table, the impression is that everybody is equal and the makeup of the panel becomes a representation of the ongoing negotiation over the criteria for success in Israeli society. For example, ex-generals are regular guests, representing as they do the established elite. They talk on the panel with up-and-coming groups like self-made millionaires and entertainers, representing newer pathways to elite status.

Over its broadcast life, the show has continuously negotiated its approach to the political. Throughout its early years the show has focused on exposing the informal, private, sometimes sentimental, sometimes embarrassing aspects of the personalities of politicians and other celebrities. Ehud Barak, for instance, was asked to sing; the ex-head of Internal Security played his clarinet; Foreign Minister David Levy was asked to comment on the rumor that he was not circumcised because he had been born in a naturally "super Kosher" form. And another ex-general was given the task of interviewing a couple, in which the wife had undergone a sex-change operation. In the months leading up to the 1999 elections, Shilon introduced a serious critical journalist monologue at the beginning of each show. It was in the words of *Ha'aretz* (June 22, 1999) "serious, biting, and entirely unflattering" to politicians and the public. Prime Minister Netanyahu canceled his scheduled appearance on the program in response to one of these monologues. It seems that many viewers have also cancelled their attendance, and the show's ratings declined precipitously. Shilon responded by returning to the winning formula of oozing empathy, love, and flattery to the viewers, never again allowing himself to exhibit a politically critical attitude unless in a humorous fashion.

In the United States, as we have seen, it is difficult to get anyone to defend an ideological position with any amount of intensity, reducing talk shows to some form of joking or role-playing. In Israel, it was almost impossible to carry out a political debate without getting into a fight, and at times walking out. The remaining option was the Shilon formula of mixing celebrities, criminals and quirks in an intimate bubble, creating a false sense of community by closing out any social and political issues, tuning in instead to intimate confessions, and making audiences happy by offering to save their souls by donating money for today's tragedy.

Media research has shown an interest in the sociological and cultural aspects of "therapeutic" talk shows in which viewers are called to "share the pain" of studio participants. The overtly political talk did not receive similar attention. As we have seen, a comparison of the similar genre in the United States and Israel reflects the difference in the politicization of the two societies. Although in the two countries these programs are broadcast live, in the United States they are watched mostly on cable TV by a minority of "news junkies" who prefer this type of drama to the drama of sport and soap; in Israel, news junkies make up prime-time audiences. In the United States the various subgenres have distinctive characteristics; in Israel prime-time talk shows, lasting for 90 minutes or more, incorporate debates on ideology, strategy, and personality. In the United States, anchors are often after laughs; in Israel they provoke studio participants and their fans at home to get emotional, often angry (with participants walking out in the middle of the show as standard practice). U.S. talk shows are for the knowledgeable few, Israeli talk shows are for mainstream viewers, increasingly becoming a crucial space for politicians to talk to their constituencies, especially at election time. The package is American, in the anchor's combining the persona of journalist with media celebrity, in the positioning of the public to view not only as citizens (and ideological supporters), but also as individuals looking for drama, or as experts on strategic moves. Yet, even if Israelis are game to try out the various viewing positions, most of them nevertheless remain ideologically committed and emotionally involved.

10

Americanization Under Siege: New Media, Same Middle East

Each time it seems as if Israel is on its way to becoming the 51st state, a bomb goes off and we are brought down to earth with a thump. The new Palestinian uprising, which exploded on (the Hebrew calendar's) New Year, has reminded us once again that we are still a long way from achieving the ideal of a society that can afford to focus on issues concerned with the quality of life rather than with personal and national survival. The fighting that broke out between Israelis and Palestinians in the fall of 2000 is a signal that Israel is still trapped in a primordial struggle over a contested piece of land. Having instantly regressed to the state of "feuding neighbors" in the U.S. media (Gamson, 1992), we find ourselves back in a mode of a tribal collective under siege. Lost (again) is the fantasy of Israelis and Palestinians collaborating in "a new Middle East," with Israeli yuppies busily commuting between Tel Aviv and Silicone Valley by air and in cyberspace.

Harshly awakened from the American dream, we are still left with an Americanized media, that is, privatized channels, committed first and foremost to profits, not to the public, geared mainly to entertainment, not news, and still addressing viewers as individuals, even as they become worried members of a community under siege. Ironically, the only remaining publicly committed media (after the emaciated public First Channel was forced to adopt the game rules of the commercial Channel Two in order to stay in the race) are the segmented radio and TV channels, only their commitment is not to the whole of the society but to their own publics. Created to reinforce sectoral (ideological, religious, and ethnic) communities, these media have flourished in parallel with the rise of privatized and globalized mainstream media. Their mandate is to struggle, with varying types of emphases, against the twin threats of "normalization" and "Americanization." The Ultra-Orthodox and Shas realize that normalization is the craving for a refined, liberal, civil, secular society, which legitimates individual choice, social, and economic mobility, and material success. They regard the importing of popular U.S. culture as the vehicle for the infiltration of hedonism, materialism, and sexual abandon, which pollute Jewish culture and corrupt the society's moral fabric. For the (ideological) Settlers in Gaza and the West Bank, and factions of the ideological right, this craving for peaceful living and individual well-being, and the imported globalized culture that goes with it, are symptoms of the society's premature giving up on the nurturing of authentic Israeli culture and on the cultivation of the Zionist ethos, the fuel for the revolution which is yet to be won.

Thus, paradoxically, the eruption of the Palestinian–Israeli conflict model 2001 finds us with nationwide media oriented toward individual consumers, at best trying to mobilize "everybody" for having fun, and ideological "small" media, increasingly alienated, addressing segmented communities fully engaged with integrating their own constituencies. Our version of Americanized mainstream media is now put to the test, at a moment when they are called on for credible coverage of fast-changing events, for managing the debate over issues that take on a new pressing relevance, and for uplifting the national mood (what public broadcasting would call "moral strength") of a country in turmoil. Can privatized media, operating within the constraints of a market economy, rise to the occasion and act in the interest of the public at a time when Israeli's viewing mode switches from a casual search for individual entertainment to a shared, anxious, and urgent need for information, intelligent policy debates, and some sense of order and reassurance?

In what follows, I first consider a number of the practices adopted by Israel's Americanized media, those elaborated on in previous chapters, and ask how they respond to the reality of fighting, and to risks such as arousing panic, churning of populist emotions, and encouraging political cynicism. I then turn to examine the implications of the presence of global media in the field, on both sides. The idea is to demonstrate that having shaped the *political* game to be compatible with the way in which media conceive their viewers, they are now shaping *war itself* to arouse the involvement of the global audience of Americanized TV.

TELEVISION TAKES ON A NEW ROLE

It is no coincidence that the introduction of privatized media into Israel happened at about the time of the negotiation and signing of the Oslo agreements, as both were based on the notion that Israelis could now afford to be like everyone else (see chap. 2). Tired of life in the shadow of a never-ending war, it looked as if Israel was finally coming to terms with its neighbors, that Israelis could lean back to watch the world outside as casual consumers expecting to be entertained, or even (Heaven forbid) be allowed to shift away from the evening news to a guilt-free viewing of their favorite soap. (A number of local media critics have praised the Israeli public for taking time off from the daily collective assembly around the news in favor of their favorite *telenovela*.)

The intensity of the armed *Intifada* of October 2000, and the speed with which Barak's government collapsed after less than 2 years, have created a chaotic situation in terms of jeopardizing all future scenarios of coexistence, reinstating an acute sense of personal anxiety, the edge of which had been temporarily taken off by the hope of Oslo. Throughout the cycles of rising and falling tensions, people once again are turning to radio and television in search of indirect guidance on daily decisions. Once again the media are looked to as the political and military "weather man," consulted on whether it is safe enough to go shopping at the mall, leave for planned trips abroad, send children to the cinema, and, in certain neighborhoods, even whether to send one's child to school. Parents of young men doing their military duty, and wives of men on reserve duty, are on the watch for danger signs.

The reason why the ratings of the evening news have not increased has to do with the new habit of immediate updating on violent incidences. For the "index of violence," people turn to the radio (for the half hourly news flashes), and, depending on the degree of violence, they turn immediately to look for the sights on TV. Television's practice of going live in any incident in which it is "justified" by the number of victims, or the horror of the visuals, robs viewers of the incentive to watch television's evening news. The once traditional tribal bonfire has become a slightly anachronistic relic, often left to deliver ceremonial summaries of the day's events, and to recycle the by now familiar pictures. The price of immediate update—partial, inaccurate, incomplete—is the loss of aura of the news, with its sense of delivering credible information, claim for control, and promise of stability. TV itself is now drawn into the flow of events, sharing the sense of chaos with its public.

Beyond the sense of personal insecurity, enhanced by the media, Israelis experience great confusion about how to define the new situation. In the fall of 2000, as the longed for peace was gradually being perceived as unfeasible, the uncertainty was so great that even the dichotomy of "internal" and "external" has lost its meaning (Ezrahi, 2001). Israelis are uncertain about whether we are at war, who is to blame for the outbreak of Palestinian violence, where the boundary lies between our responsibility and that of the Palestinians. Although all this has put a grave responsibility on radio and TV to present a coherent picture of reality, reporters themselves are finding it objectively difficult to draw such a picture, since such a reality seems to have been smashed into a fast-turning series of ambiguous and contradictory events.

THE CHANGING MEDIA ECOLOGY: FROM *INTIFADA I* TO *INTIFADA II*

In the *Intifada* of the 1980s, the then single public channel, loyal to government policy, did the job of rallying the Israeli public around the way the conflict was handled, making sure that Israelis would not suffer any dissonance about which side was in the right. The conditions were easy. TV's schedule was never interrupted for anything less than a surprise attack such as the Yom Kippur War. The lack of equipment made it difficult to broadcast from the field, and almost impossible to broadcast live, while the military kept Israeli and foreign correspondents out of "fighting zones." Therefore, the only glimpse of the action was provided by the one-channel evening news, and the reports aired were short, edited, with low-key framing. During the first 4 months of *Intifada I,* a lame caption would regularly appear on the screen, that read *Unrest in the territories.*

The coverage of clashes between the Israeli military and the Palestinian demonstrators in *Intifada I* resembled the way in which American TV has covered the Gulf War. Depersonalized and dehumanized, Israeli TV has shown Palestinians only as an anonymous mass of wild, stone-throwing, demonic figures, their faces covered with *kafias* (to hide their identity; Liebes, 1997). There were far fewer casualties on the Israeli side, but the killings, the suffering, the funerals, the relatives in hospitals, belonged to "our" side only. Voice was given only to authority figures on the Israeli side—mostly military commanders in the field or in the studio, interviewed following the day's event. This can be excused partly by the Palestinians' reluctance to allow Israeli reporters to enter their villages and document funerals, partly by the wariness of Israeli editors and producers, should the presence of the camera incite violent demonstrations that would in turn be the cause of more Palestinian losses (Kirshenbaum, 1994), and mostly by the belief that Palestinian suffering was irrelevant to the Israeli public.

As the skirmishes of the *Intifada* were contained geographically, and did not cause an existential breakage within the Israeli collective, public debate on TV could be limited to the tactical level of which means would be most effective (Hallin, 1994). Coverage hardly ever dug deep into the roots of the uprising, to the context of the daily humiliation that Palestinians have been experiencing for more than a generation, or to the self-inflicted damage of conquering another people. Thus, public TV had the attention of Israelis, but failed to use its position as the society's shared arena to show the Palestinian suffering and humiliation that have led to the violence (Schiff and Ya'ari, 1990) or to frame the large policy issues raised by the Palestinian uprising.

In *Intifada II*, censorship and restricted access are no longer options. Two reasons have joined to rule out censorship in the outbreak of the Palestinian–Israeli conflict in the fall of 2000. The first is that the violence this time (what is perhaps best defined as a "war of attrition"; Marcus, 2001), cannot be sealed off, and, as mentioned previously, the home front is no less risky or volatile than the military front. The second reason has to do with the 1990s media revolution in Israel, following which Israelis had acquired access, via cable and satellite, into the news of major international channels, and with media practices that have developed in Israel's privatized TV channels. In this new environment, domestic TV channels are better equipped to transmit from the various scenes of action, less directly dependent on government, and keenly aware of the viewers' new capacity to zap among an abundance of channels offering additional coverage of what goes on in the fighting, and an escape into another melodrama, slightly less close to the skin.

Personalization of the Conflict: Identifying With the Victims

Can Israeli media at the time of *Intifada II* do better than they did in *Intifada I*? Do the nationwide media, with their Americanized practices, have the means of addressing Israelis as a collective in a situation that demands facing major issues together, beyond the immediate concerns of individuals? Compared with what we knew from the First Channel's performance in the *Intifada* of the 1980s, we are now much more aware of the human tragedy surrounding us, on our side as well as the other. Yet, although we have gained in information and in empathy, we have lost the sense of membership and the potential for deliberation. Israeli media model 2000 continue to speak to viewers as individuals, not as part of a collective in trouble.

The personalization of the suffering of individuals and families who were hit randomly continues to substitute for coping at an ideological, or policy-oriented, level. The human cost of the terrorist acts and the fighting (with slight interruptions for the Sharon/Barak election campaigns) plays as the best melodrama in town. Looking at the tragedy of real people, which occurs as we watch, or minutes or hours before, with the dread of knowing that "there, but by the grace of God, go I," is television at its most effective. We all can identify. And each of us, for now, should thank our lucky stars. Fate can always strike. Allowing viewers to experience intense empathy for the stricken victims and the grieving families takes the events out of their broader political and ideological context, and even acts as some form of escape from more active deliberation.

Television's routine following major terrorist acts may be demonstrated by an incident in which a Palestinian, employed as a bus driver for an Israeli transportation company, ran into people waiting at a bus stop (on February 13, 2001), killing 8 soldiers and civilians, and injuring more than 20. Going into the marathon mode, radio and TV both suspended their schedules and began broadcasting melancholy songs, waiting to see whether the number of casualties justifies canceling the commercials. With broadcasting back to schedule, the news programs on the day following the attack were almost exclusively devoted to a ceremonial taking leave of the dead. Dedicated to the profiles of the young women and men soldiers who had died, reporters went from one family to the next, interviewing parents who were prepared with their family albums in hand, talking to one victim's best friend, who was standing next to the dead girl at the moment the driver ran her over, her voice suffocating with tears. And, time and again, switching between the two nationwide channels, and reading in the next day's papers, we heard a friend of another dead girl's mother telling us that the mother had "felt something" and told her daughter not to go on the bus that morning. The daughter, as we knew, answered smilingly, "Would you like me to be late to the (military) base?"

On that weekend, columnist Ya'akov Rottblit (2001) described his hearing about the attack in the morning news, anticipating the familiar routine of diving into the day's personal tragedies: "Toward evening the names of the dead would be broadcast. The human stories will be heard, the shock, the crying, the sudden mourning, the suddenness of a life destroyed, and, with it, a world of individuals and families. Listen to them carefully. Who knows what tomorrow will bring? Who knows who tomorrow?" Rottblit's familiarity with the ritual steps is not accompanied by ironic distance. He remains an uncritical viewer of the ongoing narrative, engrossed by the element of Russian roulette hidden in the story, which may, at any time, turn on him, or on his readers, and drag us onto the screen.

Personalization of the Conflict: Trapped by Provocateurs

Violent, titillating juicy stories, brutal villains, suffering victims, scapegoats to hang the blame on, all receive the treatment of a disaster marathon, the ultimate format that combines and intermingles elements of entrancing drama, and/or journalistic scoops, arousing pity and fear in viewers. And *Intifada* 2000 provided disasters galore for the media to wallow in. During October and half of November 2000 alone, Channel Two interrupted its regular schedule on 9 days. The problem is that while TV cannot recreate itself, the context of reception has been dramatically transformed.

As was shown in chapter 4, interrupting the schedule to enable viewers to be out there, in real time, with the police, chasing OJ (Fiske, 1994) may disappoint a few fans of some prime-time series, but does no harm. "A relentless hybrid (format) of media circus, soap opera, and tabloid journalism," said Frank Rich (2000) of *The New York Times*, it is a conspiracy "to entertain us, and distract us." CNN's endless postelection Breaking News to trace the various legal and administrative steps taken to determine whether Bush or Gore had won the U.S. presidency, generated a lot of bad journalism. But for Americans (and the rest of the globe), there are always other channels to escape to. The difference between the routine activated by the U.S. media in the deaths of Princess Diana or John F. Kennedy Jr., and Israeli media routines triggered by terrorist attacks or other violence lies in the positioning of viewers. Viewing a disaster live, at a time of prolonged conflict in danger of further escalation, Israelis are not distracted or entertained. There is also the danger that they (we) will panic. The risk that media may cause further escalation by falling into the trap laid for them by the provocation of extremists (aimed at mobilizing media to begin with) is imminent. Deciding to go live is playing with fire; like putting a match to a barrel of gunpowder that someone has offered the channel for free.

Consider what happened when Channel Two went live to cover a group of about 30 West Bank settlers, women and children in tow, who were trapped on a holiday hike while climbing up a hill leading to a Palestinian refugee camp. Half way up, they were (so they say) genuinely surprised by Palestinians shooting from above. One member of the group called the news department of Channel Two on his cellular phone. The channel interrupted its afternoon schedule, and, for about 3 hours, turned in to live reporting from *Mount Grizim*. Viewers watched a general view of the mountain from a distance (from what turned out to be a tape shot beforehand of another side of the mountain by Palestinian cameramen, and shown in a loop), listening to the settler's telephoned report with the sound of shooting in the background. We learned then that the military was given a permit for the hike and approved its route. We also heard that members of the group were injured, that people were hiding behind rocks, that mothers could not feed their babies, and that army helicopters had failed to arrive at the scene to rescue the hikers for long hours.

The first problem presented by the very long broadcast was that we were getting the story from a single, not disinterested, source. Worse, from a journalistic perspective, are the restrictions reporters impose on themselves when interviewing victims. On the day in which a mother hears that three of her children have lost their limbs, no reporter is going to ask her if she considered whether *Kfar Darom* (a Jewish settlement in Gaza Strip) is a place to raise children. By the same token, the minute the settlers seem to be the victims, their word is unquestioningly accepted, disregarding the fact that, in the case of this particular hike, they have knowingly and intentionally put themselves in jeopardy.

A day or two later, more accurate information is provided. The army had prohibited any holiday hikes in "the territories." The officer who (with or without knowing) did give permission, did not approve the route taken by the settlers. The army helicopters, facing a complex task and trying to avoid any loss of life, had maneuvered for hours, managing to save the group with only one casualty.

Editing, based on cross-checking of sources, was sacrificed for the authentic experience (which turned out to be less authentic than it first seemed), and for the high ratings. The information transmitted in the live broadcast was delivered by the initiators of this "innocent incident," who apparently had no qualms about endangering their families for the sake of flaunting their rights. With a little less luck, they might have succeeded. But there is no reason why television should assist them in the task.

The settlers cast themselves in the position of heroic victims, convinced the channel, and were given the royal treatment—a whole afternoon of soaps canceled on Channel Two, hours of listening to reports mixed with insinuations as to the danger in which they found themselves, the inefficiency of the military, the uncertainty about the number and state of the victims. As long as they were not rescued, the story had the potential of developing into a huge disaster, perhaps a huge failure on the part of the army, and viewers could be engulfed with empathy for the trapped hikers and rage at their Palestinian attackers. When the facts of the story became clearer, the public's sympathy changed into a sense of having been manipulated by the settlers, and rage at their recklessness. Looking back, the narrative of this marathon proved false and needed rewriting. So much for live broadcasting as journalistic practice, or as good melodrama.

Personalization of the Conflict: Seeing and Hearing Palestinians

The Oslo accords have brought about a dramatic change in the increasingly common encounter with Palestinians on the screen. Israeli TV regularly reports from the Palestinian West Bank and Gaza, daily hosting Palestinians on news and talk shows, at the scene of action, in the studio and on the telephone. Throughout the fall of 2000, the suffering of Palestinians was shown, Palestinian voices were heard on the air and on the small screen, and some form of dialogue has continued. In parallel with the daily Palestinian ambushing and shooting of Israeli civilians on the roads, planting bombs in buses in Tel Aviv, Netanya, and other cities, and throughout the Israeli retaliations of closing off the border to Gaza, imposing economic sanctions, targeting and killing Palestinians in charge of terrorist attacks, Channel Two has had an Israeli Arab reporter broadcasting from Gaza during, or in the aftermath of, Israeli retaliatory attacks.

Thus, minutes after the Israeli bombing of military headquarters inside Gaza in retaliation for the lynching of two Israelis in Rammalla, Channel Two's news reporter Suleiman A-Shafi was broadcasting to Israelis live from Gaza, interviewing anxious residents, conveying feelings of fear, helplessness, and despair.

Witnessing the suffering of ordinary Palestinian victims, reminding ourselves that most of them are people who would like to lead a normal life and provide for their children, strengthens us in recognizing that we are all human beings, and to hell with ideological and political differences. We also feel the need that they do the same. Thus, for example, on the week following the explosion of a school bus in *Kfar Darom*, in which three children of one family were left with amputated limbs, Golan Yochpaz, a morning news anchor on *Galey Zahal* radio station, interviewed Muhammad Farsi, a Palestinian, member of the *Tanzim* (one of the PLO factions carrying out attacks on Israelis). Yochpaz interviewed Farsi on a number of consecutive days, trying time and again to get him to express some empathy for the Israeli victims. Rational, responsible, smart, Farsi declined. For him human suffering was part and parcel of the conflict, and had to be thought of in a broader context. In other words, Farsi refused to accept the depoliticized position which sticks to the personalization of the conflict, so that we can all be friends.

Unsurprisingly, Farsi shares this approach with the Jewish settlers, who, when interviewed following terrorist attacks, never lose sight of their mission, and knowingly accept more victims, even children, in the name of their ideological beliefs. TV moderators, however, are acutely aware of the conditions under which gathering the nation to mourn with the victims is possible. It can be done only by bracketing out the political dispute. In the present world of media, with their appeal to the gut, there can be nothing in between a screaming match, in which populist rhetoric reigns, and the unity of extending personal empathy.

Prime-time TV talk shows, frequently hosting Palestinians, continue doing what they were set up to do, that is, to create the most dramatic clashes among participants. And the Palestinians are joining the game with as much zest as their Israeli counterparts around the table, arguing sometimes with them, and sometimes among themselves, on current topics of mutual concern.

The *Politica* talk show, which aired on December 5, 2000, concerning Israel's relations with the Palestinians, is a good case in point to demonstrate that all is personal. Motivated by the finding that Israel was paying money into the pocket of Muhammad Dahlan, a member of the Palestinian Authority in charge of the exchange of goods between Israel and Gaza, the anchor raised the question of whether corruption within the Palestinian Authority should affect mutual relations. The *Muchtar* (head) of Zur Bacher, a Palestinian village south of Jerusalem, raised the allegation of corruption at the top (of the Palestinian administration). Two Israeli participants, an academic and an industrialist involved in developing joint economic ventures, protested, insisting that internal Palestinian affairs should not be of any concern to Israel. Zayad Abu Zayad, member of the Palestinian leadership, retaliated by asking the Israeli participants, "and in your government, is there no corruption?" (thereby avoiding the issue). He then attacked the Palestinian *Muchtar* as a "collaborator," and stormed out of the studio. (As noted in chap. 9, walking out in protest is not an infrequent phenomenon among Israelis participants.) The closest the debate ever touched on an issue was when the question of whether corruption in the Palestinian authority should be of concern to Israel arose. But this allegation brought out the national allegiance on the side of the Palestinian representative, causing him to protest the affront: "We only do what everybody, including you, does," rather than relate to the problem. The rest of the show consisted of a number of mutual accusations, and Zayad's walkout in protest.

The reality of killing and talking took an almost surrealist turn on a Channel Two talk show hosting Knesset members and Muhammad Dahlan, the very object of the *Politica* debate. Considered responsible for a number of terrorist attacks against Israel, Dahlan was asked to join the debate from a Gaza studio. Anchor Nissim Mish'al quoted Ariel Sharon (not a candidate for prime minister at the time), who had asked: "How come Dahlan is still alive?" Mish'al wanted to know what Dahlan himself thought of the idea (of his own assassination). Dahlan listened to the translation in his earphones and replied in Arabic, explaining why in his opinion it was not such a good idea. But upon departing, feeling less formal, he concluded in very Israeli-sounding Hebrew, "I too hope that things will get better" (*gam ani mekaveh sheyihyeh tov*).

Ironically, the depersonalization of Palestinian victims on Israeli TV in *Intifada I*, works in a similar direction to the all round personalization of Israeli TV at *Intifada II*. Just as the symbolic absence of Palestinian casualties from the screen, and the low number of victims on the Israeli side have helped in integrating Israelis around the notion that justice was on our side and precluded the need to worry about policy fundamentals, so does the celebration of everybody's pain, "even" the Palestinians', appeal to viewers' personal emotions of fear and pity, ignoring the need for collective thinking and for facing the larger context of the situation, on a policy level. The personalization of a human tragedy promises all the satisfaction of wallowing in melodrama, without any attempt to shoulder responsibility, retaining as many viewers for the channel without boring or alienating anyone or getting their backs up.

This becomes clearer when comparing the way in which the families of unintended victims express their anguish, to the rhetoric of Palestinian leaders (recall Farsi's refusal to express empathy) and of supposedly self-sacrificing heroic settlers in the West Bank and Gaza, when faced with death and injury. As mentioned, when disaster strikes, interviewers censor all moral issues (which nevertheless are on everyone's mind), in this case refraining from raising the question whether parents should endanger their children by continuing to live in places under constant ambush. But the media never initiate a serious debate about the settlers' role in the possible solutions to the conflict, unless there is an immediate emotional trigger. There is never any time. There is only room for the stories of the day. Americanized TV can choose between two poles. One is the screaming populist *Popolitica*-style match, skirting the edge of physical violence, with the anchor egging on participants to get at each other's throats, and, having succeeded, makes a show of calming them down. The other is sharing in the pain of others, and Heaven forbid if any reminder of the context raises its ugly head and blows up the idyll.

What seems like a successful attempt by Americanized media, in the period of an eruption of the Palestinian–Israeli conflict, to gather the society for deliberation around the common cause, thus stops short of success. In the individualized mainstream society, all that is left in common is to identify with the victims. Sharing an ethos, rallying around heroes, or even conducting a serious debate on our collective goals, would necessarily leave out some viewers and alienate others. Channel Two's version of shared empathy is no different from that of the U.S. networks following the TWA accident or John F. Kennedy Jr.'s death.

THE FIGHT OVER WHOSE VICTIMS SUFFER MORE

The practices of Israeli media, as we observed, are no different from those of media the globe over. They all compete over images of suffering, interviewing victims, and condemning the aggressors of the day. The most touching or shocking images have the capacity to arouse public opinion and cause a superpower to intervene by sending troops, or by withdrawing armies. Personalized images of death, injury and victimization have had a mounting effect on the conduct of war, influencing the strategy undertaken by the United States in the Gulf War, playing a role in George Bush's decision to send troops to Somalia, and giving legitimacy to Clinton's military intervention in Kosovo.

The Israeli–Palestinian fighting carries this trend one step further. As a war that cannot be won on the ground, and in which victory for either side cannot end in the total surrender of the enemy, or in the conquest of territory, it is a war in which media not only cover the fighting but are also regarded as arbitrators. Media coverage has become a means of scoring points. In a contest over which side can mount more international support to pressure the other side, capturing world public opinion on the small screen becomes vital. In this kind of contest, the fight is waged over which side can be portrayed as the victim. Naturally, the weaker side has a better chance, and, in the case of the Palestinians, strengthening their case with fabricated evidence of victimization is not ruled out.

Fighting in the Field to Win on the Small Screen

In past wars, Israeli media played an essential role on the home front, and reporting from the actual front was carefully filtered. This is the first local outbreak in which media, Israeli and foreign, play a major role in the war itself. Legions of foreign channels such as CNN, NBC, BBC news, and European news channels, employing local Israeli and/or Palestinian professional teams, transmit the sounds and the sights, sometimes live, to the rest of the globe. Arab television stations are also among the major players. The Palestinian channel competes with, and often lags behind, the *Hizaballa* channel transmitting from South Lebanon and devoting full-time to the Palestinian–Israeli struggle, and the CNN-like *El Jezira* broadcasting from Katar, all carry regular reporting and commentary on the Palestinian-Israeli story.

Clearly, this time, Israeli and international media cannot be kept out. Instead, they have become major actors in the field, transforming the rules of the war game. This is very different from two recent limited wars, the Falklands and the Gulf, in which the western democratic governments who initiated the attacks took measures to control the media. Keeping the media out was considered crucial for achieving a decisive victory in the battlefield, and for doing it as fast as possible (Ignatious, 2000). Unlike the Israeli–Palestinian fighting, both these wars set out to achieve a specific military target, were fought far away from home, within clearly demarcated areas. They were relatively short, and took place in countries with no permanent presence of international media.

Unlike these two wars, the Israeli–Palestinian fighting of Fall 2000 had no clear strategic targets, no "battlefield" to seal off. Instead, there were frontlines everywhere, overlapping and intersecting, and violence that strikes the military and the citizenry alike. Fought on both sides with the knowledge that the battle could not be won on the ground, it was conducted with an eye to the television screens around the world. The ultimate judge was public opinion, or, more precisely, the way public opinion was perceived by the world leaders who called the shots. And the war over public opinion had very different rules from the war aimed at conquering territory and defeating the enemy. As an underdog, the weak side (i.e., the Palestinians) had an overwhelming advantage to begin with, and the strong side (Israel) could make only little use of its superior force, having to minimize damages to its image by carefully targeting its military action, and by highlighting the suffering of Israeli victims.

Thus, once it became clear the media would not go away, their incorporation into the thinking of the Israeli military transformed strategic thinking. As we learned from Amir Oren (2001), a military columnist of *Ha'aretz*, instead of talking in terms of an "overall" or "existential" war, in which "the strongest will win," "a crushing victory," "unilateral determent," or "war at the front," the conflict was conceptualized in terms such as "limited confrontation," "political constraints," "limited objectives," "mutual deterrence," and "war on the home front." Moreover, instead of thinking in terms of censorship, generals now talk about "selective damage," a "media war," "the power of the weak," and "victory equals public opinion."

Who's the Cruelest of Them All? The Competition Over TV Images

If victory equals international public opinion, and if public opinion equals television, then television, as was pointed out here, equals the individualized images of human suffering and/or human brutality on the small screen. Out of the daily coverage, only very few images "take" and conquer the world, that is, are bought by channels the world over, repeatedly recycled and turned into symbols. The power of such images lies in their telling a story that ostensibly needs no words, in their immediately recognizable molested humanity, and/or in their brutalizing inhumanity. Even if the truism that a picture is worth a thousand words does not always hold (Schudson, 1996, claimed that U.S. public opinion took as long to shift to opposing the war in Vietnam as it had taken to turn against the war in Korea), these are the instances in which pictures, or short video sequences, are most effective. And their self-explanatory quality is particularly useful for viewers who are ignorant of the context.

Two images, one from each side, compete for the status of the emblematic horror of *Intifada II* (at the time of this writing). One depicts the dying moments of Muhammad A-Dura, a child caught with his father in an exchange of fire between Palestinians and Israeli soldiers at Netzarim Junction (close to Gaza) on October 1, 2000. There is no evidence in the picture as to which side the killers came from, and the results of an investigation conducted by the military were inconclusive, but the child is presumed to have been killed by Israeli soldiers. The second image is from the lynching of two Israelis in a Palestinian police station in Ramalla. The fragment shown by the camera is that of a body being tossed out of a second-floor window, and being molested by the mob waiting underneath.

Both of these images could turn into giant journalistic scoops. Like anything that makes it in the hype-world of media, they would be shown everywhere in no time, their glory lasting for days, even longer. They would be fitted into news promos, and grow familiar to TV viewers the world over.

The battle over rival images can be conducted upfront or behind the scenes. The framing of Muhammad A-Dura's killing as evidence of the Israeli army's brutality was challenged by Israeli spokespersons after it was shown. Israeli officials responded by accusing the Palestinians of "sending children to the front in order to cynically use their death for propaganda." It was a poor defense, but it was said upfront, and its validity could therefore be considered and challenged.

The Palestinian attempts to contain the damage of the lynching were conducted behind the scenes, before the images were ever aired. To prevent the transmission and airing of pictures not to their liking, Palestinians censor video footage taken by foreign reporters, never hesitating to threaten, even with death, professionals who are doing their job. The pictures of the lynching were aired only due to the insistence of an Israeli crew member, working for Italian TV, who shamed RAI into showing them (Barnea, 2000). Although Israel is generally committed to the norms practiced in Western countries, the Palestinians have no qualms about twisting the arms of foreign reporters. They also understand how global TV works, and exploit the fact that countries all over the world are always ready to show pictures of extreme human brutality or suffering. RAI's reluctance to air the lynching stemmed from its fear of Palestinian revenge, and the editors' catering to the overwhelming support of Italian public opinion for the Palestinian cause. The showing of these images, potentially damaging to the Palestinians, after all, was the result of the Israeli crew member's anger—as a human being, as a professional and as an Israeli—over the injustice of hiding the truth in this instance, after inundating world screens with the images of Muchamad A-Dura's killing.

It should be noted, then, that the RAI example raises questions about global images on TV. It turns out that behind the airing of what looks like authentic, human images, seeming to speak for themselves, there may be a process of selection and editing which has little to do with professional decisions. Under the guise of reporting the conflict as they see it, TV producers may prefer not to expose or challenge countries that censor their transmission, ending up offering a one-sided coverage of war. Moreover, their coverage of conflict may be constrained by the sympathies they ascribe to their public, causing a reluctance to let in any dissonant notes.

EPILOGUE

Written before the recent outbreak of violence between Israelis and Palestinians, the most popular song of 2000 was a lethargic, weary ballad, perhaps too old for the young singer-songwriter Aviv Geffen. There can be no doubt, however, that he has captured the mood of Israelis. The low-key melodic refrain says: *Wake up, wake up, beloved homeland, for we are very tired and in need of rest* (*uri ur, uri ur, moledet ahuva, ki anachnu ayefim meod, zekukim lemenucha*).

Looking back, it appears that the Americanized form of television, in which owners aim at maximizing profits by catering to the needs of entertainment-seeking individuals viewing in the safety of their homes, has been prematurely adopted by Israeli society, or, more precisely, by its political system. In peaceful, firmly established democracies, a commercialized system may cause only little harm, in spite of the accumulation of evidence to suggest that such a market-based media system does a poor job in its enactment of a public sphere everywhere (see a *Herald Tribune* article about the networks in the 2000 U.S. elections, quoted in *Ha'aretz* December 12, 2000). In Israel, as the outbreak of *Intifada II* has once again laid bare, the Americanized model had been superimposed on a vulnerable society, which at any moment may be thrown into a state of existential anxiety in which media carry a heavy responsibility.

In a society suffering as it is from the ills of external violence erupting periodically, and from internal strife among warring segments within, a multichannel, privatized media, could undermine the public's potential capacity to achieve rational decisions at times of crisis. The danger in this split society is twofold. Mainstream Israelis were increasingly subject to human-interest information that is geared only to keep them from zapping to another channel, not to set an agenda. The other sectors of Israelis are subject to their own ideological channels, motivated by the need to prove their moral superiority, and to increase emotional commitment to the group, taking for granted that the center would hold.

Looking for "normal" existence, rest from strife, a civil society, and a middle class lifestyle, mainstream Israelis are the target audience of privatized TV channels broadcasting nationwide and operating along the American model. Other groups—settlers, ethnics, militant Ultra-Orthodox—all strive to continue the primordial struggle within the society and/or vis-à-vis the Palestinians. Tired of the demands of collectivity, with its prospect of forever "living on the sword" and the constant need for alertness, conflict and conquest, and alienated from the religious zealots and ultra-religious ethnic groups, mainstream Israelis heartily embrace Americanized culture, with its multiple channels of escapist entertainment. The groups who oppose quiet, "normalization" and individualization, regard Americanization as the mother of all evil, reiterating an attitude that used to be central in the heyday of Zionist pioneering. Yet although Americanization was once juxtaposed with the ethos of the new Israeli Jew, it is now juxtaposed with a variety of segmented ethnic Ultra-Orthodox lifestyles (what Zionists would have regarded as "diasporic Jews"), or with the militant nationalist-Orthodox ideology of settlers in the occupied territories. Each of these groups has its own radio and TV channels (some to the exclusion of all other channels).

The problem with media that have developed the journalistic practices needed for "survival" in a commercial competitive system is that they carry the ills elaborated in the various chapters of this book. Most of these practices—the sensationalization of news, the political talk shows that promote mudslinging, the introduction of live breaking news with its appropriation of the screen for long minutes, sometimes hours, by anyone who is ready to create a violent provocation—appeal to the emotions rather than to reason. Thus these media act to undermine Israelis' ability to act responsibly as a collective vis-à-vis the Palestinian *Intifada* of 2000, and their ability to make long-term, viable, rational decisions. Regardless of the will and integrity of individual reporters and editors, the system cannot help but exploit national crises for scoops, tantalizing moments, and the latest prophets of doom. Post-Americanization Israeli media, cynically continuing to promote internal strife, encouraging extremism and escape, are still the only public space left for debating Israel's future bravely and seriously.

References

Alexander, Jeffrey. (1981). Mass media in historical, systemic and comparative perspective. In E. Katz & T. Szecsko (Eds.), *Mass media and social change* (pp. 22-42). London: Sage.

Alexander, J., & Jacobs, R. (1998). Mass communication, ritual and civil society. In T. Liebes & J. Curran (Eds.), *Media, ritual and identity* (pp. 23-41). London & New York: Routledge.

Alger, Dean E. (1994). The media elections: Evidence on the role and the impact. In D. Graber (Ed.), *Media power in politics*. Washington, DC: CQ Press.

Arian, Asher. (1996). Neither mobilized nor mobilizing. *Ha'ayin Hashvi'it*, 4. Jerusalem: The Israel Democracy Institute (in Hebrew).

Atkinson, M. (1984). *Our masters' voices: The language and body language of politics*. London: Routledge Kegan Paul.

Auer, J.J. (1962). The counterfeit debates. In D. Kraus (Ed.), *The great debates in Carter vs. Ford*. Bloomington: Indiana University Press.

Avraham, Eli, & First, Anat. (2003). "I buy American": The American image as reflected in Israeli advertizing. *Journal of Communication*.

Barnea, Nahum. (November 2000). Winds of war: The lynching test. *Ha'ayin Hashvi'it*, 29, 4-5.

Barthes, Roland. (1975). The rhetoric of the image. In *Image, music, text* (S. Heath, Trans., pp. 33-42). London: Fontana.

Bavelas, J.B., Black, A., Chovil, N., & Mullett, J. (1990). *Equivocal communication*. London & New Delhi: Sage.
Benjamin, Walter. (1985). Theses on the philosophy of history. In H. Arendt (Ed.), *Illuminations* (pp. 253-264). New York: Schoken Books.
Bennett, Lance. (1997). Introduction. *Political Communication, 14.*
Benniger, James. (1987). Personalization of mass media and the growth of pseudo community. *Communication Research, 14*(3), 352-371.
Bilmes, J. (1995, July). *Questioning in the American vice presidential debate: A study of interactional rhetoric: Part I.* Paper presented at the International Pragmatics Conference, Mexico.
Blondheim, Menachem, & Kaplan, Kimi. (1993). The evil broadcasting authority [Rashut Hashidur]: Communication and tapes in an ultra-orthodox society. *Kesher, 14,* 51-62.
Blum-Kulka, Shoshana. (1983). The dynamics of political interviews. *Text, 3,* 131-153.
Blum-Kulka, Shoshana. (2000, September). *Studying scandal as a journalistic genre: The process of entrapment.* Lecture presented at the annual meeting of the Broadcast Talk seminar, Ross Priory, Scotland.
Boorstin, Daniel J. (1964). *The image: A guide to pseudo events in America.* New York: Harper & Row.
Booth, Wayne. (1982). The company we keep: Self-making in imaginative art, old and new. *Daedelus, 111,* 33-59.
Cardiff, David, & Scannell, Paddy. (1987). Broadcasting and national unity. In J. Curran, A. Smith, & P. Wingate (Eds.), *Impacts and influences* (pp. 157-173). London & New York: Methuen.
Carey, James. (1998). Political ritual on television: Episodes in the history of shame, degradation and excommunication. In T. Liebes & J. Curran (Eds.), *Media, ritual and identity* (pp. 42-70). London & New York: Routledge.
Carlin, D.B., & Bicak, P.J. (1993). Towards a theory of vice presidential debate purposes: An analysis of the 1992 vice presidential debate. *Argumentation and Advocacy, 30,* 111-130.
Caspi, Dan. (1996). American-style electioneering in Israel: Americanization versus modernization. In D. L. Swanson & P. Mancini (Eds.), *Politics, media and modern democracy.* Westport, CT: Praeger.
Caspi, Dan, & Yechiel Limor. (1992). *The mediators: The mass media in Israel 1948-1990.* Tel-Aviv: Am Oved.
Curran, James. (1998). Crisis of public communication: A reappraisal. In T. Liebes & J. Curran (Eds.), *Media, ritual and identity* (pp. 175-202). London & New York: Routledge.
Danner, Mark. (2000). The shame of political TV. *NY Review of Books, XLVII,* 14.
Dayan, Daniel, & Katz, Elihu. (1993). *Media events: The live broadcasting of history.* Cambridge, MA: Harvard University Press.
Delli Carpini, Michael & Williams, Bruce A. (2000). Let us entertain you: The politics of popular media. In L. Bennett & R. Entman (Eds.),

Mediated politics: The future of political communication. Cambridge: Cambridge University Press.
Dewey, John. (1927). *The public and its problems.* New York: Henry Holt.
Edelman, Murray. (1988). *Constructing the political spectacle.* Chicago: University of Chicago Press.
Eliasoph, Nina. (1998). *Avoiding politics: How Americans produce apathy in everyday life.* Cambridge: Cambridge University Press.
Epstein, E. (1973). *News from nowhere.* New York: Random House.
Ewen, S. (1988). *All consuming images.* New York: Basic Books.
Ezrahi, Yaron. (2001, January). Through the kaleidoscope: On the role of journalists in a situation in which events do not make a story. *Ha'ayin Hashvi'it, 30,* 13-14.
Fallows, James. (1996). *Breaking the news.* New York: Vintage Books.
Fiedler, Leslie. (1982). *What was literature? Mass culture and mass society.* New York: Simon & Schuster.
Fiske, John. (1994). *Media matters.* Minneapolis: University of Minnesota Press.
Galtung, Johan & Ruge, Mary. (1970). The structure of foreign news. In J. Tunstall (Ed.), *Media sociology* (pp. 38-52). London: Constable.
Gamson, William. (1992). *Talking politics.* New York: Cambridge University Press.
Gans, Herbert. (1980). *Deciding what's news.* New York: Random House.
Geertz, Clifford. (1983). From the native's point of view. In C. Geertz, *Local knowledge.* New York: Basic Books.
Gerrits, Robin. (1992). Terrorists' perspectives: Memoirs. In D. Paletz & A. Schmid (Eds.), *Terrorism and the media* (pp. 29-60). Newbury Park: Sage.
Giddens, Anthony. (1994). *Modernity and self-identity.* Cambridge, UK: Polity Press.
Giddens, Anthony. (2000). *Runaway world: How globalization is reshaping our lives.* London & New York: Routledge.
Gitlin, Todd. (1980). *The whole world is watching.* Berkeley: University of California Press.
Gitlin, Todd. (1998). Problems in the theory and practice of the public sphere. In T. Liebes & J. Curran (Eds.), *Media, ritual and identity* (pp. 168-174). London & New York: Routledge.
Glasgow University Media Group. (1976). *Bad news.* London: Routledge & Kegan Paul.
Goffman, Erving. (1974). *Frame analysis.* New York: Harper & Row.
Goffman, Erving. (1975). *The presentation of self In everyday life.* New York: Doubleday.
Grice, H.P. (1975). Logic and conversation. In P. Cole & J. Morgan (Eds.), *Syntax and semantics 3: Speech acts* (pp. 43-59). New York: Academic Press.
Griffin, Michael, & Kagan, Simon. (1996). Picturing culture in political spots: 1992 campaigns in Israel and the United States. *Political Communication, 13,* 43-61.

Gross, Larry. (1998). Minorities, majorities and the media. In T. Liebes & J. Curran (Eds.), *Media, ritual and identity* (pp. 87-102). London & New York: Routledge.

Gurevitch, Zali, & Aran, Gideon. (1991). Al Hamakom (Antropologia Yisraelit). *Alpaim, 4*, 9-44.

Hallin, Dan. (Ed.). (1994). *We keep America on top of the world: Television journalism and the public sphere*. London & New York: Routledge.

Hallin, Dan. (1998). Broadcasting in the third world: From national development to civil society. In T. Liebes & J. Curran (Eds.), *Media, ritual and identity*. London & New York: Routledge.

Hartley, J., & O'Regan, T. (1992). *Tele-ology: Studies in television*. London & New York: Routledge.

Herzl, Theodor. (1902). *Altneuland*. Leipzig: H. Seeman Nacht.

Horton, Donald, & Wohl, Richard. (1956). Mass communication and parasocial interaction. *Psychiatry, 19*(3), 215-229.

Ignatious, David. (2000, December 11). Keeping the media out. *Herald Tribune*.

Iyengar, Schanto. (1991). *Is anyone responsible? How TV frames political issues*. Chicago: University of Chicago Press.

Jamieson, Kathleen. (1992). *Dirty politics*. New York: Oxford University Press.

Jamieson, Kathleen. (1996). *Packaging the presidency*. New York: Oxford University Press.

Jucker, A. (1986). *News interviews: A pragmalinguistic analysis*. Amsterdam: John Benjamins.

Just, Marion R., Crigler, Ann N., Alger, Dean E., Cook, Timothy E., Kern, Montague, & West, Darrell, M. (1996). *Crosstalk*. Chicago: The University of Chicago Press.

Katriel, Tamar. (1998). The dialogic community: "Soul talks" among early Israeli communal groups. In T. Liebes & Z. Curran (Eds.), *Media, ritual and identity* (pp. 114–135). New York: Routledge.

Katz, Elihu. (1971). Television comes to the people of the Book. In I. L. Horowitz (Ed.), *The use and abuse of social science* (pp. 27-32). New Brunswick, NJ: Transaction Books.

Katz, Elihu. (1988). Disintermediation: Cutting out the middle man. *Intermedia, 16*, 30-32.

Katz, Elihu. (1989). Journalists as scientists. *American Behavioral Scientist, 33*, 234-8.

Katz, Elihu. (1993). The end of journalism? Notes on watching the Gulf War. *Journal of Communication, 42*(3), 5-13.

Katz, Elihu. (1996). And deliver us from segmentation. *Annals of the American Academy of Political and Social Science, 546*, 22-33.

Katz, Elihu. (1998). Broadcasting holidays. *Sociological Inquiry, 68*(2), 230-241.

Katz, Elihu, & Wedell, George. (1977). *Broadcasting in the third world*. Cambridge, MA: Harvard University Press.

Katz, Elihu, Gurevitch, Michael, & Haas, Hadassa. (1997). Twenty years of television in Israel: Are there long-run effects on values, social connectedness, and cultural practices? *Journal of Communication, 47*(2), 3-20.

Kimmerling, Baruch. (1998). The new Israelis: a multiplicity of cultures without multiculturalism. *Alpayim,* 264-308.

Kirshnbaum, Motti. (1994). *The evolution of public broadcasting.* Lecture presented at the annual conference of the Smart Institute of Communication, Hebrew University.

Lazarsfeld, Paul F., & Merton, Robert K. (1948). Mass communication, popular taste and organized social action. In L. Bryson (Ed.), *The communication of ideas* (pp. 93-125). New York: Harper.

Liebes, Tamar. (1994). "What a relief": When the press prefers celebration to scandal. *Political Communication, 11,* 35-48

Liebes, Tamar. (1997). *Reporting the Arab–Israeli conflict: How hegemony works.* London: Routledge.

Liebes, Tamar. (1998). Television's disaster marathons: A danger for democratic processes? In T. Liebes & J. Curran (Eds.), *Media, ritual and identity.* London & New York: Routledge.

Liebes, Tamar. (1999). Displacing the news: The Israeli talk show as public space. *Gazette, 61*(2), 113-125.

Liebes, Tamar, & Katz, Elihu. (1993) *The export of meaning: Cross-cultural readings of "Dallas."* Cambridge, UK: Polity Press.

Liebes, Tamar, & Katz, Elihu. (1997) Staging peace: Televised ceremonies of reconciliation. *The Communication Review, 2*(2), 235-257

Liebes, Tamar, & Peri, Yoram. (1998). Electronic journalism in segmented societies. *Political Communication, 15*(1), 27-44

Lippman, Walter. (1924). *Public opinion.* New York: The Free Press.

Mancini, Paolo, & Swanson, David. (1996). Politics, media and modern democracy: Introduction. In D. L. Swanson & P. Mancini (Eds.), *Politics, media and modern democracy.* Westport, CT: Praeger.

Margalit, Avishai. (1999, August). Israel: Why Barak won. *New York Review of Books.*

McChesney, Robert W. (1999). *Rich media, poor democracy.* Urbana & Chicago: University of Illinois Press.

Merton, Robert. (1946). *Mass persuasion.* New York: Harper & Row.

Meyrowitz, Joshua. (1985). *No sense of place.* New York: Oxford University Press.

Meyrowitz, Joshua. (1994). Visible and invisible candidates: A case study of "competing logics" of campaign coverage. *Political Communication, 11,* 145-164.

Molotch, Harvey & Lester, Marilyn. (1974). News as purposive behavior. *American Sociological Review, 3,* 101-12

Murdoch, G. (1988). Talking about terrorism: Television and the context for political discourse. In P.A. Brook (Ed.), *The news media and television.* Carlton: The Center for Communication, Culture and Society, Carlton University.

Negrine, Ralf & Papathanassopoulos, Stylianos. (1996). The "Americanization" of political communication: A critique. *Press/Politics, 1*, 45-62.
Oren, Amir. (2001, February 9). IDF's media strategy. *Ha'aretz*, p. D1.
Peri, Yoram. (1988). From political nationalism to ethno-nationalism. In Y. Lukacs & A. M. Battah (Eds.), *The Arab–Israeli conflict* (pp. 79-92). Boulder, CO & London: Westview Press.
Peri, Yoram. (1995). The era of new politics. *Journalists' Yearbook 1994-5* (pp. 79-92). Tel-Aviv: Israeli Journalists' Association.
Protess, David L., Cook, Lomax, Cook, Fay, Doppel, Jack C., Ettema, James, Gordon, Maragret, Leff, Donna, and Miller, Peter. (1981). *The journalism of outrage: Investigative reporting and agenda building in America*. New York: Guilford.
Ram, Uri. (1997). The 1996 elections: Images and amulets. *Theory and Criticism, 9*, 199-207.
Rich, Frank. (2000, October 29). The age of mediathon. *NYT Magazine*, p. 58.
Rottblit, Ya'akov. (2001, February 15). Watching television. *Ha'ir*, 15-16.
Ryfe, David. (1999). Franklin Roosevelt and the fireside chats. *Journal of Communication, 43*, 1.
Sabato, L. J. (1992). Open season: How the news media cover presidential campaigns in the age of attack journalism. In M. D. McCubbins (Ed.), *Under the watchful eye: Managing television campaigns in the television era*. Washington, DC: CQ Press.
Scannell, Paddy. (1996). *Radio, television & modern life: A phenomenological approach*. Oxford, UK: Blackwell.
Schiff, Zeev & Ya'ari, Ehud. (1990). *Intifada: The Palestinian uprising—Israel's third front*. New York: Simon & Schuster.
Schudson, Michael. (1992). *Watergate in American memory*. New York: Basic Books.
Schudson, Michael. (1996). *The power of news*. Cambridge, MA: Harvard University Press.
Schudson, Michael. (1997). Why conversation is not the soul of democracy? *Critical Studies in Mass Communication, 14*, 297-309.
Shinar, Dov. (1987). *Palestinian voices: Communication and nation building in the West Bank*. Boulder, CO: Lynne Rienner.
Silj, Alessandro. (1988). *A Est di Dallas: Telefilm usa Europei a Confronto*. Rome: Rai, Vpt.
Sivan, Emanuel. (1994). Cultural enclaves. *Alpayim , 4*, 45-99.
Taub, Gadi. (1998). *Hamered Hashafuf*. Tel Aviv: Hakibbutz Hameuchad.
Teheranian, Majid. (1979). Iran: Communication, alienation, revolution. *Intermedia, 7*, 6-12.
Tolson, Andrew. (1996). *Mediations*. London: Edward Arnold.
Tuchman, Gay. (1978). *Making news*. New York: The Free Press.
Ungar, Sanford J. (1972). *The papers & the papers*. New York: E. P. Dutton.
Williams, Raymond. (1974). *Television: Technology and cultural form*. New York: Schoken Books.

Winkler, C.K., & Black, C.N. (1993). Assessing the 1992 presidential and vice presidential debates. *Argumentation and Advocacy, 30,* 77-87.

Wolfsfeld, Gadi. (1997). *Media and political conflict.* Cambridge: Cambridge University Press.

Wolfsfeld, Gadi. (1998). Promoting peace through the news media: Some initial lessons from the Oslo Peace process. In T. Liebes & J. Curran (Eds.), *Media, ritual and identity.* London & New York: Routledge.

Wolfsfeld, Gadi, & Weimann, Gai. (2001). Struggles over the electoral agenda: The elections of 1996 and 1999. In A. Arian & M. Shamir (Eds.), *The elections in Israel, 1999* (pp. 27-42). Albany: State University of New York Press.

Author Index

A

Alexander, J., 65, 74, 75, 107, 129, 205
Alger, D.E., 114, 121, 122, 205, 208
Alkinson, M., 140, 205
Aran, G., 10, 208
Arian, A., 1115, 116, 205
Auer, J.J., 133, 205
Avraham, E., 35, 205

B

Barnea, N., 202, 205
Barthes, N., 54, 56, 205
Bavelas, J.B., 141, 206
Benjamin, W., 76, 206
Bennett, L., 69, 206
Benniger, J., 154, 206
Bicak, P.J., 134, 206
Black, A., 141, 206
Black, C.N., 141, 211
Blimes, J., 134, 206
Blondheim, M., 125, 206
Blum-Kulka, S., 9, 141, 206

Boorstin, D.J., 88, 206
Booth, W., 69, 206

C

Cardiff, D., 23, 206
Carey, J., 67, 75,81, 206
Carlin, D.B., 134, 206
Caspi, D., 26, 129, 206
Chovil, N., 141, 206
Cook, F., 169, 210
Cook. L., 169, 210
Cook, T.E., 122, 208
Crigler, A., 122, 208
Curran, J., 23, 206

D

Danner, M., 68, 206
Dayan, D., 33, 48, 66, 73, 79, 81, 206
Delli Carpini, M., 166, 206
Dewey, J., 161, 207
Doppel, J.C., 169, 210

Author Index

E
Edelman, M., 68, 72, 120, *207*
Eliasoph, N., 153, *207*
Epstein, E., 58, *207*
Ettema, J., 169, *210*
Ewen, S., 183, *207*
Ezrahi, Y., 192, *207*

F
Fallows, J., 168, *207*
Fiedler, L., 89, *207*
First, A. 35, *205*
Fiske, J., 65, 70, 83, *207*

G
Galtung, J., 47, 106, *207*
Gamson, W., 189, *207*
Gans, H., 47, 68, *207*
Geertz, C., 21, 136, *207*
Gerrits, R., 77, 81, *207*
Giddens, A., 3, 6, 83, *207*
Gitlin, T., 68, 122, *207*
Glasgow University Media Group, 68, *207*
Goffman, E., 68, 105, 134, 179, *207*
Gordon, M., 169, *210*
Grice, H.P., 145, *207*
Griffin, M., 113, *207*
Gross, L., 24, 105, 122, *208*
Gurevitch, M., 32, *209*
Gurevitch, Z., 10, 32, 5\35, *208*, *209*

H
Haas, H., 32, 35, *209*
Hallin, D., 19, 49, 59, 65, 67, 68, 74, 110, 193, *208*
Harley, J., 25, *208*
Herzl, T., 1, *208*

I
Ignatious, D., 200, *208*
Iyengar, S., 65, *208*

J
Jacobs, R., 65, 75, 107, *205*
Jamieson, K., 114, 115, *208*
Jucker, A., 141, *208*
Just, M., 122, *208*

K
Kagan, S., 113, *207*
Kaplan, K., 125, *206*
Katriel, T., 73, *208*
Katz, E., 5, 20, 29, 32, 33, 35, 40, 44, 48, 58, 59, 65, 66, 73, 79, 81, 122, 126, *206*, *208*, *209*
Kern, M., 122, *208*
Kimmerling, B., 22, 28, 36, *209*
Kirshenbaum, M., 192, *209*

L
Lazarsfeld, P.F., 35, *209*
Leff, D., 169, *210*
Lester, M., 67, 68, 74, 88, *209*
Liebes, T., 5, 6, 27, 32, 33, 34, 36, 68, 99, 126, 192, *209*
Limor, Y., 26, *206*
Lippman, W., 153, *209*

M
Mancini, P., 113, 128, *209*, *211*
Margalit, A., 159, *209*
McChesney, R.W., 7, *209*
Merton, R.K., 35, 154, *209*
Meyrowitz, J., 47, 49, 114, *209*
Miller, P., 169, *210*
Molotch, H., 67, 68, 74, 88, *209*
Mullett, J., 141, *206*
Murdoch, G., 68, *209*

N
Negrine, R., 113, *210*

O
O'Regan, T., 25, *208*
Oren, A., 201, *210*

P
Papathanassopoulos, S., 113, *210*
Peri, Y., 36, 114, 121, 126, *209*
Protess, D.L., 169, *210*

R
Ram, U., 127, *210*
Rich, F., 195, *210*
Rottblit, T\Y., 194, *210*
Ruge, M., 47, 106, *207*
Ryfe, D., 156, *210*

S
Sabato, L.J., 115, *210*
Scannell, P., 23, 48, 59, 60, 70, 80, *206*
Schiff, Z., 193, *210*
Schudson, M., 114, 153, 161, 201
Shinar, D., 123, 128, *210*
Silj, A., 7, *210*
Sivan, E., 5, 123, *210*
Swanson, D., 113, 128, *209*, *211*

T
Taub, G., 13, *210*
Tehranian, M., 123, 124, *210*
Tolson, A., 136, 138, 140, *210*
Tuchman, G., 77, 107, *210*

U
Ungar, S.J., 8\97, *210*

W
Wedell, G., 20, *209*
Weimann, G., 116, *211*
West, D., 122, *208*
Williams, B.A., 166, *206*
Williams, R., 32, *210*
Winkler, C.K., 141, *211*
Wohl, R., 156, *208*
Wolfsfeld, G., 68, 116, 120, *211*

Y
Yaari, E., 193, *210*

Subject Index

A
Alper, Rogel, 8-15
Altneuland, 1-6
Americanization. *See* Broadcasting, Culture, Television
Ariel, Meir, 12-13

B
Breaking news, Action news. *See* Live broadcasting/Disaster marathons
Broadcasting
  Americanization of, 11-15,18-19, 41, 86, 114-15, 190
  Channel Two news, 8, 15, 34, 45, 63, 64, 85;
  and cultural enclaves, 5, 36-38
  and journalistic practices, 91-110
  privatized, 34
  and scandal, 89
  See also Channels, multiple; Electronic journalism; Media ecology; Radio; Television

Broadcasting, Public
  in Arabic, 30
  BBC-like, 23
  and democratic participation, 23-25
  during radio monopoly, 17-18, 25-29, 38-39
  during television monopoly, 30-34, 39-40
  in/and Hebrew, 23, 25, 38
  and ideology, 9-11, 14
  and immigration, 21-23, 27-28
  license fee, 43
  and national integration, 38-40
  and public interest, 43-44
  politicization of, 45-46
  post-monopoly, 34,-38, 44- 46
  Safra square, 50-58, 60
  and war, 26

C
Channels
  and fragmentation, 44-45

multiple, 30, 34-35, 44
public television in the era of, 43-61
Shas, 37, 124-126
radio, Second. *See also* Radio
Clinton, Bill, 152-156
Critics
  media/cultural, 8, 11-15
Culture
  Americanized, 1,2, 6, 18
  authentic, 6-7,18
  capitalist, 2, 5
  commercialized, 5-7
  cosmopolitan, 2, 5
  cultural imperialism, 6-7
  democratized, 2
  enclaves, 5, 18
  "ethnic," 28
  European, 1, 2, 3
  heritage, 2-5
  imported, 5, 18
  "Israeli," 2, 12-15, 18-19, 21-22, 25, 27, 28
  Jewish, 3-5
  local/global, 8
  multiculturalism, 19, 22-24, 28, 30-32, 36-38
  "real," "phony", 4, 8, 14, 15
  "our," 8, 15, 19
  pluralistic/segmented, 23-25, 28
  reinvention of, 4
  Yiddish 1, 5-6

E

Editors/Journalists
  and interviews/sources, 91-103
  in Public Broadcasting, 46-61
  and routine violations, 105-108
  vs. management, 43-46
  vs. politicians/government, 43-46
  and scandal, 108-110
  techniques of source trapping, 93-103
  on TV talkshows, 165-188

Eilon, Ya'akov, 12
Electronic Journalism, 64
  Breaking News/Action News
  co-opting, 81
  Disaster Marathons, 64, 66-69
  Media Events, 66
  practices of, 65
  and public debate, 60
  promos, 86-88
  scandal, 88-111
  talkshows, 165-188
See also News

G

Geffen, Aviv, 15, 203
Genres, *See* Electronic Journalism

H

Hebrew. *See* Altneuland, Radio
Heritage/"heritage", 2-5, 8-11, 23
  and Zionism, 8-11
  and "Israeliness," 28
Hobsbaum, Eric, 2-3, 3-5

J

Journalism. *See* Electronic journalism, Editors/Journalists

K

Kennedy, John F. Jr., 11-15

L

Live broadcating/Breaking news/Disaster marathons
  in bus bombings (1996), 74-77
  CNN, 64
  in "helicopters disaster" (1997), 71-72
  effects of, 77-82
  on radio, 26-27
  in terrorist attacks 74-77, 121-124, 193-199

Subject Index

See also Electronic journalism, genres of; Media events

M
Media ecology, 85
  globalization, 8
  in low-intensity war (2000), 189-201
  mainstream, 111
  New and old media, 128
  and multiculturalism, 124
  in Palestinian *intifada* (1988), 192-193
  segmention, 124-128, 190
  See also Media events; Radio; Televison
Media events, 66, 70, 81
  and the establishment, 79-80
  and trauma, 66
Multiculturalism. *See* Culture, Televsion

N
News
  action, 63-68
  American, 11
  breaking, 64
  Channel Two, 63-64
  culture, broadcast
  editing 48-50
  framing, 46-59
  item, 51-57
  "openness"/"narcotiazing," 59
  promos, 86-88
  primetime, on televison, 63
  ratings, 86
  room, 47
  routine, 67-68
  worthiness, 47
  See also Editors/Journalist, Electronic journalism, Radio, Live broadcasting

Netanyahu, Benjamin, 50-59
  on televsion debate (1996), 136-150
  on televsion debate (1999), 159-162

P
Peres, Shimon
  on televsion's debate (1996), 133-150
Politics
  Americanization of, 61
  and authenticity, 133, 151-164
  and multiculturalism, 90
  personalization of, 61
  personalized, 89
  and private space, 90
  and pseudo-gemeinshchaft, 156-158
  strict norms in, 90
  of television debates, 133-150

R
Radio
  in Arabic, 27
  and BBC, 23
  Galey Zahal, 26, 87
  and Hebrew, 25, 27
  in holidays, 29
  and immigrants, 27-28
  live, 29
  and nation building, 25-29, 38-39
  and "Israeliness," 27, 38
  pirate, 37
  television, 31, 32
  under British rule, 25, 30
  at war, 26-27, 191

S
Said, Edward, 10
Shohat, Orit, 13

Stanton, Jack, 152-156,
   and pseudo-gemeinshcaft, 156-157

T

Television, 18, 19
   in Arabic, 30
   commercial vs. public, 8-15
   critics of, 8-15
   and *Dallas*, 32
   and de-collectivization, 34-41
   in election campaign, 114-115
   electoral debate on, 134-150
   First/Public Channel, 17, 29-34, 43-61
   and Hebrew, 25, 27, 30
   as historian, 30
   history of, 25-29, 40
   and holidays
   and individualism, 35-36
   and license fee, 43
   and multicultualism, 30, 31, 36-38
   and national integration, 30-34
   public, 8-15
   as video store, 30
   See also Broadcasting, privatized; Broadcasting, public; Channels, multiple; Electronic journalism; Radio

Tradition, 2-4
   and heritage, 2-5
   reinvention of, 4

V

Vilnai, Ze'ev, 9-10

OHIO UNIVERSITY LIBRARY

Please return this book as soon as you have finished with it. In order to avoid a fine it must be returned by the latest date stamped below. All books are subject to recall after two weeks or immediately if needed for reserve.

DEC 1 5 2003

MAR 2 9 2005

CF

Printed in the United States
1074000001B